THE QUEST FOR TECHNICAL KNOWLEDGE

The Quest for Technical Knowledge

Bengal in the Nineteenth Century

SUVOBRATA SARKAR

MANOHAR
2012

First published 2012

ISBN 978-81-7304-949-1

Published by
Ajay Kumar Jain *for*
Manohar Publishers & Distributors
4753/23 Ansari Road, Daryaganj
New Delhi 110 002

Typeset by
Umesh Chand Nailwal
Delhi 110 092

Printed at
Salasar Imaging Systems
Delhi 110 035

To my teacher
Professor Deepak Kumar

Contents

Preface

The history of technology is a relatively unexplored area of historical research. Among the themes which have been taken up for specialized investigation in this project is the history of technical and engineering education. While science education, especially the contribution of renowned scientists, has drawn the attention of historians, the history of technical and engineering education and research is a relatively neglected area. Technology as a form of knowledge, sometimes referred to loosely as 'technical education' in colonial records, is important. So is the history of technical education, part of institutional history with social, economic, cultural, and developmental aspects. The more it is unveiled with all its multi-faced aspects, the more fascinating it becomes as a subject of historical research. This is true especially of Bengal, where the legacy of technical and engineering education has not received the attention it deserves.

There prevailed rich literary and cultural traditions in Bengal almost from the beginning of British rule. In the nineteenth century there were several Bengali journals in circulation, including *Digdarsana* (1818), *Samachar Darpan* (1818), *Sambad Koumudi* (1821), *Samachar Chandrika* (1822), *Sambad Prabhakar* (1831), *Sambad Bhaskar* (1839), *Vidyadarshan* (1842), *Tattobodhini Patrika* (1843), *Vividartha Samgraha* (1851), *Somprakash* (1858), *Rahasya Sandharbha* (1863), *Bamabodhini Patrika* (1863), *Bangadarshan* (1872), *Bharati* (1877), *Balak* (1885), and *Sadhana* (1891). My study explores the perceptions and responses of the Bengali intelligentsia towards modern technical knowledge in the nineteenth century, as reflected in the pages of these journals.

Discussing the various future dimensions of historical research in science, technology and medicine (STM), Deepak Kumar writes about the importance of local histories. According to Kumar the official records have luckily survived but pamphlets, tracts, journals written in different Indian languages can give better clues to how the Indians thought of STM issues.[1] The present work relies on Bengali journals to understand the development and assimilation of technical knowledge in nineteenth-century Bengal.

The study has been divided into five chapters. The first introductory chapter focuses on the major objectives of the study, the research questions raised in the context, the rationale behind undertaking such a study, the methodology, and also a detailed description of the selection of Bengali journals. The views of noted historians on technical knowledge in the colonial context are also presented. The nineteenth century was the age of innovative steam technologies, developed in Europe and then diffused to other regions of the globe. In an era characterized by 'a massive transfer of technology from the West to Africa and Asia' with colonialism as the backdrop, British India has often been taken as an ideal example of this situation. Among the new technologies which made waves in nineteenth-century India, were the printing press, steamships, telegraph, medical tools and technologies, railways and, in the last decade of that century, electricity.

The second chapter analyses how various technological inventions of nineteenth century in the West were used by the British in Bengal. There were certain plans behind their introduction by the colonial power. The chapter tries to gauge the impact of these technological tools and projects on the society, whether the relocation of European technologies on Indian soil was successful or not.

The third chapter is dedicated to technical education introduced by the British in nineteenth-century Bengal. Western technologies are significant not only as 'tools' but also as forms of knowledge, sometimes referred to as 'technical education' in colonial records.[2] How was this knowledge generated, used and transferred, and to whom? Thus the major thrust of this chapter is to analyse the impact of state sponsored technical education on Bengali people and their responses to it.

The next chapter tries to capture the vital link between technical knowledge and industrialization. The period under review is said to have been a century of arrested development for indigenous business enterprises in Bengal. This has engaged the attention of the scholars and no single agreed explanation exists to account for this situation. The chapter investigates the initiatives of Bengalis to establish business enterprises. Throughout the nineteenth century there were Bengalis who started their own enterprises. The chapter also tries to see the impact of the lead by these Bengali entrepreneurs on the 're-industrialization' of Bengal.

The concluding chapter consolidates the findings and attempts to throw light on the forces behind the development and assimilation of technical knowledge on the part of the colonial administrators as well as the people of Bengal. There emerge various questions for further research that would help evolve a more comprehensive understanding of the evolution of technical education in British India.

A study of this kind is subject to certain limitations. As the present study is based on Bengali journals, the first limitation comes from that. Preservation of journals is always a tough job, and especially about the nineteenth-century journals, the situation is easily imaginable. The main obstacle is a lack of consciousness of the past and the humid weather of West Bengal.[3] It was difficult to trace the less known journals. Many volumes of the well-known journals are missing, and the condition of the remaining journals, which have immense historical value, is not good. Many pages are in such poor condition that they are difficult to handle and read. It has been learnt that a few copies of several journals are in personal collections, beyond the reach of the investigator.

Another limitation is the Calcutta-centric character of Bengal. There were many journals which were published outside Calcutta, especially from various *mofussil* areas of Bengal,[4] in the nineteenth century. Unfortunately we do not have any record of these. The Bangiya Sahitya Parishad, National Library, Asiatic Society, and a few small libraries in Kolkata have collections of those journals which were mainly published from Calcutta. So the regional journals are lost forever. Even so, this volume provides a basic understanding of the development and assimilation of technical education in nineteenth-century Bengal.

SUVOBRATA SARKAR

NOTES

1. Deepak Kumar, 'Science and Society in Colonial India: Exploring an Agenda', *Presidential Address* (Modern India), Indian History Congress, Calicut, 28-30 December 1999. Later published in *Social Scientist*, vol. 28, no. 5/6, May–June 2000, pp. 24-46. In another article, Kumar added 'Environmental Perspectives' to STM and now the phrase is HISTEM (History of Science, Technology, Environment and Medicine). Deepak Kumar, 'Developing a History of Science and Technology in South Asia', *Economic and Political Weekly*, 7 June 2003.
2. Roy Macleod and Deepak Kumar, 'Introduction: Western Technology and British Rule', in Macleod and Kumar (eds.), *Technology and the Raj: Western Technology and Technical Transfers to India 1700–1947*, Sage, New Delhi, 1995, p. 15.
3. Bajendranath Bandopadhyay mentioned this problem in 1932: *Sangbadpatre Sekaler Katha*, vol. I, Bangiya Sahitya Parishad, Kolkata, 1932, p. 2. Most recently (2000) Swapan Basu also complained about this. See Swapan Basu (ed.), *Sangbad Samayikpatre Unis Sataker Bangali Samaj*, Paschimbanga Bangla Academy, Kolkata, 2000, p. 1.
4. Sekhar Bhoumik, 'Ancholik Patrika', in Swapan Basu and Muntasir Mamun (eds.), *Dui Sataker Bangla Sambad Samayikpatra*, Pustak Biponi, Kolkata, 2005, pp. 141-71.

Acknowledgements

This book would not have been possible without the constant encouragement and support of my teacher, Prof. Deepak Kumar. It is impossible today to sum up his contribution in a few words. I remain grateful to him not only for this book but also for shaping my entire academic engagement. He constantly reminds us to ask new questions which according to him are more important than the findings! This book is dedicated to him.

I acknowledge the lessons and encouragement I received from teachers at the Jawaharlal Nehru University, Visva-Bharati, and Raiganj Coronation H.S. School.

Prof. Sandip Basu Sarbadhikary read the entire document and made valuable suggestions, for which I am earnestly grateful.

Prof. Smritikumar Sarkar, Dr. Raj Sekhar Basu, Dr. Subhayu Chattopadhyay and Dr. Jayanta Bhattacharya have been a constant source of encouragement. I am grateful to them for their valuable suggestions.

I am thankful to Prof. Bhaskar Chattopadhyay (Retired Professor, Burdwan University), Prof. Suchibrata Sen, Prof. Chhanda Chatterjee, Prof. Bhaskar Jyoti Basu, Prof. S. Jeyaseela Stephen, Dr. Bipasha Raha, Dr. Syed Ejaz Hussain, Dr. Arpita Sen, and Dr. Arunava Das (Visva-Bharati), Prof. Ranjan Chakraborti (Jadavpur University), Prof. Arun Bandopadhyay, and Dr. Sanjukta Dasgupta (University of Calcutta), Prof. Sujata Mukherjee (Rabindra Bharati University), Prof. Arabinda Samanta (Burdwan University), Prof. Ananda Gopal Ghosh and Prof. Ratna Roy Sanyal (University of North Bengal), Dr. Ratan Dasgupta (University of Gour Banga), Dr. Asim Sarkar (Malda College), Mr. Kishore Bhattacharya (Patha-Bhavana, Visva-Bharati) and Mr. Jyotirmoy Chaudhury (Raiganj Coronation H.S. School). Their encouragement infused in me a sense of self-confidence.

I am thankful to Prof. Binod Khadria, Prof. Geetha B. Nambissan,

Prof. Dhruv Raina, Dr. Saumen Chattopadhyay, Dr. S. Srinivasa Rao and Dr. Arvind Kumar Mishra (ZHCES, JNU), Dr. Nandita Khadria and Dr. Radha Gayathri (ERRU, JNU), Dr. Padmanav Samarendra (Jamia Millia Islamia) and Dr. Sangeeta Dasgupta (CHS, JNU) for showing a keen interest in my work and for constant encouragement.

I cannot but remember with thanks the officials and staff of National Library, WB State Secretariat Library, State Archives of WB, Bangiya Sahitya Parishad Library, Birla Industrial & Technology Museum Library, Department of History Library, University of Calcutta, Jadavpur University Library (Kolkata), Postgraduate Department of History Library, Malda College (Malda); National Archives of India, Nehru Memorial Museum & Library, JNU main Library and ZHCES Library (New Delhi) for their immense help and cooperation. Mr. Nageswara (in-Charge, Rare Book Section, National Library) kindly gave me permission to take a few photographs of the nineteenth-century Bengali journals and Mr. Pratap Pal (National Library) assisted my study of these journals.

I offer my heartfelt thanks to Dr. Neelam Kumar (NISTADS, New Delhi) and Dr. Nandita Basu Sarbadhikary (Visva-Bharati, Santiniketan) for their affection without which it was really hard for me to stay so far away from my family.

I am beholden to all my friends for their care and kindness. I am indebted to Jyoti and Rashmi for their support and encouragement. I wish to thank my friends Ajeet, Anand, Debashis, Sandip, Saumen, Saurav (Puchan), Somak and Umesh for their loving company. I am grateful to Soma (Samarpita Mukherjee) and her family for their company and guidance in my initial days in Delhi.

My special thanks are due to the editor at Manohar Publishers & Distributors for help and care in publication.

My Ma, Babi, Masi, Bhai and in-laws have been always there whenever I needed them. I am grateful for their love and compassion, which helped me to sustain myself. Sneha, your love and emotional support is unforgettable. Thank you is not enough!

SUVOBRATA SARKAR

CHAPTER 1

Introduction

> The newspaper is the chronicle of civilization—the common reservoir into which every stream pours its living waters, at which every man may come to drink.
>
> BULWER LYTTON[1]

The nineteenth century was a very significant period in the history of India. It was during this period that the country witnessed the emergence of several intellectual currents, religious, social, political, economic, and cultural. For the colonial power, by the beginning of the nineteenth century, the empire had more or less been won. The job was to keep it, and to use it for profit. In order to establish their complete supremacy, British colonizers had to dethrone as well as delegitimize pre-colonial symbols and ideas, both political and cultural and at the same time present their ideas in a form that would appear attractive to the natives. They realized that colonizing the mind of the subjugated population was more important than the sword. One of the major tools of colonizing the mind was education, replacing existing indigenous knowledge systems with their own.

Another relevant point is that colonialism was not the result of mere Western superiority, but of the unleashing of overwhelming force backed by technology and at minimal cost.[2] Technological changes affected the timing and location of European conquests and thus determined the economic relations of colonialism. It made European expansion swift, complete, and cheap. The ability of Europeans in the nineteenth century to conquer foreign lands arose from a relatively few inventions like iron-hulled steam ships, improved firearms, telegraph, and railways. With these tools, Europeans brought about a shift in global relations.

The connections between colonialism and technological change is a topic that engages historians. There was a close connection between commercial interests, technological change, and government policy from the early years of British rule. Technology, whether as tools or as forms of knowledge, is not value-free. It always manifests socio-political qualities and drives the economy. In colonial conditions it acquired the contours of the colonial power, both commercial and administrative.[3] Thus in the colonial context technical knowledge is an important area of historical research.

In the nineteenth century, Bengal was the political centre of British India, the intellectual hub of the country. It was Bengal where the first serious sustained contacts were made between Western science and India's own scientific tradition. Here the first educational establishment fashioned on the Western system was set up. Bengal served as a model of this system to the rest of the subcontinent. Nineteenth-century Bengal remains a fascinating study of Bengali identity and nostalgia.

Journals, newspapers, and periodicals[4] (henceforth journals) are important sources of history. From them we can get a fair reflection of the society under study. There were rich literary and cultural traditions in Bengal almost from the beginning of the British rule. In the nineteenth century the dawn of a new era was ushered in by unprecedented creativity backed by fruitful imagination in the fields of reform movements as well as literary and artistic movements.[5] This phenomenon, sometimes referred to as the 'renaissance', was, no doubt, the result of the Western impact leading to growing awareness of the people of Bengal. So also in the field of science, rethinking and recreation were the distinguishing symptoms of regeneration. In the nineteenth century, by the blessing of printing press, there were many Bengali journals in circulation. Prominent among them are *Dig-Durshun* (1818), *Samachar Darpan* (1818), *Sambad Koumudi* (1821), *Samachar Chandrika* (1822), *Sambad Prabhakar* (1831), *Sambad Bhaskar* (1839), *Vidyadarshan* (1842),

Tattobodhini Patrika (1843), *Vividhartha Samgraha* (1851), *Somprakash* (1858), *Rahasya Sandarbha* (1863), *Bamabodhini Patrika* (1863), *Bangadarshan* (1872), *Bharati* (1877), *Balak* (1885), *Sadhana* (1891), *Sahitya Parishad Patrika* (1894), *Silpotatto O Pushpanjoli* (1897), and *Udbodhon* (1899). The present study deals with the development and assimilation of technical knowledge in Bengal through the pages of these journals.

This study will explore the technologies and technological themes that captured the imagination of the reading public of nineteenth-century Bengal, study the evolving relationships between technological ideas of development and technical education, and investigate the variety of social forces and interests that shaped the evolution of technical education in Bengal. We shall also study the emergence of various indigenous enterprises and their impact on the society of Bengal.

The current study seeks to find answers to some of the most important questions related to the history of education in India. This will contribute to a better understanding of the complex relationship between British colonialism and development of technical education in Bengal, and its assimilation by the Bengali people. How were various tools and projects used by the British in Bengal? Was the relocation of European technologies on Indian soil successful? What factors influenced the shaping of colonial policies of technical education and the subsequent establishment of technical institutes in Bengal? How did local knowledge re-shape colonial institutions and policies? The response of the Bengali intellectuals to state-sponsored technical education will be investigated, as also the emergence of indigenous enterprises and their role in 're-industrialization'.

Scholars who have done extensive research on the social history of science, technology and medicine, have given special importance to education.[6] Technical education is part of overall discussions on the colonial educational system. We have some case studies also on technical education [Dhruv Raina and S. Irfan Habib, *Domesticating Modern Science: A Social History of Science and Culture in Colonial India* (2004); Mangamma Jolepalyam, *Technical and Agricul-*

tural Education: A Study of Madras Presidency (1990); B.R. Tomlinson, 'Technical Education in Colonial India, 1880-1914: Searching for a "Suitable Boy" ', in Sabyasachi Bhattacharya (ed.), *The Contested Terrain: Perspectives on Education in India* (1998)]. A detailed study of the development of technical education in the Bengal Presidency, however, is yet to be done.

During the nineteenth century there were many English journals in circulation, such as the *India Gazette*, *Englishman*, *Calcutta Review*, *Bengal Hurkaru*, *Calcutta Gazette*, *Morning Chronicle*, *Reformer*, *Enquirer*, *Hindu Patriot*, *Bengalee*, *Indian Mirror*, and *Dawn Magazine*. Considering their numbers the contemporary journal *Friend of India* remarked that Calcutta was not only the 'city of palaces', but also a 'city of journals'.[7] But these were confined to a limited readership. People who did not know English remained outside the circle of these journals. For the majority of Bengalis one of the major sources of information were journals published in Bengali. Before the introduction of the printing press, poor Brahmin pundits moved from door to door, to relate the news of the day.[8] So a detailed study of the Bengali journals is very important.

A letter written to the editor of the famous *Somprakash* on 13 April 1863 is worth a mention.[9] One Rajendra Kumar Roy chaudhury of Baruipur near Calcutta wrote about his experience after a lecture session at the Bethune Society (Calcutta). Reverend Dr. Duff, Lalbihari Dey, Abdul Latif, and Kishorichand Mitra, had delivered the lectures. He was bewildered. The session had been attended by almost a hundred listeners. After the lecture some from the audience asked Rajendra Kumar about the lectures. As they did not know English, they were unable to understand them and were ashamed. Then they remarked that of the scholars who delivered lectures all were not Sahebs (Europeans), many of them were Bengali. If they had only uttered a few words in their mother tongue, they could at least have been understood. Rajendra Babu explained to them the subject matter of the lectures. He thought that it was painful that so many people at the lecture session could not comprehend them. The organizers should know this. They could easily arrange one or two lectures in Bengali. When so many people attended such lectures in spite of the fact that these were delivered in English, their eagerness to learn was evident. According to Rajendra Kumar the society should organize at least one lecture in Bengali at every session. He felt that not only the Bethune Society, but other scientific and literary societies of Calcutta did not think of the general people.

If the situation in 1863 was like that, so we can simply guess about the picture before that, i.e. in the first half of nineteenth century. Bengali journals were a window through which they received the glimpse of new knowledge.

Bengali journals are the main primary sources of this study. Bajendranath Bandopadhyay mentioned that about 1046 journals appeared during the nineteenth century in Bengali.[10] Later Swapan Basu added another 100 names in the list.[11] It is not possible for anyone to study all of them: most are missing. The National Library and Bangiya Sahitya Parishad Library, Kolkata have the biggest collections. Apart from these, few small libraries of Kolkata like Chaitanya Library, Joykrishna Library, and Rammohun Library preserve a few copies of these journals. The Asiatic Society and Centre for Studies in Social Sciences, Kolkata also preserved some of these in microfilm. From there the investigator chose the following samples for study: *Dig-Durshun* (1818), *Samachar Darpan* (1818), *Samachar Chandrika* (1822), *Sambad Prabhakar* (1831), *Jnananeshan* (1831), *Sambad Purnochandradaya* (1835), *Sambad Bhaskar* (1839), *Tattobodhini Patrika* (1843), *Vividhartha Samgraha* (1851), *Education Gazette O Saptahik Bartabaho* (1856), *Somprakash* (1858), *Rahasya Sandarbha* (1863), *Bamabodhini Patrika* (1863), *Grambarta Prakashika* (1863), *Amrita Bazar Patrika* (1868), *Sulav Samachar* (1870), *Bangadarshan* (1872), *Sadharani* (1873), *Vijnan Darpan* (1876), *Bharati* (1877), *Balak* (1885), *Sadhana* (1891), *Sahitya Parishad Patrika* (1894), and *Sibpur College Patrika* (?). Utmost care was taken to cover all the decades of the century.

Apart from these, the private papers and publications of the Bengali intellectuals of nineteenth century provide valuable insights regarding their viewpoint of the technical education in Bengal.

The reports of various education commissions, especially those related to technical education, give a basic idea of the nature and methods followed by the government to spread technical instruction in Bengal.

As is true for every study, in this study also, secondary sources too are important. Expert comments and scholarly views have been taken into consideration to get into the current debates and discourses on the topic. The work of those scholars who had extensively explored the area of technical knowledge, have also been utilized in the current study.

The period 1814 to 1818 deserves special attention. In 1814 Rammohun Roy (1772–1833) started residing at Calcutta permanently, leaving his job at Rangpur. He was a pioneer of the scientific approach to social problems. Hindu College was established in 1817 mainly through the initiatives of Indians to 'instruct the sons of the Hindoos in the European and Asiatic languages and sciences'.[12] In the very next year (1818) the first journal in Bengali appeared.

Nineteenth-century publications in Bengali and other Indian languages were overwhelmingly textbooks at the elementary level.[13] There were no new enquiries in the field of science and technology except at the end of the century. In an essay written in 1889, Jadunath Gangopadhyay pointed out that scientific knowledge could not be practised in the country only through translation. This required independent thought, acceptable research activity, and the evaluation of science on the basis of one's own experience.[14] The stream of science and technology introduced by the British was outside the reach of the ordinary people. It was stories of the achievements of Western science and technology that were disseminated through Bengali journals.

A variety of practices and regimes of scientific and technological knowledge had originally emerged in the West. These were re-situated in the course of colonial rule. The re-situation of these practices led to their reformulation as well. A different society, culture, tradition and existing indigenous knowledge systems provided the context in which the gradual spread of this knowledge occurred, followed by its adaptation and articulation through various reformulations.[15] One of the primary means of reformulation and dissemination of such knowledge in Bengali were the journals.

The first initiative to capture the story of Bengali journals was made by Kedarnath Majumdar, editor of *Sourav*.[16]

In 1920 P.N. Bose remarked on the utter absence of any systematic attempt to chronicle the different activities of the Bengali press. According to him although more than a hundred years had rolled away since the first Bengali journal saw the light, 'no interesting history was there to arrest the attention of the learned scholar'.[17] Along with H.W.B. Moreno he attempted a comprehensive history of Bengali journals from its inception and covered the entire nineteenth century.

One should also remember the name of Mahendranath Vidyanidhi. Although he did extensive research on the history of Bengali journals, he remained outside the limelight as he did not publish any book on this.[18] Many articles by him were published in the famous journals of the day, including 'Samayik Sahitya' (in Bengali), *Nabya Bharat*, 10/12 (Chaitra, 1299),[19] 1892; 'Bangla Sambadpatrer Itihas' (in Bengali), *Janmabhumi* (1303), 1896, (1304), 1897, and (1305), 1898; 'Bangla Bhasay Pratham Sambadpatra Bengal Gejeti' (in Bengali), *Anusandhan* (1899).[20]

In the history of Bengali journals, the work of Bajendranath Bandopadhyay deserves central place. He demonstrated that the growth of Bengali language and literature, the spread of the English education and European culture, the socio-economic-political condition of the country, in short every aspect of Bengali life in the nineteenth century, were beautifully portrayed in the journals of that time.[21] He studied the period 1818 to 1840 and compiled mainly the news of *Samachar Darpan*, the famous journal of the nineteenth century. Apart from *Samachar Darpan*, he also studied *Bangadutt*, *Samachar Chandrika*, *Sambad Purnochandradaya* and collected some important reporting on education, literature, and contemporary society. Bajendranath wanted to compile the news from the journals till 1857, but was unable to complete his project.

Another scholar, Jatindramohon Bhattacharya, extensively wrote on the society and Bengali journals of nineteenth century. Important articles written by him were 'Sambad Bhaskare Sekaler Katha' in *Prabudha Bharat*, 1/2 (1933) and 'Sambadpatre Se Juger Katha' in *Prabortak* (1937).[22]

The unfinished task of Bajendranath was mostly completed by Binay Ghose. He studied journals like *Sambad Prabhakar*, *Tattobodhini Patrika*, *Sambad Bhaskar*, *Vidyadarshan*, *Sarbosubhokari*, *Bengal Spectator*, *Somprakash* and compiled the news in four volumes.[23] Based on these four volumes, he wrote a book (vol. V) on nineteenth-century Bengal, *Banglar Samajik Itihaser Dhara*, describing the evolution of village and urban society, the emergence of indigenous enterprises, and the growth of the Bengali middle class.

Recently two scholars have presented their viewpoints on the society of nineteenth-century Bengal through the prism of Bengali journals. The first is a Ph.D. thesis of University of Calcutta submitted by Partha Chattopadhyay (1974), published as *Bangla Sambadpatra O Bangalir Nabajagoran*.[24] Here for the first time the writer vividly explored the nature of these Bengali journals along with their editors.

Most recently Swapan Basu compiled the reporting on various popular uprisings in Bengal and the changing status of women in society evident in the pages of nineteenth-century Bengali journals.[25] He nicely describes the evolution of Bengali journals, along with some contemporary English journals.

NINETEENTH-CENTURY BENGALI JOURNALS: A BRIEF OVERVIEW

Journals are a mirror of their time. Sidney Kobre remarked that journals are inseparable part of the society,[26] and to understand the nature of a particular journal, one should know the politico-economic and social context in which it appeared.

The first journal in India was published by a European, James Augustus Hicky, in the second half of the eighteenth century. The history of the Indian press commenced with his *Bengal Gazette*

(29 January 1789). From 1789 to 1818 many English journals were published (names are already mentioned). These were the early inspiration for Bengali journals. They were named Gazette, Spectator, Prabhakar (in English 'Sun'), Darpan (in English 'Mirror'), like their English contemporaries. But these similarities or imitations are only confined to the title; the content and aim were totally different. For the English journals it was profit-making and entertainment, but the Bengali journals were dedicated to social reform and the spread of useful knowledge.[27] The journals owned by Europeans catered mostly to business interests, but in the hands of the indigenous people the Bengali journals became a medium of the dissemination of knowledge, which helped the social reform movement in a great way.

Bengal, and particularly its principal city, Calcutta, had been the first area in India to experience the impact of British rule. Calcutta, the capital of British India from 1793 to 1911 was the centre of interaction between the British and their Indian subjects. Land reforms, new economic opportunities, Western education, property laws, and a new spirit of individualism contributed to the growth of intellectual and social activities which were to affect all of India. Like any industry, the growth of journals requires infrastructural support, for example, growth of educated population, development of printing press, good communication, proper advertisement, etc. By the last half of the eighteenth century these facilities became available at Calcutta, although in a slow pace.

The most important agent for the development of a new middle class and of social change was Western education. Although the spread of Western education was desired by calculating Englishmen who wanted to fill the lower levels of the bureaucracy, it was also eagerly sought by middle-class Hindus who perceived it as a vehicle for professional mobility and the means by which they could learn the secrets of the technologically superior Western world.

The 1820s and 1830s were optimistic decades for idealist Englishmen and Western-educated Bengalis, as the 1840s and 1850s were decades of disillusionment. Bengalis continued to be influenced by Western values and ideologies, but there was a shift in the focus of their criticism which 'began to be levelled against the British government, the operation of British justice and the methods of British industrial and commercial enterprises'.[28]

Disenchantment with British rule was closely related to economic and professional frustrations. The educated class held high aspirations which could not possibly be met with the limited number of jobs. They were further frustrated by the fact that high salaried jobs were reserved for the Europeans. In the entire civil service with 7,000 posts in 1857, the 900 'covenanted' positions went only to Englishmen, and of the 5,298 lesser posts, 3,082 were filled by Englishmen, only 2,846 by Indians.[29] The other professions open to Western-educated Indians–law, medicine, education, and engineering–also favoured Europeans. These grievances were expressed in petitions emanating from associational meetings and published in Bengali journals which were rapidly increasing in number.[30]

The Western-educated class in Bengal searched for new social and political models. While they were not rejecting aspects of Westernization to which their education had introduced them, their earlier desire to imitate Western social and religious institutions declined. There was a new spirit of criticism. Bengali society moved towards a synthesis of the old and the new, the Indian and the Western. A new intellectual and moral maturity was becoming discernible.[31] The most important characteristic of mid-nineteenth-century Indian thinking was an unprecedented emphasis on cultural synthesis. Numerous Bengali journals of the period (*Sambad Prabhakar*, *Tattobodhini Patrika*, *Vividhartha Samgraha*, etc.) claimed this objective. The idea of cultural synthesis enabled them to absorb an alien culture and also promised a possible opportunity to transcend the barriers imposed by colonialism.[32] The nineteenth-century Bengali journals were in this way witness to the evolution of Bengali society and its people.

According to some scholars, the weekly *Bengal Gejeti* edited by Gangakishore Bhattacharya published in 1818 was the first Bengali journal, while some others think that the first Bengali journal was the monthly *Dig-Durshun.*[33] As no single copy of *Bengal Gejeti* is available now, we'll begin our discussion with *Dig-Durshun.*

Dig-Durshun (Monthly)

Dig-Durshun was published by the Serampore Missionaries during April 1818 and was edited by John Clarke Marshman. There were scientific discussions in this journal. It contained notes or news items on physics, geography, geology, astronomy, biology and chemistry. A somewhat inscrutable article on the magnet and compass was published in the first issue. In the sixth issue (September 1818) gravitation of earth was discussed with reference to Newton's law and 'Lightning and Thunder' was another topic in this issue. In its ninth issue (December 1818) the properties of the magnet and the history of its use were elaborated.

Realizing its potential as a teaching aid, the Calcutta School Book Society (estd. 1817) purchased many copies of *Dig-Durshun* and requested the editor to publish its English version.

Contemporary English journal *Friend of India* observed in December 1818:

> It has been suggested that certain articles in the monthly *Dig-durshuna*, might not be wholly uninteresting to our youth in general. As it appears reasonable, therefore, that nothing should be with held from our Indian youth from which they can derive the slightest information, it is proposed in future to publish separately an English translation of each number. . . .[34]

Samachar Darpan (Weekly)

This journal too was published by the Serampore Missionaries (from 23 May 1818) and lasted for a quarter of a century. J.C. Marshman was the editor of *Samachar Darpan*, was ably assisted by Sanskrit scholars like Joy Gopal Tarkalankar, Tarini Charan Shiromoni, etc. After the establishment of the Hindu College (1817), the demand for English education was very high. *Samachar Darpan* was thus published in both Bengali and English from 1829 onwards. In the first phase the journal continued till 1841. Under the editorship of Bhabani Charan Chattopadhyay of Calcutta the journal again appeared in January 1842 and lasted for two years.

The contemporary journal, *Friend of India* said, 'The *Sumachar Durpun* was discontinued in 1841, or rather transferred to a native editor in Calcutta, in whose hands it soon dropped or died.'[35]

In the third and final phase the initiative was again taken by the Serampore Missionaries and *Samachar Darpan* again started on 3 May 1851. After two years (1853), however, its circulation finally ended. Another Bengali journal of that time, *Sambad Prabhakar*,[36] mentioned the closure of *Samachar Darpan* which had had a permanent place in the history of Bengal. Partly this was because one of the objects of this journal had been to reproduce in Bengali the articles about new discoveries and industrial developments published in books in England and Europe.

Sambad Kaumudi (Weekly)

It was edited by a conservative Hindu scholar Bhabani Charan Bandopadhyay (4 December 1821). Both James Long and Bajendranath Bandopadhyay considered Rammohun Roy to be the key voice from 1822, after Bhabani Charan left the journal. A good number of articles were written here by Roy and Dwarakanath Tagore.[37] Translations of articles, news or letters published earlier in English were reprinted. According to James Long, Rammohun used this journal as a vehicle of social reform. Rammohun and Dwarakanath highlighted the 'favourable' socio-economic consequences of indigo cultivation by the Europeans. They also desired permanent settlement of the Europeans in India with a view of paving the way for the application of Western technology in economic fields. The *Kaumudi* was in favour of European medical science. No copy of the journal is available at present.

Samachar Chandrika (Weekly)[38]

Bhabani Charan Bandopadhyay started this journal (on 5 March 1822), after he left the editorship of *Sambad Kaumudi*. This journal represented the conservative section of the Hindu community. It opposed widow-marriage, female education, and the abolition of sati. From 1830s *Chandrika* became the mouthpiece of the Dharma Sabha.

After the death of Bhabani Charan (1848), his son Raj Krishna Bandopadhyay edited the journal. By that time journals like *Sambad Prabhakar*, *Sambad Purnochandradaya*, had became popular and it was difficult for *Chandrika* to compete with them. Later the ownership of this journal was handed over to Bhagabati Charan Chattopadhyay.

Sambad Prabhakar (Weekly)

Sambad Prabhakar (28 January 1831) acquired an important place in Bengali culture. Iswar Chandra Gupta, known as a conservative poet, was its editor. Financial assistance came from Jogendramohon Thakur of Pathurighata.[39] After the death of Iswar Chandra (1859), his brother Ram Chandra Gupta became the editor. But due to bad health he could not perform the duty very long. Later, Gopal Chandra Mukhopadhyay became the editor of *Prabhakar*.

In its first phase, the journal showed conservative viewpoints, but gradually changed its stand regarding female education, widow-marriage, etc. In the 1840s and 1850s *Prabhakar* was the ardent supporter of various social reform movements. The journal criticized the British government on several occasions.[40] Popular uprisings including the revolt of 1857 were vehemently criticized by *Prabhakar*.

Iswar Chandra was in favour of introducing modern technology in agriculture. He was also an advocate of the development of factories and technical instruction in India. *Prabhakar* boldly asserted in 1849 that the introduction of railways might be considered a revolutionary event ushering in a new age.

Sambad Purnochandradaya (Monthly)

Purnochandradaya appeared as a monthly on 8 June 1835 and the editor was Harachandra Bandopadhyay. In 1836 it became a weekly.[41]

Harachandra was the editor of *Purnochandradaya* for three years. From 1838 onwards Udaychandra Adya, Aditya Chandra

Adya, and Gobindo Chandra Adya became the editors. *Sambad Purnochandradaya* was an excellent journal and was published for almost 73 years.

Sambad Bhaskar (Weekly)

In the 1840s various liberal ideas continuously flowed through the pages of this journal and Bengali people were very much influenced by it. *Bhaskar* first appeared in March 1839 and Sreenath Roy was the editor until November 1840. But the real force was Gouri Shankar Tarkabagish who performed all the duties as editor.

Another famous journal of the day *Jnananeshan* wrote on Gouri Shankar: 'Previously the pundit of our journal, became the editor of *Bhaskar* and it has been performing well so far. . . .'[42]

After the death of Gouri Shankar (1859), his foster son Khetra Mohon Bhattacharya became editor. *Sambad Bhaskar* lasted for a long period.

Tattobodhini Patrika (Monthly)

This journal was the mouthpiece of the 'Tattobodhini Sabha', established by Debendranath Tagore (1839) to promote the Brahmo religion. *Tattobodhini Patrika* appeared as a monthly on 16 August 1843 and remained a crucial agent in the evolution of Bengali society almost through the century.

Debendranath wrote in his autobiography:

> . . . many members of *Tattobodhini Sabha* are unable to attend the meetings of our organization as they are busy with their work at distinct places. They were totally unaware about the happenings of the *Sabha*, especially the lectures delivered by Ram Chandra Vidyabagish. The books written by Rammohun on Brahmo religion and philosophy deserve proper circulation. Apart from that the subjects which enrich the knowledge of our people should reach to them. Considering these things, I decided to launch *Tattobodhini Patrika* in 1843. . . .[43]

He continued,

> . . . there were very few journals in circulation at that time and none of them were involved in any healthy discussion. *Tattobodhini* was

the first journal which started serious discussion on various branches of knowledge. . . .[44]

Although religious discussion was high on the agenda of the journal, many articles on literature, philosophy, science, archaeology, sociology, and politics and even economics appeared in *Tattobodhini.* For example, an article published in 1870 lamented the fact that Bengalis were not involved in international trade (*Bharatbarshio Banijjer Unnati,* Jaistha, 1792 Saka, i.e. 1870). On issues like female education, education through mother tongue, science education, etc., too, *Tattobodhini* showed great concern.

Akshay Kumar Dutta was the editor of the journal for 12 years (1843–55). Under his editorship *Tattobodhini* became the best journal of the day.[45] Then the following persons became editor: Nabin Chandra Bandopadhyay (1855–9), Satyendranath Tagore (1859–62), Ajyodha Nath Pakrashi (1865–7, 1869–72), and Hemchandra Vidyaratna (1867–9, 1877).[46]

The editorial team of *Tattobodhini* deserves special attention. Iswar Chandra Vidyasagar, Rajendralal Mitra, Debendranath Tagore, Rajnarayan Roy, Ananda Chandra Vidyabagish, Akshay Kumar Dutta, were in the five-member editorial body at various times.[47] So we can see almost all the dignitaries of nineteenth-century Bengal were involved with the journal. The *Calcutta Review,* a contemporary journal, remarked:

> To those, who are wise enough to know what the expressiveness of the Bengali language means, we would recommend the perusal of the *Tatwabodhini Patrika,* a monthly publication in Bengali, which yields to scarcely any English publication in India, for the ability and originality of its articles.[48]

Vividhartha Samgraha and *Rahasya Sandarbha* (Monthlies)

Today ideal places for the practice of science are research laboratories and institutions. But in the nineteenth century, educated people believed associations were capable of fulfilling this role because only in such associations was there adequate exchange of knowledge and experience.[49] The establishment of societies and the publication of journals as organs of these societies led to the foundation of such publications as *Vividhartha Samgraha* and *Rahasya Sandarbha. Vividhartha Samgraha* (October 1851) was published with the financial assistance of the 'Banga Bhasanubadok Samaj' or Vernacular Literature Committee, founded in December 1850 with the aim of publishing good books. Iswar Chandra Vidyasagar, Rajendralal Mitra, James Long and others were associated with it. *Vividhartha*, with beautiful line engraved pictures, was edited by Rajendralal Mitra.

The variety of subjects, styles of presentation and quality of illustrations contributed to the journal's ability to win over readers, a fact testified to none other than Rabindranath Tagore. He wrote in his autobiography that this journal had greatly influenced him in his childhood.[50]

Rajendralal Mitra edited this journal from 1851 to 1859. During that time many technological innovations were mentioned there (e.g. on electric telegraph, vol. 3, 1775–6, Saka, i.e. 1853). The publication of *Vividhartha* was, however, somewhat irregular. In 1861, with the seventh volume, Kaliprasanna Sinha became its editor. Two years later the journal stopped publication.

After *Vividhartha Samgraha* stopped circulation, under the initiative of Rajendralal a new journal named *Rahasya Sandarbha* was launched to fill the vacuum. The new journal was published with the financial assistance of the 'Calcutta School Book Society' and 'Vernacular Literature Society' in January 1863. The first editor was Rajendralal himself. *Rahasya Sandarbha* was as popular like its predecessor. Due to the illness of Rajendralal, Prannath Dutta became the editor and under his guidance the journal operated for another few years.

Education Gazette O Saptahik Bartabaha (Weekly)

The journal appeared on 4 July 1856 with the financial assistance of the Education Department and Reverend O'Brien Smith was the editor. All the responsibilities of editing was done by Rangolal Bandopadhyay.

About the beginning of the year under report, a newspaper in Bengali, called the *Education Gazette*, was established, under the editorial charge of the Reverend O'Brien Smith, under the auspices and patronage of this Department, assisted by a Government Grant of Rupees 200 a month. The object is to supply the people in the interior of the country with a newspaper cheap in price and healthy in tone.[51]

In March 1866 Pari Charan Sarkar, Assistant Professor of English Literature of Presidency College, became editor. But due to differences of opinion with the government, he left the job in July 1868. In the same year (December 1868) Bhudev Mukhopadhyay became the editor and the ownership of the journal was also handed over to him. Till 1885 he was associated with the journal. Many scholarly articles written by Bhudev were published in *Education Gazette*. After his death (1885), his son Kumardeb Mukhopadhyay was editor. As a journal sponsored by government, *Education Gazette* was the supporter of many government policies, including the Vernacular Press Act (1878).

Somprakash (Weekly)

Somprakash was first published on 15 November 1858 and from the beginning it was popular. Dwarakanath Vidyabhusan was the editor of the journal and Pundit Iswar Chandra Vidyasagar was closely associated with it. The contemporary journal *Hindu Patriot* was to say,

The *Shome Prokash* was first projected by Pundit Eswar Chunder Vidyasaghur, and we believe the first number was written by him. But he fell sick and made over the paper to Pundit Dwarkanauth, under whose able management the paper attained the foremost place among the Bengalee newspapers.[52]

Somprakash was the first to start political analysis among the Bengali journals. According to Bhudev Mukhopadhyay, Dwarakanath, the editor showed the way to run a Bengali journal with authority. His political and sociological analysis were an inspiration for other editors of contemporary Bengal.[53]

Grambarta Prakashika (Monthly)

Harinath Majumdar, headmaster of a Bengali Pathshala, started this journal in 1863 as a means of drawing attention to the miserable condition of the poor villagers. He was forced to stop several times due to scarcity of funds, but re-started on every occasion with great enthusiasm.[54]

Regarding social reform, Harinath followed the middle path. Although he was sympathetic about female education, he was not in favour of university education system for them. Confused about the liberty of women, at the same time Harinath supported widow-marriage. Throughout his life he wrote against the oppression by zamindars of the peasantry.

Bamabodhini Patrika (Monthly)

Bamabodhini appeared in August 1863 under the editorship of Umesh Chandra Dutta. It was an initiative by the Brahmo Samajis to elevate the position of women.[55] The degree of liberation was, of course, decided by the men! Now for the first time Bengali women started writing about their own problems. *Bamabodhini* supported female education, but regarding female liberation it showed a very conservative mentality. Some articles on the science of elementary nature were published here to make them aware about various scientific achievements of the day.

Here we should mention about the first Bengali journal for and by women was *Banga Mohila* (1870), Mokkhodayini Mukhopadhyay[56] was the editor. The journal survived for a year.

Amrita Bazar Patrika (Weekly)

The year 1868 is very important in the history of the Bengali press. On 20 January 1868, under the brilliant editorship of Sisir Kumar Ghosh, *Amrita Bazar Patrika* began publication. Poet Nabin Chandra Sen termed the journal and its editor pioneers of Indian nationalism.[57]

In the beginning *Amrita Bazar* was only published in Bengali, but from 1869 onwards in both Bengali and English. In 1871 Sisir

Kumar shifted the journal to Calcutta, earlier it was published from the ancestral village of the Ghosh family, Magura, in Jessore district.

How the government of the day viewed *Amrita Bazar* will become apparent from the following note which appeared in the Bengal Administration Report in 1872:

> The *Amrita Bazar Patrika* is believed by some to be more extensively read than others. The language of its articles is occasionally rough, but it has the merit of discussing social and agrarian subjects both from the tenant's as well as from the landlord's point of view.[58]

The journal came to be appreciated in England also. Towards the beginning of 1872, Babu Girija Sankar Sen, who was then in England, wrote to his father in Bengal, 'Please ask the proprietors of the *Amrita Bazar Patrika* to send their paper to the East Indian Association (London). Many people here may subscribe to the paper. I have seen many extracts from the *Amrita Bazar Patrika* in London papers.'[59]

After the Vernacular Press Act (14 March 1878), the *Amrita Bazar Patrika* was converted to the English language fully on 21 March 1878.

Sulav Samachar (Weekly)

Sulav Samachar was published by Kesab Chandra Sen's 'Bharat Sanskar Sabha' in 1870 (1 Agrahayan, 1277 B.S.). In its first issue the editor mentioned that the journal was not for the rich and affluent but the toiling masses.[60] The price was only 1 paisa. Its language too was simple. *Sulav Samachar* was published for nineteen years.

Bangadarshan (Monthly)

Bangadarshan was edited by Bankim Chandra Chattopadhyay and appeared in the literary arena of Bengal in 1872 (Baishak, 1279 B.S.). Major writers of Bengal occasionally wrote here. Bankim was the editor till 1882 and after him, Sreeschandra Majumdar.

Bharati, Balak and *Sadhana* (Monthlies)

These three journals were entirely run by the Tagore family. Each became popular under the editorship of Rabindranath. Not only was the major portion of these journals written by him, we can assume that the *Bharati, Balak* and *Sadhana* prepared the ground for young Rabi to become the *mohiruho* (a big tree) of the literary arena of Bengal.

Cultivation of knowledge, both indigenous and Western, in Bengali was the objective of *Bharati* (1877). Dwijendranath Tagore was the editor. After him, Swarnokumari Debi, Hiranmoyi Debi, Sarala Debi, Rabindranath served this journal.[61] Contemporary eminent litterateurs of Bengal wrote for this journal.

Balak was published in 1885 (Baishak, 1292 B.S.) under the editorship of Jnanadanandini Debi who was very much interested to publish a pictorial journal for young boys. She wanted Sudhindra, Balendra, and the younger Tagore family, to write for it. Rabindranath was involved with the journal as a writer and editor. After one year this journal merged with *Bharati*.[62]

Sadhana, one of the famous journals of the nineteenth century, was published in 1891 (Agrahayan, 1298 B.S.) and Sudhindranath Tagore who was then only twenty-two, was the first editor. After three years Rabindranath became the editor of *Sadhana*.[63]

Sahitya Parishad Patrika (Thrice in a Month)

This journal was the mouthpiece of the 'Bangiya Sahitya Parishad' (estd. 1894), previously the 'Bengal Academy of Literature'. Rajanikanta Gupta was the first editor of *Sahitya Parishad Patrika* (Shrabon, 1301 B.S.; 1894).[64]

TECHNICAL KNOWLEDGE IN COLONIAL CONTEXT

In any social and cultural setting the educational policy of a state, or of private institutions or individuals, has a number of different purposes. The expansion of British political power in India was accompanied by the control, transmission, production, and reproduction of knowledge.[65] In the imperial scheme, the production of knowledge is a function attributed to the metropolitan country ruling the Empire, while the reproduction of that knowledge, its transmission and replication, is the function assigned to the system of education of the colonized. The colonial system of education can be viewed as a means of the preservation and reproduction of colonial authority, not only cognitive but also political, among the 'natives'.[66]

The first technical college (Thomason College of Civil Engineering) in India was opened at Roorkee, in UP in 1847 when Britain itself did not have a tradition of providing institutional training to engineers.[67] In Bengal a survey department was started in 1841 and a post of Professor of Civil Engineering was created at the Hindu College in 1843–4. Professorship in experimental and natural philosophy had already been instituted there. Lord Dalhousie was keen that an engineering college should be set-up in Calcutta, as well as in Bombay and Madras. The College of Civil Engineering was started in 1856 at Calcutta, with its temporary location at the Presidency College. The Civil Engineering Section of the Presidency College maintained its separate identity until it merged with the College of Civil Engineering in 1861.[68]

In India, engineering education had definite objectives. While in France and Germany, its aim was to facilitate industrialization, in India it was intended to meet the needs and requirements of the colonial government.[69] In 1854–5 a Public Works Department (PWD) was established. With the expansion of its activities, the British required trained staff in subordinate ranks on a large scale. To employ British engineers for lower jobs were not economical. From the beginning, the PWD influenced the growth of engineering education in India in several ways. Most important among them were the courses which were structured to meet the immediate requirements of the department, rather than provide training for the higher ranks of the profession. For this reason civil engineering remained the favoured subject. Indeed, all the colleges opened during nineteenth century were called 'civil engineering colleges'.[70] The other branches of engineering (electrical, mechanical and mining) remained neglected until the 1930s.

Even in civil engineering there was little scope for Indian engineers to grow: the PWD showed a discriminatory policy of recruitment, recruited its senior engineers from Britain and restricted technical training in India to lower-level jobs. By the end of the nineteenth-century Indian intellectuals had developed a vigorous critique of the colonial discourse on science and technical education. Gradually they realized the vital link between science, technical education, and industrialization.

As mentioned above, the first engineering college was established in India in 1847, while the Imperial College, London was founded in 1879. By the turn of the century there were four colleges which were giving advanced engineering training in India: Thomason Engineering College at Roorkee, the Bengal Engineering College at Sibpur near Calcutta, the Engineering College at Madras and the College of Science in Poona.[71]

The expansion of colonial power and the production of scientific knowledge were related processes and in the process India served as the arena for the construction of a large-scale scientific research system. An important point that Zaheer Baber discusses in his book is the immanent connection between instruction on science and technology and the emergence of the colonial capitalist state.[72] This required that the colonial state be innovative in the founding of formal technical institutions. Until the end of the nineteenth century, England had no formal institutions imparting technical education, and engineers received their training as apprentices, so that the engineering colleges established in colonial India served as models for replication in England and the colonial encounter contributed to the development of technical education in Britain.[73] The development of technical knowledge in Bengal and its assimilation by the Bengali people in the nineteenth century is the central theme of the present research.

NOTES

1. Quoted in P.N. Bose and H.W.B. Moreno, *A Hundred Years of the Bengali Press: Being a History of the Bengali Newspapers From Their Inception to the Present Day*, Calcutta, 1920, p. 1.
2. Daniel R. Headrick, *The Tools of Empire: Technology and European Imperialism in the Nineteenth Century*, Oxford University Press, New York, 1981, p. 10.
3. Deepak Kumar, 'Investigating the Histories of Technology and Medicine in South Asia', *Proceedings of the Indian Association for Asian & Pacific Studies*, Kolkata, 2006, pp. 32–57.
4. Journal: a newspaper or magazine that deals with a particular subject or professional activity (p. 641), Newspaper: a printed publication appearing daily or weekly and containing news, advertisements and articles on various subjects (p. 783), Periodical: a magazine, etc., that is published at regular intervals (p. 861), *Oxford Advanced Learner's Dictionary*, Oxford, 1948. The Bengali journals appeared in nineteenth century, fulfilled all the characteristics of the above-mentioned 3 categories, so now onwards I'll mention all these as Bengali Journals.
5. Arabinda Poddar, *Renaissance in Bengal: Quests and Confrontations 1800–1860*, Indian Institute of Advanced Studies, Simla, 1970, p. 35.
6. See Deepak Kumar, *Science and the Raj: A Study of British India*, 2nd edn., Oxford University Press, New Delhi, 1995; Zaheer Baber, *Science of Empire: Scientific Knowledge, Civilization and Colonial Rule in India*, Oxford University Press, New Delhi, 1998; David Arnold, *The New Cambridge History of India: Science, Technology and Medicine in Colonial India*, Cambridge University Press, Cambridge, 2000; Gyan Prakash, *Another Reason, Science and the Imagination of Modern India*, Oxford University Press, New Delhi, 2000; Kapil Raj, *Relocating Modern Science: Circulation and the Construction of Scientific Knowledge in South Asia and Europe Seventeenth to Nineteenth Century*, Permanent Black, Delhi, 2006; Roy Macleod and Deepak Kumar (eds.), *Technology and the Raj: Western Technology and Technical Transfers to India 1700-1947*, Sage, New Delhi, 1995.
7. Swapan Basu (ed.), *Sambad Samayik-Patre Unis Sataker Bangali Samaj*, Paschimbanga Bangla Academy, Calcutta, 2000, p. 4.

8. Shibnath Shastri, *Ramtanu Lahiri O Tatkalin Banga Samaj*, 2nd edn., New Age Publishers, Calcutta, 1904, p. 39.
9. *Somprakash*, 13 April 1863.
10. Bajendranath Bandopadhyay, *Bangla Samayik Patra*, vols. I and II, Bangiya Sahitya Parishad, Calcutta, 1935 and 1951.
11. Swapan Basu (ed.), op. cit., p. 4.
12. Benjamin Zachariah, Subhas Ranjan Chakraborty and Rajat Kanta Ray, 'Presidency College, Calcutta: An Unfinished History', in Mushirul Hasan (ed.), *Knowledge, Power and Politics: Educational Institutions in India*, Lotus Collection, New Delhi, 1998, p. 307.
13. See *Catalogue of Bengali Books* published by Rev. James Long, Sanders, Cones & Co., Calcutta, 1855: Buddhadev Bhattacharya, *Banga Sahitye Vijnan*, Paschimbanga Bangla Academy, Calcutta, 1960; Durgaprasad Bhattacharya, 'A Preliminary Note on Survey of Books on Science and Technology in Major Indian Languages in the Last Quarter of the 19th Century'. Paper presented at seminar on *Science and Empire*, NISTAD, New Delhi, January, 1985; Sharadindu Sekhar Roy (ed.), *Bangla Bhasay Vijnan Charcha 1818–1860*, Asiatic Society, Kolkata, 2007.
14. Jadunath Gangopadhyay, 'Banglar Chikitsak Samaj', *Chikitsa Sammilani*, Calcutta, April–June 1889.
15. Pradip Kumar Bose (ed.), *Health and Society in Bengal: A Selection from the Late 19th Century Bengali Periodicals*, Sage, New Delhi, 2006, p. 9.
16. Kedarnath Majumdar, *Bangla Samayik Sahitya*, Mymensingh, 1917.
17. P.N. Bose and H.W.B. Moreno, *A Hundred Years*, p. 2.
18. Baridbaran Ghosh, 'Bangla Sambad-Samayikpatra Charcha Prasange'; Swapan Basu and Muntasir Mamun (eds.), *Dui Sataker Bangla Sambad Samayikpatra*, Pustak Biponi, Kolkata, 2005, p. 506.
19. The Bengali calendar was introduced in Akbar's reign to facilitate revenue collection. The Bengali year is called Bangla (Fasli) San (B.S.). By adding 593 to the Bengali year one gets the corresponding Christian year.
20. Baridbaran Ghosh, op. cit., pp. 506-7.
21. Bajendranath Bandopadhyay, 'Introduction', *Sambadpatre Sekaler Katha*, vol. I, Bangiya Sahitya Parishad, Calcutta, 1932, p. 1.

22. Baridbaran Ghosh, op. cit., p. 512.
23. Binay Ghose, *Samayikpatre Banglar Samajchitra 1840–1905* (in Bengali), 5 vols., Bengal Publishers Pvt. Ltd., Calcutta, 1962–8.
24. Partha Chattopadhyay, *Bangla Sambadpatra O Bangalir Nabajagoran*, Dey's Publications, Calcutta, 1977.
25. Swapan Basu (ed.), *Sambad Samayikpatre Unis Sataker Bengali Samaj*, 2 vols., Paschimbanga Bangla Academy, Calcutta, 2000, 2003.
26. Sidney Kobre, *Development of American Journalism*; quoted in Partha Chattopadhyay, op. cit., p. 9.
27. Partha Chattopadhyay, op. cit., p. 13.
28. T.W. Clark, 'Encounter and Growth in Bengali Culture', E.C. Dimock (ed.), *Bengal Literature and History*, Michigan University Press, Ann Arbor, 1967, p. 90.
29. B.B. Misra, *The Indian Middle Class: Their Growth in Modern Times*, Oxford University Press, London, 1961, p. 316.
30. B.B. Majumdar, *History of Indian Social and Political Ideas*, Firma KLM, Calcutta, 1967, pp. 84, 88–9.
31. T.W. Clark, op. cit., p. 91.
32. Deepak Kumar, 'The "Culture" of Science and Colonial Culture, India 1820–1920', *The British Journal for the History of Science*, vol. 29, no. 2, June 1996, pp. 195–209.
33. P.N. Bose and H.W.B. Moreno, op. cit., p. 6. See also, Bajendranath Bandopadhyay, 'Introduction', *Sambadpatre Sekaler Katha*, vol. I, p. 3. Shibnath Shastri, op. cit., p. 106.
34. Quoted in Bajendranath Bandopadhyay, *Bangla Samayik Patra*, vol. I, p. 4.
35. *Friend of India*, 15 May 1851.
36. *Sambad Prabhakar*, 12 April 1853; 'Samachar Darpan Patra Sree Rampure Gangar Jale Pran Tyag Kare'.
37. Durgaprasad Bhattacharya, Ranjit Chakravarty and Rama Deb Roy, 'A Survey of Bengali Writings on Science and Technology 1800-1950', *Indian Journal of History of Science*, vol. 24(1), 1989, pp. 8–66.
38. See Bajendranath Bandopadhyay, *Bangla Samayik Patra*, vol. I, p. 21.
39. Jogendramohon Thakur was the elder son of Nandakumar Thakur, third son of Gopimohon Thakur, of Pathurighata. See Binay Ghose, *Samayik Patre Banglar Samaj Chitra*, vol. I, p. 1.

40. Swapan Basu, op. cit., p. 8.
41. Quoted in Bajendranath Bandopadhyay, *Bangla Samayik Patra*, vol. I, p. 51.
42. Quoted in *Samachar Darpan*, 23 March 1839.
43. Satish Chandra Chakroborty (ed.), *Maharshi Debendranath Thakurer Attma-Jeeboni*, quoted in Partha Chattopadhyay, op. cit., p. 55.
44. Ibid., p. 56.
45. Shibnath Shastri, op. cit., p. 131.
46. Bajendranath Bandopadhyay, *Bangla Samayik Patra*, vol. I, p. 84.
47. Partha Chattopadhyay, op. cit., p. 59.
48. 'Early Bengali Literature and Newspapers', *Calcutta Review*, January–June 1850.
49. Pradip Kumar Bose, op. cit., p. 14.
50. Rabindranath Tagore, *Jibansmriti*, Calcutta, 1912, p. 72.
51. *Report of the Director of Public Instruction for the Year 1856–57*; quoted in Bajendranath Bandopadhyay, *Bangla Samayik Patra*, vol. I, p. 142.
52. *Hindu Patriot*, 9 January 1865.
53. *Education Gazette*, 3 September 1886.
54. Bipasha Raha, 'Kangal Harinath' (in Bengali), in Debabrata Chattopadhyay (ed.), *Parikatha*, 10/2, May 2008, pp. 404–19.
55. Anindita Bandopadhyay, 'Meyeder Patrikar Jagot', Swapan Basu and Muntasir Mamun (eds.), op. cit., pp. 267–9.
56. According to Bajendranath, Mokkhodayini was the sister of W.C. Bonnerjee. Bajendranath Bandopadhyay, *Bangla Samayik Patra 1868–1900*, vol. II, Bangiya Sahitya Parishad, Calcutta, 1951, p. 3.
57. Bajendranath Bandopadhyay, *Bangla Samayik Patra*, vol. I, p. 213.
58. Paramananda Dutt, *Memoirs of Moti Lal Ghose*, Amrita Bazar Patrika, Calcutta, 1935, p. 29.
59. Ibid., p. 30.
60. Bajendranath Bandopadhyay, *Bangla Samayik Patra*, vol. II, pp. 4, 5.
61. Ibid., p. 23.
62. Ibid., p. 45.
63. Ibid., p. 62.

64. Ibid., pp. 65 and 67.
65. Nigel Crook, 'The Control and Expansion of Knowledge: An Introduction', in Nigel Crook (ed.), *The Transmission of Knowledge in South Asia*, Oxford University Press, New Delhi, 1996, pp. 1–26.
66. Sabyasachi Bhattacharya, 'The Contested Terrain of Education', in Sabyasachi Bhattacharya (ed.), *The Contested Terrain: Perspectives on Education in India*, Orient Longman, New Delhi, 1998, p. 7.
67. G.W. Roderick and M.D. Stephens, *Scientific and Technical Education in 19th Century England*, David and Watts, London, 1972, p. 18.
68. S.P. Gupta, *Modern India and Progress in Science and Technology*, Vikas, New Delhi, 1979, p. 122.
69. Arun Kumar, 'Colonial Requirements and Engineering Education: The Public Works Department, 1847-1947', in Roy Macleod and Deepak Kumar (eds.), *Technology and the Raj: Western Technology and Technical Transfer to India 1700-1947*, Sage, New Delhi, 1995, p. 216.
70. *Quinquennial Review on the Progress of Education in India*, Government Press, Calcutta, 1904, *QR India, 1897–1902*, vol. I, pp. 248–9.
71. S. Ambirajan, 'Science and Technology Education in South India', in Roy Macleod and Deepak Kumar (eds.), op. cit., p. 113.
72. Zaheer Baber, *The Science of Empire*, pp. 205–12.
73. Russel Dionne and Roy Macleod, 'Science and Policy in British India, 1858–1914: Perspectives on a Persisting Belief', *Proceedings of the Sixth European Conference on Modern South Asian Studies*, CNRS, Paris, 1979, pp. 55–68.

CHAPTER 2

Technology as Power Spectacle

> The Railway, the Electric Telegraph, the new and improved organization of large and important departments, these are but the more salient points of a domestic administration of which it is not too much to say, and History will say, that its almost every step has been either an improvement or a preparation for an improvement.
>
> Farewell address of Sir Frederick J. Halliday, Lt.-Governor of Bengal, to Dalhousie[1]

Max Weber defined power as the legitimate exercise of violence. While military or state-sponsored engineering has served power by providing the tools of violence, power, as Weber wisely suggested, also rests on legitimacy. Power may be equated with the capacity to impose one's will, but effective power, like legitimate violence, requires more. It has historically required displays of material intelligence and stewardship over nature in order to superimpose a right to rule on a capacity to rule well.[2] Technology is one of the major means of showing power; it helps to establish domination in a legitimate way.

Concerned with the problems of power and legitimation, Michel Foucault visualized the concept of power from an unusual angle: as systems of thought which control what is socially legitimated and institutional. Foucault argues that knowledge is always located in relation to its uses, in relation therefore to form a power, as power cannot be exercised without the extraction, appropriation, distribution, or retention of knowledge. According to him, power and knowledge directly imply each other.[3] There was a close connection between commercial interests, technological change, and government policy in India from the early years of British rule. Technology, whether as tools or as forms of knowledge, is not value-free. It manifests socio-political qualities and drives the economy. In colonial conditions it acquired the contours of the colonial power, both commercial and administrative.[4]

Along with technology, law and the legal apparatus, *adalat* (courts), *thana* (police stations), and *jelkhana* (prisons) were also used to legitimize the coercive apparatus of the state.[5] Foucault argues that our societies are maintained not only by the army, police or centralized visible state apparatus, but precisely by those techniques of dressage, discipline and diffused power at work in various institutions.[6] While the legal apparatus was very useful to order the native society, but the impact of Western technologies in a colonial set-up were massive and thorough.

Among the many events of the nineteenth century, two were of momentous consequence for the entire world. One was the progress and power of steam and industrial technologies; the other was the domination and exploitation of Africa and much of Asia by Europeans. Historians have analysed these phenomena separately. The connections between technology and European imperialism must, however, be approached concurrently.[7]

There have been two distinct periods when imperialism has been dominant in the modern world: the first occurred during the sixteenth and seventeenth centuries, and the second during the late nineteenth century. The earlier imperialism was motivated mainly by dynastic ambitions, religious zeal, and the desire for land and wealth.[8] The new imperialism of the nineteenth century was armed with a technological capacity to deploy forces quickly by land and sea. The new ability of Europeans in the nineteenth century to conquer other continents stemmed from a relatively few inventions. The first was the application of steam and iron to riverboats, starting in the 1820s. By the 1860s iron-hulled steamships appeared regularly in Asian and African waters. Constant improvement in firearms, from muskets to machine guns, gave small European-led units an overwhelming advantage over their African and Asian enemies.

Quinine prophylaxis reduced the death rate among Europeans in the tropics. Steamships, railways, and telegraphs allowed Europeans to control their newly-acquired colonies efficiently.[9]

The effects of these technologies were experienced almost everywhere in the nineteenth century, but particularly in India and Africa rather than Persia or China, over which European influence was exercised only indirectly.

TECHNOLOGY AND HISTORY: A BRIEF OUTLINE

Technology has been a fact of human life as long has there has been human lives. From the time that human beings emerged as a separate species on this earth, they have tried to control, manipulate, exploit, and sometimes even subdue the earth with tools. In all times and all places, human beings have attempted in some fashion to use tools to control their natural environment. This is as true of the human beings who first learned how to rub two stones together to make a spark as it is of those who subsequently created the atomic bomb.

Tools are used to produce things, but both things produced and the things used to do so are included in the term technology. Domesticated animals and plants are technologies that people created in order to secure food supplies; medications are technologies that people created in order to improve their health. Even languages are technologies: they are things that people have created so as to better control and manipulate the social environment.[10]

Technological systems are arrays of technologies. Once primitive human beings had passed beyond the use of digging sticks they had passed out of the realm of technology into the realm of technological systems. A single tool, even the most primitive of them, is usually not sufficient to get a job done. A hammer, for example, must be applied to something, which is itself a tool, in order to function as a hammer; even the original digging stick may have needed to be sharpened with a stone. All technological systems, of necessity, have people embedded in them. A hammer is not really a hammer until someone picks it up and uses it. Technological systems can, and sometimes do, become quite large and complex: the paradigm would be a personal computer which requires an entire electrical network plus software, diskettes, printers and modems—as well as programmers, trainers and manufacturers—in order to function properly.

The Greek root of technology, *techne*, means belonging to the arts, crafts or skills, and is also related to tactics. Therefore, to the ancients, technology was more than 'gadgets', it was also to do with skills, know-how, and the art of doing things.[11] Max Weber used the German word *technik*, which he used to mean both technology (machines and tools) and technique.[12] He saw technology as including both physical products and ideas (or intellectual devices). This view of technology is well summarized by Jacques Ellul,[13] who used the French word *technique* in the same way as Weber used *technik*. Thus the technical or technological elements of the production process are a diverse set of variables and can include cultural and intellectual elements.[14]

Technology was earlier defined as technical artefact and science as knowledge. Here the question arises, is technology another science? Probably the answer is 'No'. Both were historical variables.[15] Science in part is knowledge about technology and technology can be embodied knowledge. They are two sides of the same coin, enmeshed in a 'symbiotic relationship'.[16] Techno-scientific developments can be seen as a non-determined, multidirectional flux that involves constant negotiation and renegotiation among the groups and between the forces shaping history.[17] George Basalla thinks technology is erroneously defined as the application of scientific theory to the solution of practical problems. He agrees that science and technology have interacted at many points, and key modern artefacts could not have been produced without the theoretical understanding of natural materials and forces provided by science. 'Nevertheless, technology is not the servant of science', emphasizes Basalla.[18]

The historians of technology rejected the notion that science is the context of technology, or that technology is simply applied science. This then raised the question whether the relationship between technology and other so-called contextual factors, such as the political and the social, should be redefined as interactive. The same question was asked about science and its context. A way out of the constraints of contextualism and into an interactive mode is now posed by the use of the 'system' or 'networks' approach. Heterogeneous professionals, such as engineers, scientists and managers and heterogeneous organizations, such as manufacturing firms, utilities and banks become interacting entities within systems or networks. Disciplines, persons and organizations in systems and networks take on one another's functions as if they are part of a seamless web.[19] Technology forms part of a seamless web of society, politics and economics. Thus the development of a technological artefact is not merely a technical achievement; embedded within it are social, political, and economic considerations.[20]

The history of technology is an effort to recount the history of all those things, those artefacts that we have produced over the years. The social history of technology goes one step further, integrating the history of technology with the rest of human history. It assumes that objects have affected the ways people work, govern, cook, transport, and communicate: the ways in which they live. It also assumes that the ways in which people live have affected the objects that they invent, manufacture, and use. A social history of technology, in short, assumes a mutual relationship between society and technology; it also assumes that changes in one can, and have, induced changes in the other.[21]

The origins of the history of technology as a discipline can be found in the *Annales d'historie economique et sociale*, established in 1929 by Marc Bloch and Lucien Febvre. In November 1935, seven years after founding their journal, Bloch and Febvre published a special issue titled, *Les techniques, l'histoire et la vie*, a collection of empirically based articles, criticism and prescriptive and programmatic statements.[22] It is a landmark in the historiography of technology. It is important for the discipline of history of technology that the journal emerged as part of the broader Annales programme that aimed to expand the scope of historical studies and placed techniques within the same broad framework. For Bloch and Febvre, the history of techniques was intrinsic to history itself, and they provided a rich model for an expansive discipline.

As a discipline, the History of Technology, was further institutionalized with the foundation of the Society for the History of Technology (SHOT) and the creation of the journal, *Technology and Culture* in 1958. But with the exception of Daniel Headrick,[23] SHOT insiders have paid little attention to non-Western technology or to non-Western ideological perspectives on technology transfer.[24] From the last decade of the twentieth century alone have scholars over the globe paid special attention to the place and role of techno-scientific changes and developments in the colonial process in South Asia, with good emphasis on British India. Because the nineteenth century was an age of innovative steam technologies, developed first in Europe, then diffused to other regions of the globe and in an era characterized in terms of 'a massive transfer of technology from the West to Africa and Asia', and with colonialism as a conduit, India has often been taken to exemplify the momentous scale and impact of this process.[25]

According to Melvin Kranzberg, all history is relevant, but the history of technology is the most relevant.[26] As we live in a 'global village', made so by technological developments, we are conscious of the need to transfer technological expertise from the rich to the less developed nations. And here the history of technology has a great deal to say about the conditions, complexities and problems of technology transfer.

Although the transfer of technology argument duly highlights the importance of exogenous innovation and the role of technology as a 'tool of empire',[27] it can easily become an excessively one-dimensional idea, stressing the dynamism of the West but ignoring the context in which new technologies were employed. Technologies are seldom discrete bodies of knowledge, transferable wholesale, without emendation, from one society to another. Technological transfers are more likely to take the form of a 'dialogue' rather than a simple process of diffusion or imposition,[28] and this was especially the case in India, which had a wide range of existing technologies and a physical and social environment far removed from that of Europe. It needs to be recognized that under colonialism the dissemination of new technologies was constrained and conditioned by the partisan nature of political and economic control.[29] Colonial rule interrupted the 'inventive exchanges' India formally had with its Asian and Indian Ocean neighbours and created instead a near-monopoly of technological dialogue with and through the West, primarily Britain. State power was used to promote technologies that served the regime's military, economic, and ideological needs while restricting Indian access to technologies that might harm metropolitan interests. The social, political and cultural impact of technological change remained a continuing source of debate and raised several questions about the meaning and value of India's modernity.

MODERN TECHNOLOGY IN THE NINETEENTH-CENTURY BENGALI IMAGINATION

> A particular period is generally known for few special incidents. We have enough example from history that incidents like the conquest of Alexander, valour of Napoleon, invention of Newton, Luther's religious reform, religion spread by Buddha, invention of printing press, etc., made famous of that particular period of time. If anybody asks what the significance of nineteenth century is, our answer would be the development of science and technology. Like any other incidents, the sphere of influence of these two is not limited to any particular place, group, or time. The modern science first emerged in Europe and America. Now the blessings of science and technology are spreading all around the globe. The development of science and technology is definitely a major aspect of the modern world.
>
> *Arya Darshan*, Kartik 1282 (1875)[30]

The British colonization of India unleashed many forces that altered the course of Indian history. Besides the much studied politico-commercial and socio-cultural aspects of British rule, the introduction of science and technology was an important development that influenced Indian life in several ways. The early phase of British colonialism represented a period when, despite clearly defined interests and motives for specific projects, there was no explicitly formulated 'science and technology policy' and there was constant experimentation, trial and error.[31] By the mid-nineteenth century, partly as a consequence of the rapid growth of science and technology in Europe in the aftermath of the Industrial Revolution, British India proved to be a good testing ground for a number of experiments in the application of science and technology by the colonial state. What followed in nineteenth-century India was state-sponsored scientific research and development activity. As one scholar has put it, British India constituted a social laboratory or testing ground for a number of policies that could be transferred to Britain.[32]

Forging India into a productive, interlocking network of irrigational works, railways, telegraphs, mines and manufacturing, the colonial state introduced and oversaw the establishment of modern technologies. In an important sense, however, technology was not only the instrument but also the substance of state power. Increasingly, state power meant the growing technological configuration of the territory. Technology forged a link between space and state, making the newly configured India part and parcel of the institution of its technological configuration.[33]

Another important point is that colonized people were not mere objects at the hands of the colonizers. The invasion of their countries by a technologically advanced culture awakened not only the well-known movements for national independence, but also a desire to share in the benefits of Western technology.[34] The Western invasion created new desires among tropical consumers. Railways and telegraphs built by the Europeans for their own benefit were soon flooded with Indian customers. Along with the demand for devices has arisen a parallel demand for knowledge. Thus, Western technology flowed to India, first pushed by the Europeans and later pulled by the awakening demands of the Indian people.

Among the new technologies of the nineteenth century which made waves in colonial Bengal were the printing press, the steam-ship, vaccination and inoculation, the telegraph, the railway and in the last decade of this century, electrification. Possession of 'lightning strings' and 'fire-carriages' (the telegraph) inflated the self-image of the Raj to the point of invincibility, while the fire-breathing 'iron cow' (railway) became the life-line of the Empire.[35] As mentioned in the previous chapter, one of the primary means of reformulation and dissemination of Western scientific and technological knowledge in Bengali were the vernacular journals. So to explore the modern technologies which captured the imagination of the reading public of nineteenth-century Bengal, a close look at this corpus is desirable.

The introduction of steam vessel, stream railways, electric telegraph, printing technologies and a host of other inventions began to arrest the attention of the indigenous population. The continued display of new and improved technology by the British, aimed at the consolidation of their power in India and to increase the productive resources, also evoked a considerable amount of interest among Indians. The journal *Samachar Darpan*, tried to explore the various technological aspects of the steam engine:

> The Steam Engine is applied to an infinity of purposes. It is used for pumping up water, for working corn mills, oil mills, and the like, for expressing the juice of sugar canes, for spinning thread, for printing newspaper, for sawing timber, for impelling boats and ships on water, and carriages on land, and for innumerable other works. The steam engine, however, does not perform all these operations of itself. For them all, it serves merely the same purpose as a bullock in a Bengali oil mill; that is, it sets the machinery in motion which is to do the work. The same work which it does, might be done by water wheels, or wind mills, or by the strength of oxen, or horses, or men. But it is the cheapest, the most powerful, and the most convenient of all moving powers.
>
> There are several kinds of steam engines; but we shall content ourselves with describing that which is most commonly used, and is

called 'Watt's Double Acting Steam Engine'. Even in describing this it will not so much be our object to explain every minute part of its structure, as to make plain to our readers, how the steam is applied in it for the production of motion.

The essential parts of the steam engine are the boiler, the cylinder and the beam. In the boiler, the steam is produced; in the cylinder it exerts its force; and that force is communicated by the beam, to whatever machinery is to be moved by it. . . .[36]

India was conquered by a chartered commercial monopoly and not by the Crown of England; but political power was the prerequisite for trade and commerce. To consolidate its increasing territorial conquests and its commercial hegemony, the East India Company needed an efficient system of transport and communication. Steamboats and locomotives were introduced and the electric telegraph was brought to India as soon as their value had been demonstrated in England.[37] These not only denuded India economically by opening up the country but also strengthened military subjugation. These were all later utilized for purposes beyond the original intention for facilitating, establishing or speeding up communication, both for material (coal and cotton) and information, communication for the sake of trade, or mobilization of the army.[38] A close look of these innovations along with printing press, vaccination inoculation, and electrification would provide a better understanding.

The Printing Press

The history of the introduction of printing in India dates to the middle of the sixteenth century. India's first printing press appeared in Goa in the year 1556 almost 100 years after the historic printing by Gutenberg of the holy Bible. Along with the press arrived Joao de Bustamante, renamed Joao Rodrigues, a Spaniard trained in the art of printing, who thus holds the distinction of being the first printer in India.[39] The first Indian effort to set-up a press was that of Bhimjee Parekh of Bombay. In 1670 he approached the East India Company to send from England a printing press along with an expert printer. His intention was to publish Sanskrit books. But in the absence of a suitable type cutter, his efforts did not materialize.[40]

It was, however, not before the fourth quarter of the eighteenth century that the printing press made any headway in India. The impetus came primarily from two sources, first, the necessity to propagate the Bengali language among the civil servants under the East India Company in Bengal (and other Indian languages in other presidencies), and second, the advent of journals. The printing of books in Bengali type was pioneered by two civil servants, Nathaniel Brassey Halhed and Charles Wilkins. Halhed prepared a Grammar of the Bengali Language and Wilkins cast the Bengali movable types for the printing of the book at Hooghly.[41] Panchanana Karmakar, an Indian blacksmith, learnt from Wilkins the art of type-casting and played an important part in the history of early printing in Bengal.

The establishment of a press by the Serampore Mission constituted another landmark in the history of press in Bengal. William Carey of the Baptist Mission prepared a Bengali translation of the New Testament. Due to very high cost of printing, he decided to buy a press and was able to purchase one offered for sale in Calcutta, at a sum of Rs.400.[42] He was also able to procure the services of Panchanana Karmakar for his press. While Panchanana was working in Calcutta, Carey noticed his genius in the art of Bengali type-casting. In a letter written on 1 April 1799, Carey mentioned Panchanana. 'We have a press and I have succeeded in procuring a sum of money sufficient to get types cast. I have found a man who can cast them and the person who casts for the Company's press; I have engaged a printer in Calcutta to superintend the castion.'[43]

Thus equipped, Carey and his associates published between 1801 and 1805 many Bengali books, prominent among them were the Bengali Bible, *Dharma Pustaka*, Ram Ram Basu's *Raja Pratapaditya Charita*, Kashi Ram Das's *Mahabharata*, etc. After the death of Panchanana (1804), his son-in-law Manohar Karmakar[44] accompanied Carey in his project. Manohar joined the printing press of Serampore when Panchanana was alive. He was associated with the

Serampore press till his death in 1853. Manohar was the real flag-bearer of his teacher and father-in-law, Panchanana. He created type-casting at least in 15 different languages. Apart from that, Manohar established his own press, 'Chandradaya' at Serampore in 1837. His son Krishna Chandra took over charge of the press after Manohar's death. Following the printing machine of Serampore, Krishna Chandra built the first iron-made printing machine of 'Chandradaya'. The journal *Friend of India* mentioned Krishna Chandra and his printing machine in 1846: 'The most popular Almanack is that published in this town by our spirited punch cutter, who has cut his own punches, cast his own types, manufactured his own iron press, and engraved with his own hand the veritable effigies of the gods and goddesses which adorn his work.'[45]

Later on the Serampore Missionaries extended their labour in the field of journal literature and brought into existence *Friend of India* (1817), *Dig-Durshun* (1818) and the *Samachar Darpan* (1818). In the diffusion of scientific knowledge, the *Dig-Durshun* played an important role in Bengal. The journal reported in August, 1818:

> Of the origin of printing–If the printing machine was not discovered, the dawn of the new knowledge which emerged in Europe, then would definitely disappear. By the invention of printing press, the work of the European scholars become permanent, the price of the books become less, the lay-persons now can use these to upgrade them. The cultivation of knowledge is largely benefitted by the printing press. With the blessing of this, human civilization attains a distinct place.
>
> Among the various inventions of human being, the printing press deserves an important place. Several European countries very much benefitted by it, they accumulated higher degree of knowledge than others. The Asian and African countries are submerged in deep ignorance so far. Among the various steps taken for the betterment of these people, the introduction of printing press is one of the needed one. In short, we can say the benefits of the printing press are countless and the knowledge acquired by the European nations in various fields was not possible with out the printing technology. (*Dig-Durshun*, no. V, August 1818)[46]

The Story of Goluk Chunder

Goluk Chunder, a Bengali blacksmith of Titagar, can be acclaimed the first engineer if we abide by the original significance of the word 'engineer'. Engineer was a post-James Watt connotation and literally meant one who builds or erects steam engines. Goluk Chunder did build a steam engine in 1828.[47]

The first self-contained industrial complex of Bengal, set-up in Serampore by the famous trio of Carey, Marshman and Ward, included a foundry for type making, printing presses and even a paper manufactory. In Serampore paper making began in the first decade of the nineteenth century, but the real breakthrough came in 1820 with the introduction of steam power.[48] The 12 horse-power steam engine of Thwaites Hick and Rothwells imported from England was an object of wonder. As *Calcutta Gazette* reported on 27 May 1824:

> Even the Steam Engine although it has been in operation for four years does not cease to draw crowds of natives to inspect it from week to week, who, passing on the river from various parts of the country, leave their boats, quietly inspect it at leisure, and departed convinced that all knowledge was not engrossed by their fore-fathers, to whose ideas they have hitherto so tenaciously adhered.[49]

George Smith, the biographer of William Carey observed: 'The machine of fire as they called it, brought crowds of natives to the mission, whose curiosity fired the patience of the engineman imported to work it, while many a European who never had seen machinery driven by steam came to study and copy it.'[50] It was no European but Goluk Chunder who ultimately produced a prototype.

The steam engine made by Goluk Chunder was put on display during the Annual Exhibition of the Agri-Horticultural Society at the Town Hall of Calcutta in January 1828. The *Calcutta Gazette* reported on 17 January:

> A curious model of a Steam Engine, made by Goluk Chunder, Black-smith of Tittaghur, near Barrackpur, without any assistance from

European artists, was likewise exhibited; and although not coming within the immediate sphere of the society's exertions was considered so striking an instance of native ingenuity and imitative skill as to deserve encouragement. A donation of fifty rupees was, therefore, presented to the ingenious Blacksmith.[51]

George Smith wrote about the incident:

Resolved at the suggestion of the Rev. Dr. Carey, the permission be given to Goluk Chunder . . . to exhibit a steam engine made by himself without the aid of any European artist . . . the steam engine was useful for irrigation of lands made upon the model of a large steam engine belonging to the missionaries at Serampore.[52]

Nothing more about the life and achievements of Goluk Chunder is known. There is hardly any reason to believe that further research may unearth more. The Serampore paper mill which up to 1865 competed with English paper in Asian market as the only centre for mechanized paper-making in India, was 'gradually crushed by the expensive and unsatisfactory contracts made at home by India Office'.[53]

In the *Education Gazette O Saptahik Bartabaho* there appeared, on 26 February 1858, a report:

Before the introduction of printing press, knowledge about science, craft was largely confined into a particular class. Those who were not belonging to that particular section remained outside of the arena of scholarly activities. By the introduction of printing technology in Europe, knowledge about religion, politics, science, etc., are very much within the reach of the common people. The curse of superstition, the darkness of ignorance is removed largely by the blessings of printing press. Now in Europe, those who do not have sufficient wealth, but are extremely intelligent, can hold any prestigious position in the society. Education is within the reach of the poor by the invention of printing. During the past hundred years those who excelled in various branches of knowledge in England, came from very poor family background. People like globe trotter James Cook, inventor of steam engine James Watt, renowned chemist Humphrey Davy all were the product of self-education and a strong desire for success. These were possible due to the invention of printing machine.[54]

Steam Navigation

Discoveries and inventions remain simple curiosities until society is ready to benefit from them. The synthesis of steam engines and paddles wheels producing steam boats came as a conscious application of technology to the aid of capitalistic production.[55] On 17 August 1807, Robert Fulton's steam boat first ran on the Hudson River. Political favour, financial credit and technical skill fetched him commercial success and he is now generally referred to as the 'inventor' of steam-boats. Fulton who may well have been the first to think of introducing steam-boats in India,[56] but he did not live to see his vision come true.

Ghazi-ud-din Haidar, the Nawab of Oudh (1814–27), was the first to possess and launch a steam-boat in India on the river Gomati near Lucknow in 1819. Being fond of mechanical inventions, he asked Henry Jessop, the founder of Jessop & Co., to build a steam-boat for him. The plans of the boat and a single cylinder 8-horse power steam engine were imported from England. The boat was build by William Trickett who accompanied Jessop at Lucknow in the building of an iron bridge. The first steam-boat of India served only as a toy in the hands of its whimsical pleasure-seeking owner.[57]

The first article on steam navigation appeared in the pages of *Dig-Durshun* a year before the launch of the first steam-boat by the Nawab of Oudh. The journal observed:

> The power of steam is successfully used by the Europeans to perform various activities. Steam engine is a complex machine, but many problems can be solved easily by it. Few years ago a man in America realized to row a boat without oars, steam engine was the remedy. So he worked accordingly and made a boat without oars fitting a steam engine at the middle of the boat. He placed two wheels at both sides of the boat and connected these two with the machine. Now the man set oars with the wheels and started the engine. With the force generated by the steam, the wheels along with the oars became movable and so also the boat. Now steam-boats are very famous in Europe and America. A few boats are very big in size that at least two hundred people can easily board on these. The mileage of steam-

boats is six miles per hour against the tide and wind. The journey on such boats is very comfortable.[58]

In 1817, Captain Davidson of the Bengal Engineers brought to Calcutta an engine of 8-horse power 'to remove silted earth from the bed of the Hooghly River'.[59] But his plan did not work out and the engine was disposed in a Calcutta godown until the Company purchased it in 1822. The *Pluto*, the name it afterwards bore, was furnished with a double set of buckets to dredge on both sides.

The first steam boat to navigate the Hooghly was launched by Messrs. Kyd & Co. from the Kidderpore dockyard in 1823. Her name was given to correspond with a figurehead of the goddess Diana, which accompanied the English frame. *Diana* was a steam paddle boat with sails. The engine and frame of this vessel were first carried to China by one Mr. Roberts but later transmitted to Calcutta, where they were purchased by the agency houses.[60] She worked as a 'passage boat' on the Hooghly for one year, surprising the curious villagers with her smoke and speed.[61] In April 1824, soon after the commencement of the Burmese War, *Diana* was sold to the government.

In 1825, a small steam-assisted paddle-steamer, the *Enterprise* arrived in Calcutta, 113 days after leaving England. It had sailed from Falmouth under James Henry Johnston, opening a steam communication route between India and England via the Cape.[62] While from a commercial point of view the *Enterprise* expedition did not receive much applause, she certainly took permanent place in the history of steam navigation in India as the first steamship from England.

As *Samachar Darpan* reported on 10 December 1825,

> We are happy to announce that yesterday the first steam-ship arrived at Kolkata from England. It took three months and twenty-two days to complete its voyage. As it is the first journey of such kind, so the extra time taken by the vessel to finish the route, is understandable.[63]

In December 1824 the British East India Company and the kingdom of Burma were at war. All the three steamers, the *Pluto*, *Diana*, and *Enterprise*, had disappointed the owners and the government alike, but the outbreak of the war decided the fate of the steam vessels. Burma was separated from Bengal by almost impassable mountains. So the war was carried on chiefly along the banks of the Irrawaddy River. All three steamers were employed to move British troops across. These steam vessels played a decisive role, especially the *Diana*.[64] In the capture of Rangoon on 11 May 1824, *Diana* played an instrumental role as a rocket firing vessel.[65] This little vessel was the first case of the use of a steam vessel as part of a fighting force.[66] Till the last days of the war, *Diana* rendered great service in various actions, towing men-of-war-boats to the attack and assisting light vessels to take their stations when bombarding enemy stockades.

Samachar Darpan reported on 2 April 1831:

> The steam vessel, *Diana* has arrived here last week. She is the first steam vessel that arrived in Indian water. She was built before the Burmese war. Later on *Diana* was bought by the government. She gave an excellent service in the Burmese war. Being the first steam vessel used in a war, *Diana* is very popular among the people.[67]

An interesting episode concerning the awe created by *Diana* is found in a letter written by William Ash, chief engineer of the *Enterprise*, to Henry Maudslay, the famous engineer who had built the engine of *Enterprise*. Ash wrote:

> She being generally the first vessel to open the fire as they made as a rocket vessel of her firing from the bow of her. . . . The Burmese have a large bell in their empire they prophesied some years ago that their country would never be conquered till the bell was taken from and a vessel to go up the river without oars or sails which is very large and has been done by the Diana and is called by them the *Mertembo*, the fire devil. . . .[68]

Thus the services of the steam vessels in the Burmese war removed all apprehensions about the practicability of steam-boats. The Company no longer regarded steamers as just yet another type of vessel, but an entirely new technology destined to enhance their power.

The famous journal of the day, *Samachar Darpan*, mentioned on 16 May 1832, that:

> The Captain of the Enterprise, the first steamship which came to India from England, Mr. Johnston planned to commence steam navigation on Indian rivers, and that the Court of Directors had given the necessary permission.[69]

An important change in the building of steam vessels took place in the early 1830s with the introduction of iron steamers in India. The iron boats could be built in new shapes and dimensions difficult to achieve in wood. It is to iron that later ships owed their incredible diversity and specialization.[70] Said the *Samachar Darpan* on 9 March 1833,

> We are delighted to announce that the iron-bodied steam vessel is ready for navigation in Indian rivers. Captain Johnston is behind the successful completion of the steamship and it has achieved the standard set before it. The name of the steamship is *Lord William Bentinck*.[71]

The successful application of steam tugs down the river led the Company to employ steamers to navigate up the rivers. This was an attempt to strengthen the power and position of British power in India. The facility of conveying large bodies of troops from one part to another part of the country could lead to an amazing increase in the stability of the empire.[72] It could also transfer Company treasures with greater security and less expense.

Samachar Darpan mentioned on 10 July 1833:

> . . . two iron steam vessels and a considerable number of assistants arrived here from London last week on board the *Larkins*. They have come in pieces, and will be put together in some convenient spot in or near Calcutta; they each carry a single sixty horse power engine. They will shortly followed by two other iron boats, without engines, to be tugged by the steamers which are intended to carry troops, passengers, treasure, stores, or merchandize. . . .[73]

In addition to the introduction of steamboats on rivers, steam navigation on the high seas was opened in the late 1830s. There were three possible routes: around Africa, via the Persian Gulf and the Euphrates, and via the Red Sea.[74] The Calcutta lobby under Johnston had favoured the Cape route. But the *Enterprise* expedition had shattered their hopes. The Euphrates route was the brain child of Thomas Peacock and F.W. Chesney.[75] The latter made a survey of the Euphrates route but his expedition too failed to clinch the matter. The Bombay lobby favoured the Red Sea route. The government of the Bombay Presidency launched the steamer *Hugh Lindsay* on March 1829 'with mails for England via the Red Sea route'. A Select Committee of the House of Commons met in 1834 to examine witnesses from all the parties. The Committee recommended the Red Sea route and resolved that measures should be immediately taken on this project.

Contemporary Bengali journals were very much aware of this issue and occasionally expressed their opinions. *Samachar Darpan* observed on 15 November 1834:

STEAM COMMUNICATION WITH ENGLAND

We have received by the last ships a more detailed account of the proposal made to Parliament by Mr. Charles Grant respecting the establishment of a regular communication by steam between England and India.

During the last three or four years steam navigation had been carried on, on a small scale between Bombay and Suez, quite sufficient to show the practicability of the plan.

He stated that there were two routes open for consideration; one way of the Red Sea, the other by the Euphrates; and it would be for the Committee to examine which of these routes was to be preferred.

Now the parliament has taken up the matter in good earnest, we have no longer any doubt of success. The establishment by Government of a regular line of steam packets will form a new era in the history of this country, and confer incalculable benefits on the millions of India.[76]

From the above article we can capture the entire story of steam navigation between Britain and India. Thus the nineteenth-century Bengali journals comprised sources of information for the populace about the world.

Now we will observe a slightly different kind of reporting which appeared in the *Education Gazette O Saptahik Bartabaho* on 17 July 1857. As this year takes a permanent place in the history of India and this journal was famous for its loyalty towards the British government, its opinion is of interest.

> . . . Just imagine the improvement of India under the British Government in the last hundred years, is threatened by the rebellion of the native sepoys. If the proposed steam communication line between London and Kolkata was ready, then within 15/16 days 20–30 thousand British soldiers would come and repress the rebellion of the ungrateful sepoys.[77]

Anyway the essence of the article was similar with the view points of the contemporary middle-class Bengali intelligentsia regarding the revolt of 1857.[78]

The speed and reliability of steam navigation were vital to the British in north India at a time when overland communications remained uncertain and slow, and a reliable mail service along the Ganga was a high priority for a government that had its headquarters far away in Calcutta. The steam service on the Ganga was from the beginning a political enterprise, a means of consolidating the British presence on the plains. However, steam navigation had many limitations in India. The Ganga was not navigable by upstream of Allahabad and beyond Mirzapur. The wide seasonal variations in the height and speed of the river, along with its numerous sandbanks, shoals and other hazards, and the high cost of freight and passenger traffic, discouraged the more extensive development of this means of transport. In Bengal it was railways, not steamers that ultimately supplanted the old river boats and ferries.[79]

H.T. Bernstein argues that the introduction of steam boats in India, among other things also led the people 'to look on the English as wonderworking people akin to the demi-gods of the

Hindu Pantheon'. He says one cannot measure 'how much the British position in India rested on this point in the psychology of the people . . . '.[80] Steam not only signified to the British the dynamism of their own civilization, it also expressed the vast cultural and technological distance they saw between themselves and an India they perceived as backward and ridden by superstition.

In the mid-1830s the great essayist Thomas Babington Macaulay celebrated the uniqueness of the industrial revolution and Britain's distinction in having initiated it. He confidently judged that the English were the 'greatest and most highly civilized people that ever the world saw'. In support of this sweeping assertion he drew attention to Britain's vast empire and its powerful maritime fleet, which, he argued, could 'annihilate in a quarter of an hour the natives of Tyre, Athens, Carthage, Venice and Genoa together'. He also stressed as proof of Britain's greatness her advances in medicine, transportation and 'every mechanical art, every manufacture . . . to a perfection that our ancestors would have thought magical'.[81]

The story continues. As one of the characters of William Arnold's novel *Oakfield* (1854) remarks to a fellow passenger on a Ganges steamer, there appeared to be an 'inconceivable separation . . . between us few English, silently making a servant of the Ganges with our steam engine and paddle-boats, and those Asiatics, with shouts and screams worshipping the same river'.[82]

Rajnarayan Ray, in his autobiography, described his experience of a steamer ride in the *Lotus*, owned by Ramgopal Ghosh. The incident took place during his college days in 1843. Rajnarayan recalled,

> While our steamer was moving through the Mahananda, the villagers were shouting 'the fire-machine has come' and gathered at the bank of the river to watch the *Lotus*. Before this no steam vessel ever entered in the water of Mahananda. The villagers were terrified and considered us aliens with supernatural power. . . .[83]

So we can see the accounts of the Europeans are true, but only partially so: if we judge by the numbers of Indians who rapidly began to travel by steamboat and later on by railway, or who greeted steam as an agent of their own modernity, it is unlikely that the cultural gulf was as wide as Macaulay or William Arnold imagined.

The Telegraph

For all its limitations and imperfections, the technology of large-scale construction and engineering works was one of the ways in which the colonial state came to stamp its authority on the Indian landscape and to reduce India's vast area and varied terrain to manageable proportions. To an even greater degree than the railways, the rapid spread of the telegraph indicates the importance of the military and political impetus behind technological change in nineteenth-century India.

As rapid communication with the head of the government was of great commercial and political importance for the British they had made considerable attempts to foster the travel of news ever since the days of Clive.[84] Their early efforts were, however, directed to the reformation and organization of the traditional dak system. The introduction of telegraphs, first visual and later electric, was the first major technological innovation in this field. The first proposal for a visual telegraph line was made in 1767 by Thomas Barnard 'to give warning of invasion of the Carnatic by Haider Ali's horsemen'.[85] Then in 1788, a project of this kind was submitted to Sir Archibald Campbell, Governor of Madras, again for warning the countryside in case of an invasion. But these proposals failed to evoke interest among the Court of Directors.

Robert Ezra Park has pointed out the obviously fundamental and vital connection between communication and rational social process.[86] In a similar fashion Harold Innis has developed in a masterly way the theme that communication occupied a crucial position in the organization and effective administration of governments and empires.[87] As the most spectacular innovation in communication in its era, the electric telegraph fulfilled these roles perfectly.

Steamboats and railways were largely initiated and financed by private merchants for the expansion of trade, while the telegraph was entirely financed and managed by the government. In England, the telegraph grew as a commercial adjunct to railways, but in India it came ahead of the railways. Political and military necessities outweighed social and economic considerations in the development of the electric telegraph.[88] Externally, overland and sea routes had to be made invulnerable to any hostile, putative Russian advance. Internally, the successive annexations of local states had considerably expanded the range of imperial activities. So the authorities felt the pressing need for an electric telegraph system in India.[89]

In 1813 William Boyce of Bombay offered to establish visual telegraphs from one end of India to another. Both the Bengal government and the Court of Directors promptly accepted it.[90] George Everest, then a young artillery officer, was given charge of the survey work from Calcutta to Chunar, which he completed by October 1818. Pillars, 18 feet square and 30 feet high, were constructed at intervals of 20 miles and the signals by means of a rotating triangle were made with the use of telescope.[91] The telegraph was working between Calcutta and Chunar on one side and Calcutta and Sauger on the other. This visual telegraph continued until the electric telegraph was introduced.

Samachar Darpan observed on 4 July 1831:

> We came to know that the telegraph communication between Calcutta and Ganga-Sauger is almost finished and within two months it will be ready for use. This telegraph line is entirely sponsored by the government, but the merchant community of Calcutta will bear its monthly expenses. Anybody can imagine the usefulness of telegraph. Now at least 24 hours is necessary from Khajuri and Ganga-Sauger to get the news of the arrival of a ship in Calcutta. But after the introduction of the line, one can get such news within a few minutes. Not only that, confusion regarding the direction of the ships like 'coming up or proceeding down' the river, can be solved through the telegraph within minutes.[92]

The same journal reported about the functioning of such telegraphs:

Semaphore–The work done by telegraph, i.e. to send news at a distant place swiftly, is conducted by semaphore. These are arranged in a row so that from the first semaphore one can observe by a telescope the second one. The semaphores are made of 'movable wooden sticks' and these are arranged in such a way that movement of these parts has particular prerequisite meanings. By observing the movement of these parts from one pole to another one can send information to a long distance.[93]

This system had largely resulted from the original experiments of Dr. William Brooke O'Shaughnessy,[97] Professor of Chemistry in the Calcutta Medical College. He may rightly be regarded as the father of Electric Telegraph in India.[95] O'Shaughnessy erected an experimental line of 26 miles between Calcutta and Diamond Harbour, half overhead and half underground (including the crossing of a broad river) in May 1839. He observed that 'the experiments removed all reasonable doubts regarding the practicability of working electric telegraph'.[96] The whole system, however, remained at an experimental stage and it was only in 1849, when Dalhousie as Governor-General was engaged in continuous conflict with the Indian states, that the electric telegraph was officially proposed.[97] The very next year, O'Shaughnessy was asked to set up an experimental line between Calcutta and Chinsura.

Contemporary journal, *Sambad Bhaskar* mentioned on 16 April 1850:

> The government has decided to establish a telegraph line up to Hooghly in an experimental basis. The half of the line would be underground. The cost would be Rs. 500 for per 6 miles. After the completion of the proposed telegraph line, communication would be very fast, like an electric current.[98]

The first experimental line between Calcutta and Chinsura was opened in 1851. One half of this line was underground and the other aerial so as to save the cable from 'birds, monkeys and the danger arising from the exposure of the metal to thunderstorms'.[99] The lines from Calcutta to Diamond Harbour (30 miles), Bishtupore to Mayapore (11 miles), Kukrahata to Kedgeree (25 miles) and the shorter section including the cable across the Hooghly (16 miles), were constructed by 1852.[100] At this juncture, the role of Governor-General Dalhousie became crucial in the matter of establishing a system of telegraphs to serve all of India. He made available to O'Shaughnessy all the men, money, and equipment needed for the experimental line.

Dalhousie wished to leave behind a legacy of spectacular achievements. He was interested not only in expanding the Company's territory, but also in introducing administrative reforms, and in bringing the fruits of Western technology to India. He personally inspected the line between Calcutta and Diamond Harbour, called it 'safe, cheap, practicable and profitable',[101] and urged the Court of Directors of the East India Company to authorize large scale installations immediately. He sent O'Shaughnessy to London and asked approval of a reward for him of Rs.20,000 and his appointment as superintendent of telegraphs.

On 16 April 1852, the *Sambad Purnochandradaya* reported:

> The government and the business community of Calcutta are largely benefitted by the establishment of electric telegraph in Bengal by Dr. O'Shaughnessy. Although the government was appointed him for the purpose with all the monetary and material helps, but by the successful completion of telegraphs brings lots of utility for the society as a large. The government has rewarded him with twenty thousand rupees when he has been leaving for England. The purpose of the visit is the telegraph communication with other parts of India, especially with Bombay and Madras. The government is very much interested in the matter. So they have sent O'Shaughnessy to consult with the Court of Directors regarding the same.[102]

1853 marked the end of the experimental stage and the beginning of large-scale construction of telegraphs. The Court of Directors approved the proposal for installation of telegraphs in the other parts of India.

The selection of telegraph routes across India was largely dictated by political and military considerations. The first major section to be completed was the 800 miles from Calcutta and Agra. Then the entire network from Calcutta to Agra, Bombay and Madras, with a branch to Attock in the Punjab, was encompassed with the flying line and was in working order by 31 December 1854.[103] During the next three years, Calcutta was connected with Benares, Allahabad, Ambala, Lahore, and Peshwar. By 1857 there were about 4,500 miles of electric telegraphs in India.[104]

Notwithstanding the inadequacies which were to be expected in introducing a revolutionary technological innovation into a colonial environment, this improved mode of communication had a truly spectacular effect on the minds of the people. Once established the telegraph lines served a growing volume of domestic traffic. Both English and Indian traders used it extensively. When the lines were thrown open to the public, business houses and private persons, rather than the government, became the main users. Much of the revenue of the Telegraph Department thus came from bankers, merchants, opium traders, fund-holders and newspapers.[105] Telegraph rates were much lower than in Europe or America. At first at Re.1 per sixteen-word message for every 644 km, the Re.1 fee was later made uniform throughout India regardless of distance.[106] *Amrita Bazar Patrika* mentioned on 16 January 1869:

> By the suggestion of Cornell Robinson, Director of the Telegraph Department, the government has agreed to reduce the charge. According to new rate, it will cost 1 rupee per ten-word message to send anywhere in India. Although the government suffered a loss of Rs.8,000 in the first month (October) as per new rate, but from the second month they started making profit.[107]

The telegraph played a crucial role when the large-scale revolt of 1857 broke out. This was perhaps the first 'telegraph war'.[108] In a campaign lasting over a year, thousands of telegrams were transmitted. Although there were many social, political and cultural factors which contributed to English victory, a new technology was once again on the side of the victors. The telegraph tracked the mutineers' movements, helped resolve policy matters, and for some time even replaced the postal services. Robert Montgomery, the Judicial Commissioner of Punjab, wrote in the midst of the mutiny: 'Under Providence, the electric telegraph saved us.'[109] Edwin Arnold cited a mutineer who, on his way to execution, pointed to a telegraph line and muttered 'the accursed string that strangles me'.[110] Finally, there is the statement of Sir John Lawrence, Chief Commissioner of the Punjab during the mutiny and later Governor-General of India: 'The telegraph saved us.'[111]

The revolt of 1857 turned a strong interest among Britishers in communications between Britain and India. Promoters and the Indian government pushed several schemes at once without waiting for the technology to mature. In the process, many mistakes were made and much money was wasted, but the efforts hastened the evolution of telegraphic technology. Once submarine cables were completed between India and Britain in 1870, the telegraph integrated India more completely than ever into the administrative, military, and commercial network of the Empire.[112]

The role of the newly established telegraph in speeding up communications was noticeable in political, military, economic and social spheres throughout all of British India. This resulted in a tightening of control, a uniformity of enforcing justice, and a unity of official action which previously could not be imagined. The telegraph had woven its way into the political, social and cultural fabric of the conqueror and conquered.[113] The history of the telegraph illustrates how rapidly, given special conditions, a Western technology can be diffused.

Shiv Chunder Nundy: The First Electrical Engineer of India

In the age of industrial revolution to cope with the ever-increasing need to speed up communication abreast of steamships and railways, the new science of electricity found the first practical and large-scale application in the telegraph. It was with the introduction of the electric telegraph system that the profession of electrical engineering came into existence.[114] Although the railway used contractors, the Telegraph Department always depended on its own work parties, and so the history of the telegraph in India is replete with instances of heroism and ingenuity, especially at the lower staff level. The first Indian electrical engineer Shiv Chunder Nundy[115] came from the field of electric telegraph.

Shiv Chunder was born to a poor family in Calcutta in June 1824. His rise in the professional career shows that he was entirely a self-made man. In 1846, at the age of 22, he joined the Refinery Department of the Calcutta Mint. His technical aptitude came to the notice of O'Shaughnessy, the chemical examiner of the Mint, and Nundy was selected as his 'personal assistant'. Together they carried out several experiments in O'Shaughnessy's laboratory.

When in 1852 the Company Bahadur authorized the construction of the first telegraph line in India and selected O'Shaughnessy to lead the task, the Irishman placed his Indian protégé 'in charge'.[116] Nundy's association with the telegraph thus dates to the first line constructed, that between Calcutta and Diamond Harbour and Kedgeree on the Hooghly. Thus the mint-man became a telegraph-man, a transformation which would last the rest of his life. It was Nundy who sent the inaugural message from Diamond Harbour, received in Calcutta by Lord Dalhousie and O'Shaughnessy. Immediately afterwards, Nundy was appointed as 'Inspector' in-charge of the line. He had also to instruct and train other signallers. He was afterwards given the additional charge of the Post Office at Diamond Harbour. Subsequently he constructed about 900 miles of lines, from East Barrackpur to Allahabad, from Benares to Mirzapur, from Mirzapur to Seonee and from Calcutta to Dacca.[117]

During the construction of the Calcutta–Dacca line, it became necessary to lay 7 miles of underwater cable cross the river Padma. With no steamer company willing to lend their vessels for the work at less than Rs.10,000, an exasperated Nundy got it done by hiring country fishing boats.[118]

There are reproductions of some beautifully executed coloured lithographs of the telegraph posts innovated by Nundy, in the possession of the National Archives, New Delhi. These drawings along with an accompanying letter which he sent to O'Shaughnessy on 30 September 1855[119] are sufficient to secure for Nundy the distinction of an engineer proper.[120]

The year in which Nundy wrote the letter also saw the publication of the first treatise on the electric telegraph in Bengali by Kalidas Moitra of Serampore. Though the English sub-title humbly offered it as 'The Telegraph Office Assistants Manual', there is little doubt that the author had first hand knowledge about the progress of work in India. Moitra even put forward his proposal for sending messages in Bengali. The book contains a chart illustrating a Bengali keyboard as an alternative arrangement.[121]

During the revolt of 1857 O'Shaughnessy was away on leave. Colonel Stewart was officiating. During his frequent absences from Calcutta for inspection the disturbed districts in 1857–8, Shiv Chunder Nundy was in-charge of headquarters. In order to secure the communications between Calcutta and Bombay, he laid down a portion of the alternative line from Mirzapur to Seoni via Jubbulpur.[122] He became an Assistant Superintendent of the Indian Telegraph Department in 1866 and retired on a special pension in 1884, in which year he was made an Honorary Magistrate. Nundy was awarded the title of 'Rai Bahadur' on 28 February 1883.

The Statesman commented on 25 April 1902, 'A Rai Bahadurship seems to have been a poor reward for his excellent services.'[123]

The Railways

The nineteenth century may be called the era of the railway. The three decades from 1830 to 1860 were a time of experimentation and rapid growth in Britain, western Europe and the eastern United States. From 1860 to 1914, the web of steel spread through the world and so did the political, financial and engineering techniques that evolved along with it. If the non-Western people resisted the spread of railways, as often happened, the railway promoters knew how to apply guile and force, just as they knew how to overcome natural obstacles with bridges and tunnels.

Railways were the most important single innovation introduced into South Asia during the colonial era. Between 1853 and 1947, more than 40,000 route miles of track were laid in India, and of these, 35,406 miles were constructed and opened by 1920.[124] Building the railroad system became the most monumental project and it involved the largest international capital flow of the nineteenth century, producing the fourth longest rail network on earth, behind only those of the United States, Canada and Russia.[125]

There was an even more powerful ideological message attached to railways than there was to steamships. Locomotives and the railway network seemed to the British to furnish irrefutable proof of their material superiority and their commitment to 'civilizing' and 'improving' India. In 1848, before railway construction had even begun, the Governor-General of the day, Lord Hardinge, remarked, 'if we can proceed with our railways through the heart of the country, we shall make rapid strides in wealth and stability–for stream here would be the greatest instrument of civilization for the people, and of strength for the Government'.[126] The *Times* observed, 'for purposes political and military, as well as commercial, for economy, for safety and good government, the establishment of railways became a duty and necessity which the Government of India is bound to recognize and obey'.[127]

Bengali journals were aware of developments in England. As early as 1831 the *Samachar Darpan* reported,

> We came to know from the newspaper of England that the first train ran on an iron-made road between Manchester and Liverpool with tremendous speed. Our readers can better understand this if we say in that speed it would take only two hours from Calcutta to Murshidabad.[128]

Sambad Purnochandradaya reported on 16 April 1850:

> For the advancement of the country, especially for trade and business purposes, railways and telegraph are very important. The railway especially deserves special attention, because it can revolutionize the transport system. Railway has been operating in England from long

past. After strengthening their Empire in India, the British government now should introduce railway in this country also.[129]

It was Lord Dalhousie's ambitious public works programme that produced the momentum for what can be called the governmentalization of the state.[130] As the British Empire expanded (to embrace Sind in 1843, Punjab in 1849, and Awadh in 1856), and new threats of rebellion or invasion arose, so the need for prompt and reliable communication between Calcutta and the rest of India, and between a proliferating number of provincial centres, correspondingly grew. Dalhousie, wrote in 1853 that

> a single glance cast upon the map recalling to mind the vast extent of the Empire we hold ... will suffice to show how immeasurable are the political advantages to be derived from a system of internal communication which would admit of full intelligence of every event being transmitted to the Government under all circumstances, at a speed exceeding five-fold its present rate.[131]

The most important project in the technological reconstitution of India and the colonial state was the railways, which attracted approximately 150 million pounds of British capital during the nineteenth century, making it the single largest sphere of investment within the British Empire.[132] Though the capital was British, it was Indian taxpayers who bore the risk of investment, because the East India Company guaranteed a 5 per cent return to the investor.[133] Under this system, the work begun in 1849 with approval for the construction of two experimental lines. As Dalhousie viewed, 'the object of that experiment is to prove not only that it is practicable to construct railways in India as engineering works, but that such railways when constructed, will as commercial undertakings, afford a far remunerative return on the expended money'.[134]

Sambad Bhaskar, a popular journal, observed on 20 November 1850:

> We are hopeful by the initiatives taken by the government to establish railways in our country. Communication and business will be mostly

benefitted by this. Government has ordered to take over any land on the proposed railway routes without the consent of the owner. The railway companies made all arrangements for the purpose and the government has agreed to pay interest on the funds raised by them. Many rich Britons are interested in the project after observing the utilities of railways in their country. Orders were placed in London for the necessary machineries and equipments which are not available in India.[135]

Sambad Purnochandradaya reported on 24 December 1852:

We don't have any particular information when the railway will start in our country. Construction of railway is an enormous project. But the Englishmen are very enthusiastic and hardworking in nature. When they decide on a particular task, they take on the rest only after its completion. They have taken up the railway project with the same kind of determination.[136]

The Court of Directors decided that the first railway should be from Calcutta to Delhi through Mirzapur.[137] Construction work on the first section from Howrah to Raniganj began in 1852. It was then decided that the main line to the North-West Provinces should proceed via Rajmahal.[138] Although construction work had first begun in Bengal, the first locomotive, the *Lord Falkland*, was flagged off in Bombay 'amidst the loud applause of a vast multitude and to the salute of 21 guns' on 16 April 1853 on the 21-mile long Bombay–Thana line.[139] In Bengal, the first division of the experimental line from Howrah to Hooghly was opened for passengers on 15 August 1854, and in 1855 it stretched 195 km to the Raniganj coalfields.[140]

Sambad Prabhakar thus reported on 19 August 1854:

The railway is in full operation from last Tuesday. A huge number of people approach in a daily basis to Mr. R. Macdonald, the manager of the railway company, for tickets to Bally, Sreerampur, Chandannagor and Hooghly. But Mr. Macdonald is unable to satisfy them all. Because there is a seat capacity and the tickets are prepared according to that. We have heard that more trains will be introduced very soon.

There are three kinds of compartments in a train. The first class is well decorated and very comfortable. In the second class, not as well furnished like the previous, passengers can sit at their respective seat. But there is no roof or sitting arrangement in the third class. The railway authorities are thinking to cover up the third class with a roof to end the difficulties of the passengers.

Governor-General Lord Dalhousie will acquire fame for the introduction of railways in India.[141]

Indian railways developed, as a contemporary observer wrote, into an 'organic system, a sort of chain-work, well connected in all its links and proceeding upon one definite design',[142] because they were designed to serve the interests of the colonial state. As Dalhousie departed from India in 1856, he boasted that he harnessed India to the 'great engines of social improvement, which the sagacity and science of recent times had previously given to Western nations—I mean Railways, uniform Postage and the Electric Telegraph'.[143]

A year after Dalhousie's departure, north India exploded in the 1857 rebellion. The rebellion suspended the construction of public works, but it also demonstrated the military value of telegraphs and railways, as Dalhousie had predicted. No longer did the officials think of them as a commercial innovation imposed by London lobbyists on a reluctant East India Company.[144] With the demise of the Company in 1858, railway construction became an imperial priority as well as a shrewd investment. The British after that took up the construction of railways with renewed vigour.

The operating route miles totalled 838 in 1860 and by 1900, the railways of India with 23,672 route miles formed Asia's largest railway network. Railroad density, though lower than in the United States and Europe, was higher than in South America, Africa, Canada, and the USSR.[145] Thus it was reported in *Somprakash* on 28 September 1863:

Gradually the whole country is coming under the nexus of railways. Previously there was a dense forest at the east and south-east part of Bengal. It was beyond anybody's imagination that one day there could be a railway route. But by the European perseverance and their expertise in science-technology, now these places are also coming into the orbit of railways. Our readers know about the East Bengal Railway and Calcutta South-East Railway. Now these are spreading branches all over Bengal.[146]

The railways were, moreover, 'a British show',[147] and despite Karl Marx's confident prediction that railways would be 'the forerunner of modern industry' in India,[148] most of the technological and economic benefits accrued to the world's first industrial nation. In the early decades, rails, sleepers and pre-fabricated bridges, along with the engines and even their drivers, were imported from Britain,[149] and though in the 1880s and 1890s Indian workshops produced small numbers of locomotives, pressure from Britain thwarted the development of Indian competition. Between the 1850s and 1940s, more than 14,000 locomotives were sold to India, compared with barely 700 made there; British engineering firms profited at the expense of India's productive capacity.[150]

The railways were to provide the means for an efficient and speedy exercise of power; they were to render the immense space of India manageable, knitting together its vast and disjoined territory and people into a 'network of iron sinew'.[151] The fire-breathing 'iron cow', introduced into a pre-industrial environment, served the Raj both as a symbol and as an essential strategic, defensive, subjugatory, and administrative tool. There is little doubt that the introduction of the railways drove the state into seeking security in a different order of things. The health and vigour of the Empire was now sought in transforming the territory with technics, in instilling values of rationality, precision, calculability, speed, and productivity in the population.[152]

Vaccination and Inoculation

Colonial hegemony rested upon differences, real or assumed, giving the stamp of supremacy. Medical discourse was an important tool to achieve this end and at the same time 'a critical site of interaction and conflict'.[153] It was a double-edged weapon; it could 'distance' and 'universalize' simultaneously; one side emphasized the intrinsic difference between the two cultures while the other worked for a 'scientific' hegemony.[154]

Before 1800 Europeans commonly sought the help of local physicians, partly because so few of their own were available, partly from a conviction that they were likely to be better acquainted with the diseases and remedies of the place. During the course of the nineteenth century, however, Europe took a radical step away from medical pluralism. A growing conviction of the unique rationality and superior efficacy of Western medicine began to possess European doctors and laymen alike. One factor in this was the momentous discovery by Edward Jenner in the 1790s of cowpox vaccination: this was the first clear demonstration that man could master a major disease and it was a European innovation that was rapidly and confidently exported to the non-European world.[155] Vaccination was welcomed as a demonstration of the superiority of West over East, science over superstition.

Vaccination in the Indian context made smallpox uniquely subject to Western medical intervention at a comparatively early date. To many nineteenth-century British medical officers, smallpox was a 'scourge', responsible for 'more victims than all other diseases combined', outstripping even cholera and plague in its 'tenacity and malignity'.[156] Jennerian vaccination was introduced to India in 1802.[157] But smallpox brought the British face to face with a traditional method of treatment, that is, variolation, which entailed inoculation with live smallpox matter in order to induce a more manageable presence of the disease in the body.[158]

In the nineteenth century variolation was widely practised in Bengal in religious association with the deity Sitala. Sitala as the deity of smallpox, both as 'protector and prosecutor', reigned in north India[159] with a multitude of rituals for her propitiation. Although some Hindus relied upon worship of Sitala alone, for many variolation was itself a religious ritual. This variolation was practised by a section of Brahmins known as *tikadar*s or mark-makers and annually, in spring (February to May, so that smallpox was often known as *basantaroga*) came to the towns and villages from such faraway places like Benares, Allahabad and Vrindavan to inoculate children on a mass scale.[160] These inoculators were paid for their services by the people.

Although British medical men displayed some sympathy for the practice of variolation prior to the introduction of vaccination, later it was regarded with hostility and derided as inefficient and dangerous.[161] Such was the intensity of British hostility that in 1831, W. Cameron, the Superintendent-General of the day, dubbed variolation a 'murderous trade' and called its suppression 'indispensable to the interests of humanity'.[162] The 25 July 1832 issue of *Samachar Darpan* supported vaccination:

> Dr. Cameron has sent one copy of his report on vaccination in Bengal to us. Vaccination was introduced in our country in 1802 and became very much popular. Many people are already benefitted by this. There are 61,680 people who were vaccinated at Calcutta between 1828 and 1829. When many people will suffer from smallpox in Bengal, these inoculated lucky few will lead healthy lives.[163]

Sambad Bhaskar reported: 'Vaccination is much safer than variolation. In a village a thousand boys were variolated, but 300 boys died among them of smallpox. In another case 25 boys died among thousand who were vaccinated.'[164]

Smallpox broke out in epidemic form several times in Bengal. The death toll was so high that people were confused as what to do. In one side they had variolation which was sanctioned by religion and other side vaccination which was strongly recommended by the European physicians. This dilemma was clearly visible in the pages of contemporary journals.

Sambad Bhaskar, which had previously supported vaccination, observed on 30 April 1850:

> Our government has made a committee to prevent smallpox which has taken a disastrous form. Many dignified people of the town are included in the committee. But they have not come out with any solution so far. We came to know that the committee is going to

recommend vaccination strictly in place of variolation. But in reality many people died in spite of vaccine inoculation. So we think vaccination is not the only preventive measure against smallpox.[165]

In a situation where smallpox was almost universal, variolation was practised on a scale the British were unable to match until late in the nineteenth century.

Chikitsak-o-Samalochak, a famous medical journal of the day, reported:

There has been a major outbreak of smallpox in Calcutta these days. Though the summer, this year, has already become oppressive cholera has not yet made its appearance on a big scale. The number of deaths caused by smallpox, however, is on the increase. Poor people are rushing to Campbell Hospital at Sealdah for treatment, but there is almost no space to accommodate them. Suggestions are being mooted for setting up a new ward. It appears that it may very soon be needed.... Many people are taking vaccinations for fear of smallpox, in some cases this is yielding results, in some cases the vaccines are being rejected by the body, and in others, those who are being vaccinated are falling prey to pox as soon as they get vaccinated. However, those who have not yet got themselves vaccinated should better not take it now, for quite a few people have succumbed to smallpox after taking the vaccine.[166] (February–March 1894)

In British eyes, however, variolation was not a harmless religious ceremony. It was perpetrated because there was no shortage of 'bigots to mislead the ignorant Hindus, and to prejudice their credulous and simple minds, against whatever may be falsely represented to them as an innovation, or an interference with their religious privileges'.[167] In 1865 variolation was banned in Calcutta and its suburbs, and in 1866 the prohibition was extended to surrounding villages as well. A battle ensued to suppress variolation and replace it with vaccination. Converting the inoculators (*tikadar*s) to vaccinators, the government steadily increased the number of annual vaccinations in British India from 3,50,000 in 1850 to 8 million by the end of the century.[168] But while the number of vaccinations had increased considerably, there was no corresponding decrease in mortality from the disease.

For many nineteenth- and early twentieth-century European administrators, reformers and physicians the hazards and depredations of disease were an established part of a hostile and yet untamed tropical environment. Asia and Africa were seen to have fatal and incapacitating diseases, and only through the superior knowledge and skill of European medicine was it thought possible to bring them under effective control. In that view European medical intervention represented progress towards a more 'civilized' social and environment order.[169] The arrival of vaccination marked a new and critical stage in the development of Western medicine in India.

Medicine was taken as a prime exemplar of the constructive and beneficial effects of European rule, and thus, to the imperial mind, as one of its claims to legitimacy. It gave expression to Europe's faith in its own superiority, its mastery over man as well as nature.

The Electrification of Calcutta

The last decade of the nineteenth century saw the electrification of Calcutta, the principal city of Bengal. Until then oil and gas lights were used for the purpose.[170]

In the 1830s, O'Shaughnessy lit charcoal lights by battery;[171] but it was only with the advent of the steam-run dynamo that electric lighting became practicable. The first breakthrough in Calcutta was made by Carl Louis Schwendler, Superintendent Electrician of the Government Telegraphs and also a founder of the Calcutta zoo.

In 1877 Schwendler was asked by the government to make a detailed investigation of the possibilities of lighting Indian railway stations by electricity. His remarkable report, based on trial runs, appeared in 1881. With a second hand 25 horse-power slow-speed steam engine, Schwendler ran four 'dynamo electric machines' at Howrah Station, each of which lit a carbon arc lamp for two goods sheds. Its zinc reflectors lined with silvered glass gave a light often equal to candles per 100 square feet.[172] In 1881, Schwendler achieved another remarkable feat by setting up an electric railway for joy-rides in the zoo.[173] This was just two years after Werner Siemens's first demonstration of an electric railway at the Berlin Exhibition of 1879.

A point which Schwendler emphasized in his report on station lighting was the efficiency and ingenuity of the 'native mistri'. He mentioned the engine-driver who set right the irregular speed of a dynamo, with the help of a mercury speedometer. This optimism was borne out by the Bengali entrepreneuring firm of Dey, Sheel and Co., 'Electricians, Electrometallurgists and Brass Founders'. Apart from arranging for lights at meetings, parties, and wedding processions they manufactured a wide range of apparatus: carriage lamps lit by batteries of their own device, sewing machines, and table fans worked by electric motors. These were displayed at important gatherings, including the second national Congress of 1886 and the 1888 annual conversazione of the Mahomedan Literary Society, and won high praise from eminent scientists as well as the Viceroy himself.[174]

The Government of Bengal passed the Calcutta Electric Light Act in 1895. The first license was for a period of 21 years and covered an area of 5.64 square miles. On 7 January 1897 Kilburn & Co. secured the Calcutta electric lighting license as agents of The Indian Electric Co. Ltd. which was registered in London. A month later the company changed its name to The Calcutta Electric Supply Corporation Limited. They supplied electricity on a trial basis to the Bank of Bengal, later the State Bank of India, to the Bengal Club at Chowringhee, and to several private residences on 6 December 1898. The first generating station was erected at Emambagh Lane, near Princep Street, on 17 April 1899 heralding the beginning of thermal power generation in India.[175] The public distribution of electricity generated from thermal stations, began on 30 May 1899. Then in succession, came stations at Alipur (March 1902), Howrah (May 1906) and Ultadanga (September 1906). The electrification of Calcutta took place 17 years after New York (1882) and 11 years after London (1888).[176] Calcutta Tramways switched to electricity from horse drawn carriages in 1902. The first electric tram between

Esplanade and Kidderpore ran on 27 March 1902. By December 1902 the electrification of Calcutta Tramways was complete, making the horse-drawn carriage a symbol of the past.[177]

The rapid progress of Western technology was a major determinant of imperial expansion.[178] Steamships and cannons facilitated colonial conquest, while the printing press, the telegraph, and the railways established the communication and transportation links necessary for efficient government. Vaccine inoculation had great practical importance and served to demonstrate the growing sense of superiority of Western medicine over indigenous practice. The electrification of Calcutta was another such move to establish the superiority of the Englishmen over Asians. Electrification led to a rapid urbanization in the twentieth century.

For the British, large-scale construction schemes and engineering works were monuments to their power and munificence. In stone, steel and steam they embodied the idea of the British Raj as a technological empire, able by its grand works and feats of engineering to master the forces of nature that had defied and enslaved Indians for centuries.

THE TRANSFER OF TECHNOLOGY

Langdon Winner, a leading scholar of Science and Technology Studies (STS), once asked the question, 'Do Artefacts have Politics?'[179] His answer was that technology is intertwined with our culture and has values embedded within it that help shape society. This idea of technology shaping society is often referred to as technological determinism. The countervailing position within the field of STS is called social construction.[180] Together, social construction and technological determinism make two extremes within the field of STS. For most STS scholars, it is not one extreme or the other. Technology affects society and in turn society affects technology. Most would agree with Winner that technology and human culture are inextricably linked.[181] On the politics of technology, Winner argues that the values embedded within technology come from those who design technology. In most cases this is a small elite, who because of their position can shape society as a whole. When we put the transfer of technology into the Indian context, we understand this better.

The successful transfer of technologies depended on more than just an immediate transfer or diffusion mechanism. In addition, such mechanisms were affected by a wide range of social, economic and cultural factors. British scientific activities in India and the introduction of new technologies, though aimed at the fulfilment of colonial interest, evoked a great amount of interest among the local people. But the standard trope projects forces of traditionalism within Indian society as offering resistance to the advent of modern science and technology. The slow diffusion of a new technique was commonly explained by contemporary observers in terms of 'native character'. The differences in the rate of diffusion according to cultural anthropologists are explainable in terms of the nature and structure of the recipient culture. Taking up the case of Western technologies introduced into India, Sabyasachi Bhattacharya shows that resistance to efficient and costly machines arose from the unwillingness to 'accept the separation of the use and possession of the implements of production'.[182] The ownership of the machines resided with those who could invest in them, not in those who used them. Consequently, as and when there was resistance it was prompted by entirely economic and social considerations, having to do with the uncertainties in the transformation of the 'life worlds' of the concerned communities. As Bhattacharya puts it, 'it was not always rejection of change itself, but rejection of a change for the worse'. This reveals a lack of trust between the colonizers and colonized.[183]

Unfortunately technology transfer under colonial relations in India offered very little scope for the adaptation of these technologies by the Indian people. In fact, almost all the machinery came packed from outside, often along with technicians to handle it. The characteristic British policy was not to encourage technological development, but to increase the productive resources of the country through the agency of imported technology. The colonial officials favoured the geographical relocation of technology over its cultural diffusion.[184]

The various technological innovations, especially railways, in nineteenth-century India remained mere 'technological projects', but they had no significant impact on the nature of 'technological system'.[185] For the development of technology systems in the subcontinent, the colonial policy advocated total import and adaptation of proven technology: machineries, techniques and engineers, not only at the top level but also at the intermediate level. Local innovations were allowed only in 'low-tech' areas, that too in a marginal capacity. The subcontinent was primarily used for thc supply of raw materials and for receiving the finished product and technology.

This situation presents a sharp contrast with what happened in Japan after the Meiji Restoration in 1867 when the government adopted a vigorous policy of introducing Western science and technology.[186] There the earliest railway lines were financed and supervised by English bankers and engineers in the 1870s. Under foreign supervision, these lines were constructed by Japanese (unskilled and semi-skilled) labour. But the Japanese believed in 'learning and adapting by doing'. By the mid-1880s surveying, engineering and construction work on new projects were predominantly Japanese, engines and offices were managed by them and maximum machinery was manufactured in Japan. But in India the enormous amount spent on railways did not bear fruit in the form of significant, evolutionary impacts upon the Indian technological system. Those technologies which might have led to the growth of import-substitution industries in British India were generally avoided by the colonial masters. Loss of political and economic sovereignty is what Ian Inkster holds responsible for India's underdevelopment, especially in the field of technological development.[187]

The force of imperialism behind technology transfer was a double-edged sword. On the one side, a strong feeling of cultural supremacy brought a promise of social progress and justice to the colony, and on the other side, the urge to protect economic interests at 'home' stalled the establishment of an independent technology culture on the soil. Saroj Ghose rightly argues, 'A boon and an impediment–that was the destiny of technology transfer to the subcontinent'.[188]

So the 'relocation of European technologies' in India, in the true sense of the term, was not successful. It is not correct that Indians were averse to technological innovation itself. One should remember the enthusiasm with which the Bengali *bhadralok* took up the use of steamboats, railways and telegraphs. Among the urban middle classes in particular, the technology the West cherished as its own was often seen as the common heritage of the modern age.[189] But the British blamed the natives for their 'in-built cultural bias against technology'. This was 'not an explanation but an excuse, or even a weapon'.[190] A very important point is that technical education was not encouraged by the colonizers to support Indian technological systems.[191] Colonial government policy was not in favour of creating institutions which could provide a large cadre of engineers and skilled workers for service in industrial or technological projects. The rulers educated their subjects only up to a point. Beyond that they withheld the culture of technology. Actually the British did not want to upgrade Indian society. They used various technological innovations to rule and exploit India. Here one should remember the argument of Winner about the 'small elite'. Although the numerical strength of the British was less than their Indian counterpart, they ruled India for almost 200 years. The reason behind this is that their command over technology.

Yet many Bengali people saw Western technology as their key to power and prosperity, and they sought more machinery and knowledge than the Europeans offered them locally. Dissatisfied with a system of education which was 'solely for gaining money, and not for intellectual progress',[192] some enlightened Bengalis demanded a rigorous training in European science and technology. The *Sambad Prabhakar* wrote on 2 December 1853:

> Behind the marvellous achievements of the English people, the scientific and technical education deserves the central place. There should be separate schools and colleges for the cultivation of European sci-

ence and technology in India also. It is the duty of our rulers to teach the people of this country the secret of science and technology for which they are worshipped everywhere.[193]

NOTES

1. Scottish Record Officer, Dalhousie Papers, 218, pp. 7-8; quoted in Russel Dionne and Roy Macleod, 'Science and Policy in British India, 1858-1914: Perspectives on a Persisting Belief', *Proceedings of the Sixth European Conference on Modern South Asian Studies*, CNRS, Paris, 1979, pp. 55–68.
2. Max Weber, *From Max Weber: Essays in Sociology*, tr. H.H. Gerth and C. Wright Mills, Oxford University Press, New York, 1946.
3. Michel Foucault, *Power/Knowledge: Selected Interviews and Other Writings, 1972–7*, Harvester Press, Brighton, 1980.
4. Deepak Kumar, 'Investigating the Histories of Technology and Medicine in South Asia', *Proceedings of the Indian Association for Asian and Pacific Studies*, Kolkata, 2006, pp. 32–57.
5. Ranjan Chakrabarty, *Terror, Crime and Punishment: Order and Disorder in Early Colonial Bengal, 1800-1860*, Readers Service, Kolkata, 2009.
6. Michel Foucault, *Discipline and Punish: The Birth of the Prison*, Pantheon, New York, 1977.
7. Daniel R. Headrick, *The Tools of Empire: Technology and European Imperialism in the Nineteenth Century*, Oxford University Press, New York, 1981, p. 4.
8. R.A. Buchanan, 'The Diaspora of British Engineering', *Technology and Culture*, vol. 27, no. 3, 1986, pp. 501–24.
9. Daniel R. Headrick, *The Tentacles of Progress: Technology Transfer in the Age of Imperialism, 1850–1940*, Oxford University Press, New York, 1988, p. 6.
10. Ruth Schwartz Cowan, *A Social History of American Technology*, Oxford University Press, New York, 1997, p. 2.
11. David Rooney, 'A Contextualizing, Socio-Technical Definition of Technology: Learning from Ancient Greece and Foucault', *Technology and Culture*, vol. 27, no. 3, 1998, pp. 27–44.

12. Max Weber, *The Rational and Social Foundations of Music* (1921), D. Martindale, J. Riedel and G. Neuwirth (trs. & eds.), Southern Illinois University Press, Carbondale, 1958, p. 1.
13. Jacques Ellul, *The Technological Society*, J. Wilkinson (tr. & ed.), Vintage Books, New York, 1964, p. 4.
14. David Rooney, op. cit.
15. Otto Mayr, 'The Science Technology Relationship as a Historiographic Problem', *Technology and Culture*, vol. 17, no. 4, 1976, pp. 663–73.
16. Barry Barnes, 'The Science Technology Relationship: A Model and a Query', *Social Studies of Science*, vol. 12, no. 1, 1982, pp. 166–72.
17. Wiebe E. Bijkar, Thomas P. Hughes and Trevor J. Pinch (eds.), *The Social Construction of Technological Systems: New Directions in the Sociology and History of Technology*, The MIT Press, Cambridge, 1987, p. 13.
18. George Basalla, *The Evolution of Technology*, Cambridge University Press, Cambridge, 1988, pp. 27–8.
19. Thomas P. Hughes, 'The Seamless Web: Technology, Science, Etcetera, Etcetera', *Social Studies of Science*, vol. 16, no. 2, 1986, pp. 281–92.
20. Trevor Pinch, 'The Social Construction of Technology: A Review', in Robert Fox (ed.), *Technological Change: Methods and Themes in the History of Technology*, Harwood Academic Publisher, Amsterdam, 1996, p. 23.
21. Ruth Schwartz Cowan, op. cit., p. 3.
22. Pamela O. Long, 'The Annales and the History of Technology', *Technology and Culture*, vol. 46, no. 7, 2005, pp. 177–86.
23. Daniel Headrick, *The Tools of Empire: Technology and European Imperialism in the Nineteenth Century*, op. cit., and *The Tentacles of Progress: Technology Transfer in the Age of Imperialism, 1850-1940*, op. cit.
24. John M. Staudenmaier, 'Recent Trends in the History of Technology', *The American Historical Review*, vol. 95, no. 3, 1990, pp. 715–25.
25. Daniel Headrick, *The Tentacles of Progress*, p. 6.
26. Melvin Kranzberg, 'Technology and History: "Kranzberg's Laws" ', *Presidential Address*, SHOT, Henry Ford Museum in Dearborn, Michigan, 19 October 1985.

27. See Daniel R. Headrick, *The Tools of Empire.*
28. See Arnold Pacey, *Technology in World Civilization: A Thousand Years History*, MIT Press, Oxford, 1990.
29. David Arnold, *The New Cambridge History of India: Science, Technology and Medicine in Colonial India*, Cambridge University Press, Cambridge, 2000, p. 92.
30. *Arya Darshan* (Bengali Journal) first published in 1874 and the editor was Jogendra Nath Bidyabhusan. The journal lasted for 11 years. See Bajendranath Bandopadhyay, *Bangla Samayik Patra*, vol. II, Bangiya Sahitya Parishad, Calcutta, 1951, p. 13.
31. For more information see Deepak Kumar, *Science and the Raj: A Study of British India*, 2nd edn., Oxford University Press, New Delhi, 1995; Satpal Sangwan, *Science, Technology and Colonization: An Indian Experience 1757–1857*, Anamika Prakashan, Delhi, 1991.
32. Roy Macleod, 'Scientific Advice for British India: Imperial Perceptions and Administrative Goals, 1898-1923', *Modern Asian Studies*, 1975, vol. 9, no. 3, pp. 343–84.
33. Gyan Prakash, *Another Reason: Science and the Imagination of Modern India*, Oxford University Press, New Delhi, 2000, p. 160.
34. Daniel R. Headrick, *The Tentacles of Progress*, p. 7.
35. Roy Macleod and Deepak Kumar (eds.), 'Introduction: Western Technology and British Rule', in *Technology and the Raj: Western Technology and Technical Transfers to India 1700-1947*, Sage, New Delhi, 1995, p. 16.
36. *Samachar Darpan*, 25 April 1832. A fine diagram of the Steam Engine indicating all its parts (boiler, cylinder, piston rod of cylinder, steam pipe connecting boiler with cylinder, condenser, etc.) appeared with the article. See Appendix.
37. Deepak Kumar, *Science and the Raj*, p. 45.
38. Amitabha Ghosh, 'Colonial Constraints and Technology: Marginalized Indian Attainments', in Arun Kumar Biswas (ed.), *History, Science and Society in the Indian Context*, The Asiatic Society, Calcutta, 2001, pp. 159–60.
39. S.N. Sen, *Scientific and Technical Education in India 1781–1900*, INSA, New Delhi, 1991, p. 112.
40. Chittaranjan Banerjee (ed.), *Dui Sataker Bangla Mudrana O Prakashana*, Ananda Publishers, Calcutta, 1981, p. 18.

41. S.K. De, *History of Bengali Literature 1800-1825*, University of Calcutta Press, Calcutta, 1919, p. 78. See also A.K. Priolkar, *The Printing Press in India: Its Beginning and Early Development*, Marathi Samsodhan Mandala, Bombay, 1958, pp. 51–3.
42. S.N. Sen, *Scientific and Technical Education in India*, p. 114.
43. Siddhartha Ghosh, *Kaler Shahar Kolkata*, Ananda Publishers, Calcutta, 1991, p. 51.
44. Ibid., p. 52.
45. Chittaranjan Banerjee (ed.), *Dui Sataker Bangla Mudran O Prakashan*, pp. 55–6, 84–7.
46. In another issue of *Dig-Durshun*, no. VII, October 1818, the article on the printing press again appeared.
47. Siddhartha Ghosh, *Karigari Kalpana O Bangali Udyog*, Dey's Publishing, Calcutta, 1988, p. 30.
48. Sunil Kumar Chatterjee, *William Carey and Serampore*, Ghosh Publication, Calcutta, 1984, pp. 37–52.
49. Anil Chandra Das Gupta (ed.), *The Days of John Company: Selections from Calcutta Gazette 1824-1832*, West Bengal Govt. Press, Calcutta, 1959, pp. 13–15.
50. George Smith, *The Life of William Carey: Shoe-Maker and Missionary*, Everyman's Library, Calcutta, 1885, p. 232.
51. Anil Chandra Banerjee (ed.), *The Days of John Company*, pp. 272–3.
52. George Smith, *The Life of William Carey*, p. 231.
53. Ibid., p. 232.
54. *Education Gazette O Saptahik Bartabaho*, 26 February 1858.
55. Amitabha Ghosh, 'Introduction of Steamboats in India', *Bulletin of the Victoria Memorial*, vol. IX, 1975, pp. 32–44.
56. Robert Fulton papers to Thos. Law, 10 April 1812; quoted in Amitabha Ghosh, ibid.
57. Siddhartha Ghosh, *Kaler Shahar Kolkata*, p. 54.
58. *Dig-Durshun*, no. II, May 1818.
59. Satpal Sangwan, *Science, Technology and Colonization*, p. 81.
60. W.H. Carey, *The Good Old Days of Honourable John Company*, Quins Books, Calcutta, vol. II, 1906, pp. 18–19.
61. G.A. Prinsep, *An Account of the Steam Vessels and of Proceedings Connected with Steam Navigation in British India*, Calcutta, 1830, p. 7.
62. David Arnold, *The New Cambridge History of India*, p. 104.

63. *Samachar Darpan*, 10 December 1825.
64. Daniel R. Headrick, 'The Tools of Imperialism: Technology and the Expansion of European Colonial Empires in the Nineteenth Century', *The Journal of Modern History*, vol. 51, no. 2, 1979, pp. 231–63.
65. William Ash to Henry Maudslay, Josua Field papers (Manuscript); quoted in Amitabha Ghosh, 'Introduction of Steamboats in India', op. cit.
66. Capt. E.C. Smith, 'The Centenary of Naval Engineering', *Newcomen Society Transaction*, vol. 2, 1921–2, p. 102; quoted in Amitabha Ghosh, ibid.
67. *Samachar Darpan*, 2 April 1831.
68. William Ash to Henry Maudslay, op. cit.
69. *Samachar Darpan*, 16 May 1832.
70. Daniel. R. Headrick, 'The Tools of Imperialism: Technology and the Expansion of European Empires in the Nineteenth Century', op. cit.
71. *Samachar Darpan*, 9 March 1833.
72. Satpal Sangwan, *Science, Technology and Colonization*, p. 82.
73. *Samachar Darpan*, 10 July 1833.
74. Daniel R. Headrick, *The Tools of Empire*, pp. 23–6.
75. Report of the Select Committee on Steam Navigation to India, Parliamentary Papers, 1834, vol. XIV, pp. 378–9; quoted in Satpal Sangwan, *Science, Technology and Colonization*, pp. 84, 110.
76. *Samachar Darpan*, 15 November 1834.
77. *Education Gazette O Saptahik Bartabaho*, 17 July 1857.
78. R.C. Majumder, *The Sepoy Mutiny and the Revolt of 1857*, Calcutta, 1963, pp. 383–432. See also Benoy Ghose, 'Bengali Intelligentsia and the Revolt', in *Rebellion 1857: A Symposium*, New Delhi, 1957.
79. David Arnold, *The New Cambridge History of India*, p. 104.
80. H.T. Bernstein, *Steamboats on the Ganges: An Exploration in the History of India's Modernization through Science and Technology*, Orient Longman, Bombay, 1960, pp. 174–5.
81. Michael Adas, *Machines as the Measure of Men: Science, Technology and Ideologies of Western Dominance*, Oxford University Press, New Delhi, 1990, p. 136.

82. William Arnold, *Oakfield*; or, *Fellowship in the East*, London, vol. I, 1854, pp. 13–14, 128; quoted in Michael Adas, ibid., pp. 172–3.
83. Rajnarayan Ray, *Atma-Charita*, Calcutta, 1961, pp. 19–23.
84. Satpal Sangwan, *Science, Technology and Colonization*, p. 90.
85. R.H. Phillimore, *Historical Records of the Survey of India*, vol. 1, p. 311; quoted in Satpal Sangwan, ibid., p. 112.
86. Robert Ezra Park, 'Reflections on Communication and Culture', *Canadian Journal of Economics and Political Science*, vol. 6, 1940, pp. 135–52.
87. Harold A. Innis, *Empire and Communications*, Dundurn Press, Toronto, 1950, pp. 3, 6.
88. Saroj Ghose, 'The Introduction and Development of the Electric Telegraph in India', Ph.D thesis, Jadavpur University, 1974, p. 71.
89. Deepak Kumar, *Science and the Raj*, p. 46.
90. Satpal Sangwan, *Science, Technology and Colonization*, p. 90.
91. Krishnalal Shridharani, *Story of the Indian Telegraph: A Century of Progress*, Post & Telegraph Department, New Delhi, 1953, pp. 1, 2.
92. *Samachar Darpan*, 4 July 1831.
93. Ibid., 1 August 1832.
94. J.A. Bridge, 'Sir William Brooke O'Shaughnessy, M.D., F.R.S., F.R.C.S., F.S.A.: A Biographical Appreciation by an Electrical Engineer', *Notes and Records of the Royal Society of London*, vol. 52, no. 1, 1998, pp. 103–20.
95. Krishnalal Shridharani, *Story of the Indian Telegraph*, p. 10.
96. M. Adams (ed.), *Memoir of Sir William O'Shaughnessy Brooke, Kt.*, Indian Telegraph Department, Shimla, 1889, p. 8.
97. Saroj Ghose, *The Introduction and Development of the Electric Telegraph in India*, p. 88.
98. *Sambad Bhaskar*, 16 April 1850.
99. Krishnalal Shridharani, *Story of the Indian Telegraph*, pp. 10–11.
100. M. Adams (ed.), *Memoir of Sir William O'Shaughnessy*, p. 12.
101. Suresh Chandra Ghosh, 'The Utilitarianism of Dalhousie and the Material Improvement of India', *Modern Asian Studies*, vol. 12, no. 1, 1978, pp. 97–110.
102. *Sambad Purnochandradaya*, 16 April 1852.

103. Saroj Ghose, 'Commercial Needs and Military Necessities: The Telegraph in India', in Roy Macleod and Deepak Kumar (eds.), *Technology and the Raj*, pp. 157–8.
104. M. Adams (ed.), *Memoir of Sir William O'Shaughnessy*, p. 14.
105. Saroj Ghosh, 'Commercial Needs and Military Necessities: The Telegraph in India', p. 172.
106. Daniel R. Headrick, *The Tentacles of Progress*, pp. 121–2.
107. *Amrita Bazar Patrika*, 16 January 1869.
108. Saroj Ghose, 'Telegraph in Indian Mutiny', *The Introduction and Development of the Electric Telegraph in India*, pp. 168–94.
109. William Muir and William Coldstream (eds.), *Records of the Intelligence Department of the Government of the North-West Provinces of India during the Mutiny of 1857*, vol. I, Edinburgh, 1902, p. 491; quoted in Saroj Ghose, 'Commercial Needs and Military Necessities: The Telegraph in India', pp. 161–2, 174.
110. Edwin Arnold, quoted in Saroj Ghose, ibid., pp. 168, 175.
111. M. Adams (ed.), *Memoir of Sir William O'Shaughnessy*, p. 15.
112. *Amrita Bazar Patrika*, 7 April 1870.
113. Mel Gorman, 'Sir William O'Shaughnessy, Lord Dalhousie, and the Establishment of the Telegraph System in India', *Technology and Culture*, vol. 12, no. 4, 1971, pp. 581–601.
114. J.D. Bernal, *Science in History*, Watts: London, 1954, p. 390.
115. See Siddhartha Ghosh, *Karigari Kalpana O Bangali Udyog*, pp. 44–55.
116. Krishnalal Shridharani, *Story of the Indian Telegraph*, p. 13.
117. Ibid.
118. Hemendraprasad Ghosh, 'Shivchandra Nundy', *Masik Basumati*, (Kartik, 1360) 1953, pp. 107–14.
119. Krishnalal Shridharani, *Story of the Indian Telegraph*, p. 14.
120. Amitabha Ghosh, 'Colonial Constraints and Technology: Marginalized Indian Attainments', in Arun Kumar Biswas (ed.), *History, Science and Society in Indian Context*, p. 168.
121. Kalidas Moitra, *Electric Telegraph Ba Tarit Bartabaha Prakaran: Electric Telegraph for the Telegraph Office Assistant's Manual etc.*, Serampore, 1855 (see Appendix).
122. Krishnalal Shridharani, *Story of Indian Telegraph*, p. 15.
123. *The Statesman*, 25 April 1902.

124. Ian Derbyshire, 'The Building of India's Railways: The Application of Western Technology in the Colonial Periphery 1850–1920', in Roy Macleod and Deepak Kumar (eds.), *Technology and the Raj*, p. 177.
125. Daniel R. Headrick, *The Tools of Empire*, p. 181.
126. David Arnold, *The New Cambridge History of India*, p. 109.
127. *The Times*, 28 December 1853; quoted in Satpal Sangwan, *Science, Technology and Colonization*, p. 86.
128. *Samachar Darpan*, 13 August 1831.
129. *Sambad Purnochandradaya*, 16 April 1850.
130. Gyan Prakash, *Another Reason*, p. 161.
131. Edward Davidson, *The Railways in India: With an Account of their Rise, Progress and Construction, Written with the Aid of the Records of the India Office*, London, 1868, p. 3; quoted in Daniel Headrick, *The Tools of Empire*, pp. 182–3, 190.
132. Ian J. Kerr, *Building the Railways of the Raj, 1850-1900*, Oxford University Press, Delhi, 1995, p. 4. Although scholars disagree on the amount, there is a general agreement that it was the largest single investment within the British Empire. See pp. 4, 17–18.
133. 'Bharatbarsha Railway', *Amrita Bazar Patrika*, 16 September 1869.
134. Extracts from Dalhousie's Minute, 4 July 1850, P.W.D. (Rly.) Proceedings, 2 August 1850, nos. 39-51; quoted in Satpal Sangwan, *Science, Technology and Colonization*, pp. 87, 111.
135. *Sambad Bhaskar*, 20 November 1850.
136. *Sambad Purnochandradaya*, 24 December 1852.
137. Edward Davidson, *The Railways of India*, pp. 58–60; quoted in Satpal Sangwan, *Science, Technology and Colonization*, p. 87.
138. G. Huddleston, *History of the East Indian Railways*, Calcutta, 1906, p. 12; quoted in Daniel Headrick, *The Tentacles of Progress*, p. 62.
139. L.C. Hunter, *Indian Railways: One Hundred Years, 1853-1953*, Railway Board, New Delhi, 1953, pp. 1–15.
140. Daniel R. Headrick, *The Tentacles of Progress*, p. 62.
141. *Sambad Prabhakar*, 19 August 1854.
142. Framjee R. Vicajee, *Political and Social Effects of Railways in India*, London, 1875, p. 15; quoted in Gyan Prakash, *Another Reason*, pp. 166, 268.

143. Final Minute by Dalhousie, 28 February 1856; quoted in Ramsay Muir, *The Making of British India, 1756-1858*, Manchester University Press, Manchester, 1915, p. 365.
144. For more information see Daniel Thorner, 'The Pattern of Railway Development in India', in Ian J. Kerr (ed.), *Railways in Modern India*, Oxford University Press, New Delhi, 2001, pp. 80–96.
145. Daniel R. Headrick, *The Tentacles of Progress*, p. 55.
146. *Somprakash*, 28 December 1863.
147. Daniel Thorner, 'The Pattern of Railway Development in India'.
148. Karl Marx, 'The Future Results of British Rule in India', *New York Daily Tribune*, 8 August 1853, p. 5.
149. Daniel R. Headrick, *The Tools of Empire*, p. 188.
150. Fritz Lehmann, 'Great Britain and the Supply of Railway Locomotives to India: A Case Study of "Economic Imperialism"', *Indian Economic and Social History Review*, no. 2, 1965, pp. 297–306.
151. Edward Davidson, *The Railways of India*, p. 369; quoted in Gyan Prakash, op. cit., p. 166.
152. Michael Adas, *Machines as the Measures of Men*, pp. 221–36.
153. David Arnold, *Colonizing the Body: State Medicine and Epidemic Disease in Nineteenth Century India*, University of California Press, Berkeley, 1993, pp. 240–89.
154. Deepak Kumar, 'Medical Encounters in British India, 1820–1920', *EPW*, vol. 32, no. 4, 1997, pp. 166–70.
155. J.Z. Bowers, 'The Odyssey of Smallpox Vaccination', *Bulletin of the History of Medicine*, vol. 55, 1981, pp. 17–33.
156. Annual Report upon Vaccination in the North-Western Provinces, 1866-77, p. 4; quoted in David Arnold, 'Smallpox and Colonial Medicine in Nineteenth Century India', in David Arnold (ed.), *Imperial Medicine and Indigenous Societies*, Manchester University Press, Manchester, 1988.
157. Report on the Introduction and Progress of Vaccine Inoculation in Bengal, 1804; quoted in O.P. Jaggi, 'Diseases as Seen by Early European Physicians in India', in D.P. Chattopadhyay and Ravinder Kumar (eds.), *Science, Philosophy and Culture: Multi-disciplinary Exploration*, Pearson Longman, Delhi, 1997, p. 89.
158. Poonam Bala, *Imperialism and Medicine in Bengal: A Socio-Historical Perspective*, Sage, New Delhi, 1991, p. 104.

    Variolation involves giving a person the actual disease. It is derived from the name of the smallpox virus, variola. Vaccination involves giving a weakened or killed version of the disease (on a toxin) in order to provoke an immune response against the pathogen. In the case of smallpox, this involves giving a patient a completely different pox virus vaccinia (known as cowpox).

159. Ralph W. Nicholas, 'The Goddess Sitala and Epidemic Smallpox in Bengal', *Journal of Asian Studies*, XLI, 1981, pp. 24–39.
160. Anil Kumar, *Medicine and the Raj: British Medical Policy in India, 1835-1911*, Sage, New Delhi, 1998, p. 162.
161. Mark Harrison, *Public Health in British India: Anglo-Indian Preventive Medicine 1859-1914*, Cambridge University Press: New Delhi, 1994, pp. 82–3.
162. *Report of the Smallpox Commissioners*, Calcutta, 1850, p. 54; quoted in David Arnold, 'Smallpox and Colonial Medicine', pp. 51, 64.
163. *Samachar Darpan*, 25 July 1832.
164. *Sambad Bhaskar*, 20 April 1850.
165. Ibid., 30 April 1850.
166. Pradip Kumar Bose, *Health and Society in Bengal: A Selection from Late 19th Century Bengali Periodicals*, Sage, New Delhi, 2006, pp. 245–6.
167. *Report of the Smallpox Commissioners*, pp. 54–5; quoted in Gyan Prakash, *Another Reason*, p. 138.
168. David Arnold, *Colonizing the Body*, p. 141.
169. David Arnold, 'Introduction: Disease, Medicine and Empire', in D. Arnold (ed.), *Imperial Medicine and Indigenous Societies*, p. 3.
170. For more information see Sarmila Sarkar, 'The Urbanization of Calcutta in the Nineteenth Century: A Case Study of City-Lighting', M.Phil dissertation, Jadavpur University, 1991.
171. W.B. O'Shaughnessy, *Notes of Lectures on Natural Philosophy, 1st Series: On Galvanic Electricity*, Baptist Mission Press, Calcutta, 1841.
172. Sidhartha Ghosh, 'Calcutta's Industrial Archeology', in Sukanta Chaudhury (ed.), *Calcutta: The Living City*, vol. I: *The Past*, Oxford University Press, Calcutta, 1990, p. 253.
173. *The Statesman*, 3 January 1881 reported: 'ELECTRIC RAILWAY: The Public are respectfully informed that Railway Car-

riages, propelled entirely by Electricity, will run in the Zoological Gardens, from 11 a.m. to 6 p.m. Tomorrow and subsequent days.'

174. *The Statesman* reported on 1 January, 1887: 'The evening party given by the Indian Club on Tuesday last was a very great success, a large number of the delegates to the Congress being present on the occasion. . . . Messrs. Dey, Sil & Co. exhibited electric apparatus of their own manufacture. The instruments were generally admired by Father Lafont, Mr. Eliot, and others who saw them. The company also illuminated the place with the electric light.'
175. P. Thankappan Nair, 'Civic and Public Services in Old Calcutta', Sukanta Chaudhury (ed.), op. cit., p. 237.
176. See Thomas P. Hughes, *Networks of Power: Electrification in Western Society 1880-1930*, Johns Hopkins University Press, Baltimore, 1983.
177. P. Thankappan Nair, op. cit., p. 235.
178. Rondo Cameron, 'Imperialism and Technology', in Melvin Kranzberg and Carroll Pursell (eds.), *Technology in Western Civilization*, Oxford University Press, New York, 1967, I, p. 693.
179. Franz A. Foltz, 'Technology within Society', *The Journal of the Technology Studies*, vol. 12, no. 1, 1991, pp. 23–9.
180. See Wiebe E. Bijker, Thomas P. Hughes and Trevor F. Pinch (eds.), *The Social Construction of Technological Syatems: New Directions in the Sociology and History of Technology.*
181. Langdon Winner, *The Whale and the Reactor*, University of Chicago Press, Chicago, 1986, p. 82.
182. Sabyasachi Bhattacharya, 'Cultural Constraints on Technological Innovation and Economic Development: Some Case Studies', *Indian Economic and Social History Review*, vol. 3, no. 3, 1966, pp. 240–67.
183. Jan af. Geijerstam, *Landscapes of Technology Transfer: Swedish Iron-makers in India: 1860-1864*, quoted in 'Introduction', S. Irfan Habib and Dhruv Raina (eds.), *Social History of Science in Colonial India*, Oxford University Press, New Delhi, 2007, p. xxii.
184. Daniel R. Headrick, *The Tentacles of Progress*, p. 382.
185. Ian Inkster, 'Colonial and Neo-Colonial Transfers of Technol-

ogy: Perspectives on India before 1914', in Roy Macleod and Deepak Kumar (eds.), *Technology and the Raj*, p. 35.

186. Tanaka M. Hermann, 'The Situation and Role of Science and Technology in Transitional Period from the Feudal to the Modern Society of Japan', *11th International Congress of the History of Science*, Warsaw and Cracow, 1965; quoted in S.N. Sen, 'The Character of the Introduction of Western Science in India during the 18th and the 19th Centuries', *Indian Journal of History of Science*, vol. 1, no. 2, 1966, pp. 112–21.
187. Ian Inkster, 'Prometheus Bound: Technology and Industrialization in Japan, China and India prior to 1914: A Political Economy Approach', *Annals of Science*, vol. 45, 1988, pp. 399–426.
188. Saroj Ghose, 'Technology: What is it?', in Jyoti Bhusan Das Gupta (ed.), *Science, Technology, Imperialism and War*, vol. XV, part 1, *History of Science, Philosophy and Culture in Indian Civilization*, General Editor D.P. Chattopadhyay, Pearson Longman, New Delhi, 2007, p. 251.
189. David Arnold, *The New Cambridge History of India*, p. 124.
190. Daniel R. Headrick, *The Tentacles of Progress*, p. 309.
191. Frustrated by the British policy of technical education, P.N. Bose, a noted geologist and science-enthusiast, remarked, 'In regard to higher technical education, progress during the last two decades has, I regret to say, been practically nil in Bengal.' P.N. Bose, *Essays and Lectures on the Industrial Development of India*, Newman & Co., Calcutta, 1906, p. 87.
192. 'Note on Education', by K.M. Dey, a student of Hooghly College, *The Englishman*, 22 January 1852.
193. *Sambad Prabhakar*, 2 December 1853.

CHAPTER 3

Demand for Technical Education

> . . . practical mechanics or engineering forms no portion of native education. From the pathsala to the college they have no more practical idea of manufacturing than they have of the old women in the moon. The end and aim of their education is to make them either accountants or letter writers. India is full of raw materials which are mouldering in neglect for want of men to work them into forms and fashions. The resources of the country will never be developed unless the children of the soil learn the way to develop them.
>
> *Hindu Patriot*, 6 April 1854

Concepts such as educational dependence, cultural imperialism, and neo-colonialism abound in recent writings on the development of educational systems in the former colonies of metropolitan powers.[1] Educational systems such as were left when the imperial powers withdrew, evoked two responses. One treated them as a valuable legacy, left by the former rulers solely for the benefit of the former colony.[2] The other saw in it as yet another instance of the metropolitan power's deliberate objective of keeping down the hapless colony for its exclusive benefit. The educational system in India was successful in producing men to run the colonial administration and in directing the economy for exploitation by Britain. But the question remains whether the system was planned and erected solely for this aim, or whether there were other forces that brought about the same results.

The Indian educational system experienced a haphazard and unplanned growth because of many different agencies involved in building it. It lacked adequate primary/secondary educational facilities, and made limited provision for technical education. At the same time, there was a fairly wide development of liberal arts education at the tertiary level. Colonization being a complex process, means that it is not only technology as a tool that is important. Technology as a form of knowledge[3] is much more important. What factors influenced the shaping of colonial policies of technical education and the subsequent establishment of technical institutes in Bengal? Equally important, what was the response of the Bengali people towards state sponsored technical education?

The word 'technical education' covers a spectrum of activities, and their meaning has changed over time to cover every sort of work-oriented learning. In opening the Finsbury Technical College in 1883, Sir Philip Magnus said that in all discussion about technical education it was customary to commence with a definition.[4] He called that education or instruction 'technical' which had a direct reference to the career of the person who received it; but he explained that in practice the term had the narrow significance, which applied to the training of the engineer or chemist rather than to that of the surgeon or lawyer. In England in 1897, technical education became practically any course of study prescribed by the Science and Art Department, while in Germany it has been described as the study of the principles underlying every kind of human craftsmanship. The Shimla Educational Conference held in 1901 defined technical education as (a) the study of the scientific methods and principles underlying the practice of any handicraft, industry or profession and (b) the application of those methods and principles to the practice of the handicraft, industry and profession.[5] E.W. Collin pointed out the vagueness attached to the term 'technical education'.[6] Pramatha Nath Bose, a noted geologist and science-enthusiast, defined technical education as training for the industries.

industries dependent upon science, or science industries, such as dyeing, tanning, sugar-refining, soap-making, glass-manufacture, electro-engineering, mining, etc., and industries which have a very remote, if any connection with science and which may be called art-industries such as engraving, modelling, carpentry, shoe-making, etc.[7]

TECHNICAL EDUCATION IN NINETEENTH-CENTURY BENGAL

The Raj was founded on 'the right of conquest', but its continuance depended more upon how much acquiescence and consent it was able to elicit from its subjects. The Raj was more than just the army or the bureaucracy; it represented a culture and a way of life substantially different from the way of life of those it had subordinated.[8] The colonial imperative was to make this difference more visible, more transparent, in order to show the 'utility' of the one and the 'absurdity' of the other. Education was an important tool in this project. It masked the intensions and controlled the results.[9] It established Western hegemony in a way no army could have done.

Since every European traveller and observer harped on the deficiencies of the native character, 'character formation' was projected as the main purpose of education and the content was expected to revolve round it. Elphinstone reiterated, 'there is no way to improve the morals of the people, except by improving their education'.[10] The system led to the acquisition of literary rather than scientific knowledge. As one civil servant noted, 'The study of physical and mathematical science is rendered more subordinate to the grand object of cultivating sound principles of practical morality and provident habits.'[11]

However, in the wake of the consolidation and extension of the Empire the training of local youth in some useful branches of science became inevitable. Thus consolidation of the Empire brought in its wake certain building activities which in turn required a continuous supply of a less expensive but skilled and trained class of overseers, assistant engineers, mechanics, and surveyors. The introduction of Western science and technology thus involved the task of creating through English education a middle class who might act as agent of colonial economy and administration.[12] Naturally, the government paid more attention to engineering than to other branches of science. A plan was formulated in 1840 to prepare a subordinate class of Indian civil engineers who would materially aid the European engineer, and enable him to extend the sphere of his operations.[13]

From the rulers' point of view, administering a colony and increasing its production of export commodities required new technologies and new forms of labour, hence a certain amount of basic technical education was inevitable. Yet the colonial rulers also wanted to preserve the social *status quo*, which they feared was threatened by contact with the West. This apprehension led them to favour the teaching of crafts and agrarian skills over academic education.[14] The colonized, however, demanded an academic education based on higher level of science and technology rather than training only in crafts.

From the point of view of technical education, India is probably the most interesting colonized area. Conquered earlier than other territories, India went through its colonial evolution sooner. The case of India shows more clearly than any other the dual nature of technical education: as a response to a demand for technically trained people and as a means of developing the economy for the future. In a colonial setting, education responded to economic and political pressures from both the colonizers and the colonized. These pressures were not cumulative but often contradictory.[15]

A constant in the history of technical education in British India was the contrast between the government's oft-repeated policy of educating Indians in Western science and technology and its hesitation to carry it out. Europeans held the managerial and higher technical jobs, Eurasians the mid-level skilled and supervisory positions, and Indians were in the unskilled jobs.

Frustrated by the British educational policy, some Indian luminaries took up the question of technical education because they thought it was a precondition for economic development. The turn of the nineteenth century saw education suddenly politicized in the struggle between British authority and an awakening Indian nationalism, with technical education as one of the themes. The belief of Indian officials, from the viceroy down, was that technical education was only meant to meet existing demands, and anything more would only flood the labour market with unemployed graduates.[16] However, Indians had a much more positive view of technical education. Many nineteenth-century educationists of India veered to the view that the educational system must develop a technical-scientific bias for the industrial development of the land. Otherwise 'we were bound to go down in the face of competition with the outer world, and remained bogged down in the sluggish quagmire of the past',[17] they said.

A detailed study of technical education introduced by the British in nineteenth-century Bengal would provide a better understanding of the topic of our discussion.

The Beginning

In the early part of the nineteenth century education was neither widespread nor designed to promote science, technical arts, or crafts. The 1830s were important, but not only for medical and general education purposes. Talk about steamers, telegraphs, drains and railways and the expansion of survey and revenue operations had brought to the fore the necessity of raising a subordinate class of surveyors, mechanics, and overseers. Trained local youth were obviously cheaper than technical personnel from abroad. At this juncture, imperial interests played a most vital role. During the last Anglo–Maratha war (1817–18), Maitland had noticed how difficult it was to secure the services of local artificers.[18] So in 1840, he on his own, without government assistance, set-up in Madras a school for ordnance artificers. But in Bengal it was the government that took the initiative and an engineering class was instituted at the Hindu College in 1843. In the very next year, the idea of recruiting a Professor of Natural and Experimental Philosophy was revived. But controversy arose whether the emphasis was to be on pure science or applied science. One section of the Council of Education felt that 'the course of the Natural Philosophy would be only such as is considered necessary as a branch of general education without being specially adapted to or intended for professional men'. The other section thought that 'the course should be a combined experimental and mathematical course . . . without which it is quite impossible for the engineer, surveyor, navigator or mechanist to become proficient men in their several departments'.[19] There was certainly a need for a class of surveyors and mechanics to serve the fast-growing survey and public works departments.

Training in Surveying

The government's attention was first drawn to the need for training Indian youth in modern methods of surveying. Madras had a survey school towards the close of the eighteenth century, started (1794) by Michel Topping, the East India Company's astronomer and geographical marine surveyor at the Presidency of Fort St. George.[20]

The Bengal government had no previous such experience and it approached the Madras government and its survey establishment for advice on 'an establishment for the instruction of boys in the principles of geometry, mensuration, and drawing with a view to the employment of them as land surveyors'.[21] In 1829, by which time the whole subcontinent was open to survey (for which formidable task, cheap Indian labour was indispensible) Bentinck had to acknowledge: 'It is by a more enlarged employment of native agency that the business of Government will be at once more cheaply and efficiently transacted.'[22] Under this policy the surveyors took a more lively interest in the training of Indian youth and a few of them even started schools. Gradually the idea spread beyond government establishments and the small circles of surveyors. As prospects of employment brightened, the educational institutions started thinking seriously about introducing a course of surveying in their general curriculum.

In Bengal teaching in surveying was introduced at the Hindu College and the Calcutta Madrasa. Mr. Rowe, the teacher in surveying proved successful in this job. The good start made in this technical education is reflected in the General Committee's report of 1835.[23] Thus the Hindu College showed the way and in time produced young Radhanath Sikdar, a brilliant student of that college, who was picked up for his talents in mathematics by Colonel George Everest and was in the service of Trigonometrical Survey of India as the highest paid Indian in government service before 1857.[24] Radhanath suggested a mathematical method to Waugh, the Surveyor General, through which the heights of all the distinct Himalayan peaks including Mt. Everest were measured.[25]

Establishment of Engineering Schools and Colleges

With the expansion of public works in the various parts of the country, a new interest was generated in schools and colleges devoted exclusively to the teaching of engineering and technical sciences. The country offered great scope for constructing irrigation facilities. This in turn gave rise to a need for civil engineers who could construct and maintain canals and other irrigation works.[26] Since irrigation canals were not common in England, the Company had to provide for the training of engineers for this purpose and consequently had to provide for the study of the technical aspects of irrigation. Other engineering projects including the building of harbours and docks, fortification, roads, the improvement of river navigation, telegraphs, railroads, and since the Company wanted to know what it governed, it commissioned several surveys culminating in the Great Trigonometrical Survey of India.[27]

The Corps of Engineers, the only agency at the disposal of the government, was insufficient to meet growing requirements.[28] The Company thus prepared a subordinate class of local civil engineers on a small scale. For its calculated exploitation of the natural resources of India and also for the maintenance of its own personnel on the one hand and political as well as economic influences on the other, the Company could not but establish the minimum number of engineering institutions. Accumulation of engineering equipment and workshops at various sites after the completion of projects sometimes provided an excellent ground for starting these and in a position to make the best use of these equipment.[29] Maitland's School of Ordnance Artificers, Madras (1840) and the Thomason College of Engineering, Roorkee (1847) owed their existence to such circumstances.

The success of the Thomason College of Engineering at Roorkee showed that for the purpose of training persons capable of carrying out great public works plans, and to qualify Indians for the exercise of a profession, similar institutions should be established in other parts of India.[30] Dalhousie wished to establish engineering classes in each of the Presidencies. Thomason College could not meet the demands of the vast Presidency of Bengal. Besides, it was not desirable for the students of the North-Western Provinces to be employed in lower Bengal, for they were unfamiliar with the language, climate, and habits of Bengal. On the other hand, Bengali students were reluctant to go to Upper Provinces to learn engineering and a majority of the Board at Lahore was not inclined to encourage the employment of Bengalis in that province.[31]

Engineers, particularly the Royal Engineers, were in fact major proponents of the application of science and technology in both India's development and in support of British rule in India. They saw the benefits to India and its government to be derived from increased public works. An early champion of increased engineering applications, Sir Arthur Cotton thought that the improvements which would result from increased public works would be the most 'legitimate way of consolidating our power' in India.[32]

There was thus a tremendous pressure for the opening of more engineering institutions in other parts of India, especially in Calcutta and Madras. The idea of providing technical education to the people of India was first mentioned in Sir Charles Wood's Educational Despatch of 1854. It stated:

> Our attention should now be directed to a consideration if possible, still more important, and one which has hitherto, we are bound to admit, been too much neglected, namely, how useful and practical

knowledge suited to every station in life may be best conveyed to the great mass of the people who are utterly incapable of obtaining any education worthy of the name by their own unaided effort.[33]

In the context of the urgent need for engineers, the Thomason College of Engineering provided a model for similar institutions, and such a development was in accord with government policy as enunciated in Wood's Despatch. Referring to the College, the despatch specifically recommended that 'now that the system of railways and public works is being rapidly extended . . . it is expedient that similar places for practical instruction in civil engineering should be established in other parts of India.'[34]

Contemporary Bengali journals were very much aware of such developments. *Sambad Prabhakar*, famous journal of the day, observed:

We came to know that the Court of Directors approved the appeal of Lieutenant Governor of the North-Western Provinces Mr. Thomason to establish Roorkee Engineering College. Subjects like civil engineering, canal irrigation, bridge building, etc., would be taught there. Such an institution should be opened at Calcutta also. We have heard that Lord Dalhousie started considering the matter.[35]

Another journal, *Sambad Purnochandradaya* mentioned on 24 September 1852:

We came to know from a reliable friend that a Civil Engineering College will open very soon at our capital Calcutta. The brilliant students of Bengal will study there free of cost. Lord Dalhousie has agreed on that and the officials of the Education Council have also concentrated to it. In the beginning a Government Engineer would officiate as Principal of the College and two other Engineers would assist him. Lord Dalhousie has written about the project to the London authorities and we hope affirmative response would come very soon.[36]

In May 1854, Lt. Col. H. Goodwin, Chief Engineer of Bengal, strongly advocated the idea of opening an engineering school in

Calcutta 'as a nucleus and preliminary adjunct to the future parent institute'.[37] Lord Dalhousie conceded that one engineering college was not sufficient for the whole Presidency of Bengal and that another college of a similar character was urgently required.[38] He later recommended Goodwin's plan for establishing a training school in Calcutta for artisans and working engineers.[39] This school was required to teach the theory or science of engineering as a perfect nursery for higher training. He also favoured a scheme for establishing a college of civil engineering in Calcutta for the practical and theoretical instruction of persons to be employed in public service. The Court of Directors approved the plan and in November 1856, the Calcutta College of Civil Engineering opened at the Writers' Building.

Bengal Engineering College

The foundation of the Bengal Engineering College (12 November 1856) was soon followed by the establishment of the University of Calcutta. The initial efforts of the organizers were directed to framing suitable regulations and bye-laws and courses of study so that civil engineering could develop into a respectable branch of professional studies. But the hopes were not fulfilled until the early 1860s. For the first five or six years the College continued in its own way, training assistant engineers, surveyors and overseers for the Public Works Department (PWD).

The course of study involved a careful consideration of the actual amount and the nature of the knowledge that should be imparted to a would-be civil engineer as also of the tests laid down for the various grades of appointment under the PWD. The following subjects were arranged for instruction: mathematics, civil engineering, architecture, surveying geodesy, astronomy, natural philosophy, mineralogy and geology, chemistry and botany, landscape drawing, geometrical projection, mapping including projections of the sphere, physical geography, and photography.[40]

In the initial period apart from the shortage of teaching staff, the textbooks posed a problem. It was not that good books were not available. It was the prohibitive price of such books especially in civil engineering, which practically rendered them beyond the reach of the students. Keeping the price in mind a careful selection of text-books was made, and book-sellers were requested to procure them from England. The teachers were requested to give their own notes and extracts from reference books kept in the library. Other problems included absence of workshop facilities and a want of apparatus, models, and machinery of all kinds, necessary for a school of engineering.[41]

The Bengali journals of the period were enthusiastic about the development of engineering education in the Province. They carried advertisements for admission at the Civil Engineering College. Thus *Somprakash*, the leading journal of nineteenth century:

ADVERTISEMENT: CIVIL ENGINEERING COLLEGE

From 25th May Monday, the admission at the College will start. Those who want to take admission there, have to apply before 23rd May. The admission form will be available till that day at the College counter from 10 a.m. to 4 p.m. The candidates have to clear the entrance examination of the University; otherwise their applications will not be entertained. The outsiders can also apply, but they have to submit a character certificate and pay Rs. 45 in advance for the course fee of one year.

Principal, Civil Engineering College.[42]

When the Company relinquished its rule to the Crown in 1858, it left a legacy of government activities, objectives, institutions, and supporting attitudes which the Crown accepted and built upon.

From their very inception the three premier universities of Calcutta, Bombay, and Madras introduced each a faculty of engineering leading to the award of university degrees in this professional studies.[43] Initially the University of Calcutta introduced the Degree of Master of Civil Engineering (MCE) and later the Licentiate in Civil Engineering (LCE). Meanwhile, Calcutta University had set a very high standard in its examinations, both in MCE and LCE. In 1862 it made an FA the minimum qualification for appearing for the LCE examination. The result was that no candidate could be found eligible for the LCE.[44] So in November 1864 this college was abolished and its classes were transferred to the Presidency College. This proved to be a mistake.

In England three years were found sufficient to train an engineer; at Roorkee even two years sufficed;[45] but in Calcutta the students were asked to undergo two years' practical training after completing a three-year theoretical course. This had a detrimental effect. Bhola Nath Das, an alumnus of the Bengal Engineering College expressed his suspicion about that.[46]

The civil engineering department of the Presidency College functioned for about fourteen years from end of 1864 to 1879. In 1878 the Bengal government appointed a committee to consider the question of establishing a practical training institution for engineers at Calcutta in connection with the Workshops of the PWD. The committee saw the merit of such integrated instruction and recommended the removal of the department to the vicinity of the training workshops in Howrah.

The government accepted the recommendations of the committee and the Bengal Engineering College was restored to its former status of independent existence, this time in association with extended workshop facilities indispensable for its very functioning. The government had already acquired a large area of land in Sibpur near Howrah for purposes of constructing the workshops and manufactories of the PWD, and now proceeded to purchase the old premises of the Bishop's College for accommodating the engineering college.[47] On 5 April 1880, the civil engineering department of the Presidency College moved to the premises of the Bishop's College with its new designation 'Government Engineering College, Howrah'. A contemporary journal reported:

> Calcutta Civil Engineering College has shifted from Calcutta to Bishop's College, Sibpur on 5 April. Those who want to take admission in civil and mechanical engineering, have to pass the entrance examination. For overseer class, there will be a different examination. The course is for five years.[48]

Four classes were opened at the College, for civil engineers, mechanical engineers, civil overseers, and mechanical overseers. The Lieutenant-Governor laid special emphasis on the establishment of a small class for the sons of artisans and *mistris* to enable them to pick-up some shop experience and 'earn an honourable livelihood in a profession for which they are well adapted'.[49]

The courses were revamped in 1882. The civil engineering branch had papers in mathematics, natural science, engineering construction and drawing. Mathematics had differential calculus, integral calculus and hydrostatics, while the paper on natural science concentrated only on geology, mineralogy and metallurgy. Engineering construction called for a knowledge of the construction of buildings, bridges, roads, canals and machines like turbines, steam engines, etc. The mechanical branch had a paper on machinery in place of the natural sciences and it dealt with different types of machines and workshop appliances.[50] The whole course stretched over four years and this was followed by one year of practical training.

An apprentice department was also opened to train foremen, overseers, etc. A class of photography was added in 1892, a mining laboratory was sanctioned in 1894, and the very next year a full practical course in electrical engineering was introduced.[51] With these openings, the Bengal Engineering College of Sibpur speedily established itself as a reputed engineering institution. The demand for engineering education at all levels gradually showed marked increase.

Technical Education at School

The nineteenth century witnessed the establishment of a number of technical and industrial schools also for training in industrial arts and manufacture. These schools owed their origin to private initiative to provide for some opportunities for employment. As early as 1839 a Mechanical Institute was set-up in Calcutta but this was short-lived.[52] The *Sambad Prabhakar* lamented,

> The Lord Almighty has created the world and gifted a precious gift to us in the form of industrial art which is flourishing everyday. Today

the industrial art has attained a distinct place by human intellect. So everybody should try to upgrade the industrial knowledge. The Mechanics Institute was established in this city to impart industrial education free of cost to Bengali youth. The Chief-Justice of the Supreme Court, Sir John Peter Grant, was associated with the project along with other intellectuals of the city. But a few days ago the institute was closed due to a general lack of interest. It is very surprising that while the European countries are endeavouring to gain industrial knowledge, here the Bengalis are showing a disinterest.

The English people import raw cotton from this country by which their textile industry is flourishing day by day. Indians are the main purchaser of British manufactured clothes. But they were not interested to learn the secret of textile technology. They consider industrial education to be humiliating for them. The rest of the world believes the industrial education as the prime ladder for their advancement, but the Bengalis think the opposite.[53]

School of Industrial Arts, Calcutta

A School of Industrial Arts was opened in Calcutta on 14 August 1854 under the auspices of a society formed in the city with the object of establishing a school of education of a practical kind.[54] It was started in the house of Raja Pratap Chandra Sinha; later the school moved to a new building made available by Babu Hira Lal Seal, a successful businessman of Calcutta. The sponsors expected that the school would maintain itself from the sale of articles made by its own pupils, but this expectation did not materialize.

Three subjects were taken up for teaching, (1) elementary drawing, drawing from models and natural objects and architectural drawing; (2) etching and engraving on wood, metals and stone; and (3) modelling and pottery. Later, lithography, photography and photographic printing were introduced when experts were available.[55] A number of European gentlemen interested in technical education were associated with the Society of Industrial Art. Henry Scott, Professor of mathematics at the Bengal Civil Engineering College was its honorary secretary. On 9 May 1854 *Sambad Prabhakar* reported:

The industrial school will be open very soon. Raja Pratap Chandra Sinha has donated a building for the purpose at Chitpur. Mr. Rigwood will teach pottery and Mr. Agiar will deliver lectures on drawing. It is decided that Mr. Henry will join the school to teach wood-work and Mr. C. Grant who will come from England shortly, will instruct in copper-work. This school will definitely help the people of Bengal to secure employment.[56]

After completion of the elementary course at the school, the students could proceed to any of the following courses: (1) modelling and moulding, (2) engraving and lithography, and (3) higher drawing and painting.[57] A certain number of students with superior skills and diligence were selected to become apprentices in the workshop. They had the advantage of receiving a part of the profits from the sale of articles.

Initially the School occasioned considerable public enthusiasm, and handsome donations were received for its development and maintenance. But this enthusiasm died down and the non-official sources of finance dried up. Towards the end the School became almost entirely dependent on government support.

The engineering colleges maintained schools or junior departments for the training of overseers, surveyors, mechanical apprentices and the like. In all the four colleges the school departments proved successful. Other special schools for technical education included the schools of art, industrial schools, and apprentice schools.

Schools of Art

Schools of industrial art, or just art, first made their appearance in Calcutta, Bombay, and Madras through private initiative around the middle of the century. Education in industrial art and design formed an important part of technical education at the beginning of its history in Europe, and a similar experiment was tried in this country.[58]

Industrial-art education was a central feature of the Calcutta School of Art. It had opened classes on drawing from live models, lithography, wood-carving, and metal-chasing, and maintained general classes in other subjects. The DPI's report recorded that the School had already attained a high standard in each stage and compared favourably with any school of art in England.[59] The students completing their education in the School developed a professional competence as good as any produced by a similar English school. The work of the lithography department attracted special attention. The School was fast growing in popularity; in 1882–3 it had 96 pupils; the number increased to 157 by 1884–5.[60]

Industrial Schools

Industrial schools, as the name implied, were institutions where boys were taught one or more trades by which to earn a living. The importance of this type of school in the scheme of technical education need hardly be overestimated. Theoretically such schools were expected to contribute in a big way to the country's unemployment problem, but in practice they failed to do so for a variety of reasons. In the first place the schools were not diversified. The majority of them were aiming at producing amateur carpenters or smiths of various degrees of inefficiency. All that such schools or classes did for a student, observed Croft, was to teach him an accomplishment for his leisure hours which he never fully acquired and which he would soon forget.[61]

Bengal had in the middle of the 1880s about five industrial schools operating with varying degrees of success. As far as technical education was concerned the survey schools at Dacca, Patna and Cuttack were doing a much better job. Like the school departments of the engineering colleges, these survey schools offered a course in the rudiments of engineering, road construction, bridge building, etc., and the training was good. Their students hardly experienced any problem in obtaining employment. Simultaneously several industrial schools had also sprung up all over the province. The Principal of Sibpur College was authorized to visit and supervise them. His college now functioned as a central technical institution to which these *mofussil* schools sent their best boys for final training and from which they received their supply of teachers.[62]

Apprentice Training

In 1874 the Financial Department of the Government of India appointed a committee to consider setting up a school for apprentices in Calcutta in connection with the Mint and other government establishments employing skilled mechanical labour. The committee examined the apprentice training facilities at the following establishments: the Ordnance Department, Madras; the Futtehgurh Gun Carriage Agency; the Calcutta Dockyard, the Bombay Dockyard; the Workshops of the East Indian Railway; the Workshops of the Oudh and Rohilkhand Railway; the Sind, Punjab and Delhi Railway, etc.[63]

At the Calcutta Dockyard, an Engineering Apprentices School was established in 1862, but had to be closed down for lack of apprentices. The few boys that could be found had trained on board the steamers. At the East Indian Railway, European and East Indian boys of the age of 15 years and over were accepted as apprentices. The apprentices received thorough training in the fitting and erection of engines and promising youth were sometimes recommended for instructions at the drawing office?[64]

Observing this, the *Sulav Samachar* reported, 'Recently Government has declared that an industrial school will start at every station for the Europeans. A European teacher will instruct there with a salary of Rs. 200. Our government is very conscious about the Europeans. What about the Bengali people?'[65]

THE PUBLIC WORKS DEPARTMENT AND ENGINEERING EDUCATION

Although a number of surveys had been initiated in the early phase of colonial rule, these projects had been uncoordinated and, more often than not, local administrators had a difficult time persuading the Court of Directors of their benefits. By the mid-nineteenth century, the influence of utilitarian philosophy, structural changes initiated by colonial administration, and imperial perspectives led to the incorporation of state-sponsored public works as an integral aspect of governmental policy.[66] The first half of the nineteenth century witnessed the initiation of a number of gigantic public works, that led to state involvement in the application of science and technology, and culminated in the creation of a PWD[67] of the Government of India in 1854. This coincided with Wood's educational despatch of 1854 and indicated a shift in official policy that had previously viewed public works, as a colonial administrator put it, as 'an unavoidable evil, to be undertaken only when it could not be postponed any longer, and not, if possible, to be repeated'.[68]

From its inception, the PWD influenced the growth of engineering education in several ways. The courses of the engineering colleges were structured to serve the immediate requirements of the department, rather than provide training for the higher ranks of the profession. For this reason, civil engineering remained the favoured subject. Indeed, all the colleges opened during the nineteenth century were called 'civil engineering college'.[69]

Like other engineering colleges of the time, the Calcutta College of Civil Engineering was to fill posts in the PWD. As early as 1854, Lt. Col. Goodwin, Superintending Engineer of Bengal, had advocated a college of engineering at Calcutta 'for the general improvement of the Department of Public Works'.[70] It was to 'educate youths under 22 years of age both theoretically and practically as civil engineers, for the higher grades of the Department of Public Works'.[71] Most of its students took civil engineering, either at diploma or degree level. At the Civil Engineering College, Sibpur, the Engineering Department was meant for the training of civil and mechanical engineers for the PWD, and the Apprentice Department was for the training of upper and lower subordinates for the PWD.

Until the 1920s, only civil engineering could be studied to degree level. Electrical and mechanical engineering was introduced at the turn of the century, but remained confined to diploma courses. Even then, these additions were made primarily because civil engineers employed by the PWD needed instruction in these fields.[72]

Because the government was not clear as to which department—education, industries or public works—should manage engineering education, the PWD exercised considerable control. The PWD also exercised considerable indirect control over engineering education through such means as examinations, practical training, and the provision of teaching staff.[73] Thus the origin and growth of engineering education in Bengal had an intimate relationship with the PWD. To meet the department's needs, civil engineering was developed at the expense of other branches. For civil engineers too there was not much scope for the development of higher levels of skill, as the PWD imported its senior engineers from Britain, and restricted engineering training in Bengal to lower level jobs.[74]

TECHNICAL EDUCATION IN NINETEENTH-CENTURY ENGLAND

The educational system introduced into India by the East India Company, science education in particular, was primarily based on the British experience. Later the crown followed the same path. The educational officers, directors of public instruction, inspectors, principals, and teachers all hailed from Britain. Fundamental educational policies were determined in London. The nineteenth century was the century which saw the evolution of scientific and technical education in England, where modern sciences were born.

England, although it was first to enjoy the benefits of Industrial Revolution, remained underdeveloped in the organization of technical education for her working men.[75] Her Industrial Revolution at home coincided with her colonization and empire-building abroad. By forcing an unequal competition between factory produced goods (e.g. textiles) and those made by artisans in village industries, England destroyed India's traditional industries and built-up a prosperity that further helped her in process of rapid industrialization.[76] Moreover, England was not yet menaced by competition from European manufactures. She was therefore content with her factory system and worldwide commerce of manufactured products, which gave her a commercial pre-eminence, and was in no hurry to improve upon whatever technical education the workmen and industrial supervisors managed to have.

The consequences of complacence and neglect became evident only in the course of the series of international industrial exhibitions starting with the London Great Exhibition of 1851. But this was not the first warning. Babbage had led a 'decline of science' movement in the 1830s.[77] The Paris International Exhibition of 1867 aroused British fears of vanishing supremacy in the field of science and technology.

The government was inescapably involved in science and technology in many ways in the early and mid-nineteenth century. The first government support for technical education had come, in 1837, for art and not science.[78] Eventually in 1852, a Department of Practical Art was set up in the Board of Trade; the next year science was tacked on to it. From 1856 this Department of Science and Art came under the Privy Council Committee on Education. The Department's main object was industrial education for artisans, but it achieved almost nothing until 1859, when it launched a payment by results scheme to teach not technical skills but scientific principles.

A House of Commons Select Committee on Scientific Instruction chaired by Bernard Samuelson reported in 1868. Two years later the government appointed a full scale Royal Commission on the subject chaired by the Duke of Devonshire.[79] These Samuelson and Devonshire Reports depict in great detail Britain's scientific and technical education at the period of profound political, technological and industrial change. They showed that England in 1870, the richest country in the world, had quite remarkably little scientific and technical education. Of that little, much was inadequate in quality.

The overall picture of education by that time was not very promising: public elementary schools were about to be created to fill the wide gaps in the voluntary system; evening science classes for artisans were scattered thinly round the country; a poor secondary education system included very little science; university education was seriously deficient in quality and quantity; two higher schools of science had a mere sprinkling of students.[80]

This picture compared most unfavourably with the evidence about scientific and technical education in Europe. The star performers were the German States and Switzerland.[81] They had universal elementary education, thorough systems of secondary education and universities, often side by side with the polytechnics (technological universities), all publicly financed.

In 1882 yet another Royal Commission, this time on Technical Instruction, was appointed with Samuelson again as chairman. The commission made extensive home and foreign visits and recommended that local authorities provide secondary and technical schools. Again little action followed until in 1887 a pressure group, the National Association for the Promotion of Technical Education, was formed.[82] Between 1870 and 1900 there were developments in three crucial areas: secondary education, technical and trade education, and higher education. A network of publicly financed secondary schools for science and technology grew out of the Department of Science and Art.[83] Teaching in the science classes was largely confined to scientific principles. Applied technical education was therefore left to voluntary effort. After public pressure to apply their wealth to technical education, the city companies formed in 1878 the City and Guilds of the London Institute for the Advancement of Technical Education. A central institution, opened at South Kensington in 1885, provided advanced instruction, and grants were also given for lower level technical education. The City and Guilds, however, could not cover all of London, let alone the whole country.

Meanwhile yet another Royal Commission on Oxford and Cambridge in the 1870s led to legislation which imposed reform and a redistribution of revenues. Science now flourished exceedingly at Cambridge with its predominantly mathematical tradition and might have flourished at Oxford even with its predominantly classical tradition. Cambridge established an engineering chair in 1875 but Oxford not until 1907.[84] In 1881 the government converted the School of Mines into a Metropolitan College of Science Applicable to Industry, together with a Normal School for Science Teachers, which later became the Royal College of Science. With the City and Guilds College, they later combined to form Imperial College.

English higher education in science and technology improved greatly in the last quarter of the nineteenth century. But in the field of applied science and technology the gap between Britain and Germany or the United States probably widened.[85] The British higher education institutions remained small and few, and central and local government grants which began in 1889 were relatively low. The relative British industrial decline that began about 1870 captured the attention of historians over the globe. David Landes believes Britain's failure in the nineteenth century to develop the education system essential for national efficiency was a main cause of the decline.[86] Britain had achieved so much in the early nineteenth century with so little education that she had felt no need to create the educational infrastructure which her potential competitors were building in advance of their industrialization.[87]

TECHNICAL EDUCATION: INDIA AND ENGLAND

At the level of higher technical education there was an immanent connection between scientific and technological instruction in India and the designs of the colonial capitalist state. The changing place of Britain in the international economy required that the colonial state be innovative in the founding of formal technical institutes. The College for Civil Engineering was established at Roorkee in 1847, while Imperial College was founded in 1889. The shortfall of text-books and teaching materials for engineering schools in England was initially met by the periodically revised lecture-notes, examples and drawings, and college manuals circulated amongst students at Roorkee.[88] These books codified Indian engineering practices and were 'hailed as the most complete and satisfactory work on the subject in the English language'.[89] Institutions established in Roorkee, Calcutta, Poona, and Madras represented an innovation in the history of British technical education. As we have seen up until the end of the nineteenth century, England had no formal institutions imparting technical education, and engineers received their training as apprentices. The engineering colleges established in colonial India provided models to emulate in England in the late nineteenth century, and the colonial encounter contributed to the development of technical education in Britain.[90]

It may be argued that when Victorian England itself was lagging behind its continental competitors in science and technical education, how could its government have thought of imparting higher scientific and technical education to its dependencies?[91] It is true that Germany and America provided greater state support to science and technical education than did England. But the latter was certainly not oblivious to the need of providing techno-scientific education. Britain saw an enormous growth in its number of scientific societies from 1770 to 1870. During the 1860s the government introduced vast changes in the university system through the Royal Commissions. This effected a change from polite to professional education.[92] But in India this change did not occur.[93] Another look on the British educational policy regarding technical education in India would further clarify the point.

THE CONTESTED TERRAIN OF TECHNICAL EDUCATION

The movement for technical education gathered momentum from the 1880s, largely as a sequel to similar movements in Great Britain and the experience of growing unemployment among university-educated youth. The Educational Despatch of 1854 did not contain any special recommendation on technical education, but referred to medical, engineering, and legal education and acknowledged the need for 'useful and practical knowledge suited to every station in life'.[94]

The Education Commission of 1882 was primarily appointed to review the progress of secondary education in the light of the provisions of the Educational Despatch of 1854. Problems of technical and university education were left out of the scope of their terms of reference. But while reviewing the progress of secondary education, the Commission noticed the complete neglect of the useful and practical studies that would help students establish themselves in life. The attention of students was indeed exclusively directed to university studies, mostly in the general line, and no opportunity was offered for the development of what constituted the 'modern side' of schools in Europe, calculated to equip the boys for industrial and commercial pursuits. So the Education Commission of 1882 advised the introduction of a 'modern' side into high schools and suggested the starting of industrial schools.[95]

Although the Education Commission's recommendation spurred the government to action, it did not do much beyond emphasizing the need for technical education. The Government of India Resolution of 23 October 1884 said that: 'The bifurcation of studies suggested by the Committee is of special importance at the present time. Every variety of study should be encouraged, which may serve to direct the attention of native youth to industrial and commercial pursuits.'[96]

At the instance of Lord Dufferin, the then Viceroy, in July 1886, A.P. MacDonnell, then Home Secretary, prepared an elaborate memorandum setting forth the history of technical education in India, the actual conditions and the lines of future development. MacDonnell examined the condition of technical education in the various provinces and the steps taken by each local government to give effect to the orders of the Government of India regarding the necessity of improving practical and industrial training. He found that nowhere, except in Madras, had any practical steps been taken to give effect to these orders. As regards engineering, MacDonnell pointed out that the nature of teaching in Calcutta, Madras, and Roorkee was too theoretical and these colleges were completely isolated. Suggestions were made about the teaching of science and drawing at the primary school stage, and about starting the 'modern' side of high schools and divisional or district technical schools.[97]

Reviewing the development of technical education to 1886, Alfred Croft remarked that, apart from higher instruction in law, medicine, and engineering leading to the university degrees in these subjects, there had not developed as yet in India 'anything like a general or systematic provision of technical education, such as the needs of an advanced community would seem to demand.'[98]

Francis Spring, Under Secretary to the Government of Bengal in the PWD, submitted detailed proposals for the development of technical education in the province. His proposal envisaged the development of agricultural education, trade, technical and factory schools, survey schools, engineering colleges, and the improvement of scientific education in the general schools and colleges. For advanced technological education Spring realized the need for central institutes. No such central institute existed as yet in the Presidency, but the Bengal Engineering College at Sibpur, the science department of the Presidency College, and the Bengal Medical College, he suggested, could be made to discharge the functions of such central institutes.[99]

In 1889 E.W. Collin was deputed by the Bengal government to undertake an industrial survey of the province and submit his recommendations on the basis of its industrial status. Collin found that the industrial class in Bengal constituted only 8.75 per cent of total population, only 13 per cent of which lived in towns.[100] These figures themselves expressed the industrial backwardness of the province. Moreover, Collin reported a number of decaying industries that needed a liberal injection of capital for their revival. In this situation the establishment of a technological institute or for that matter any school for higher technical education could be met more economically by bringing in a small number of men trained in Europe as and when necessary.[101] In the meantime the government should be persuaded to encourage the establishment of new industries and manufactories. In other words, there was no point in organizing technical education before preparing the industrial base.

Nevertheless, Collin made a number of positive recommendations in specific areas where there was an immediate and ready demand for technical education. These were in the field of mining, designing, training of mechanics and workers in wood and iron, agriculture and veterinary practice, weaving, and a few other areas.[102]

The Government of Bengal considered all these proposals but as usual took little or no action. The *Education Gazette O Saptahik Bartabaho* reported on the convocation of the University of Calcutta in January 1889. From this we can assume the dilemma on the part of government regarding technical education:

The convocation of Calcutta University was held at the Senate House last Saturday. Honourable Governor-General was kindly present there. After distributing the degrees, diplomas, certificates, he delivered a wonderful lecture to the audience. His lecture was really encouraging for the Bengali people. He said, 'I am very happy that Indians are very fond of higher education. The Indian students achieved respectable position in society by their performance in the University.

But one should understand that there are differences between British universities and Indian universities. In the present situation it is very difficult to make universities here like those in Britain. The biggest problem is funds. But in near future we shall overcome the obstacles. It is also possible to convert our universities from mere examining bodies to teaching and research centres. Indian universities should follow London University, specially its curriculum. Then only the Indian universities will excel in the field of higher education.

Due to unemployment among educated Indian youths, it is a general conception that as the government is unable to provide jobs to all the educated people, it has decided to curtail the scope of higher education. I'm sorry to say this is totally wrong conception. Such policy never comes to the mind of Indian government.

Job oriented education is very necessary. The problem of unemployment can be solved by such kind of education. But such education should not hamper the progress of general education. Another conception is that the content of university education is very much literary which is far from real life situation. So people want to learn technical education and demand comes up to open technical schools. But incorporation of technical education in the university curriculum is not healthy. It will hamper the cultivation of literature which is very necessary for nation-building. The university authorities are aware of the problem, so they are reluctant to start technical education in the present context. But without hampering the current university education, I'm requesting them to consider to commence technical education separately.[103]

An expanding but not diversifying colonial economy needed craftsmen, skilled workers, and subordinate technicians, while the managerial and creative aspects of technology could safely be left to Europeans. Technical education served to meet the current demands for craftsmen, engineers, and skilled workers in the part of the natives.

So the curriculum, the instruments and the very organization of the engineering colleges were geared to meet the requirements of only subordinate grades. Seldom did private firms of repute touch the graduates of these colleges.[104] For the recruitment of superior grades in government departments, there was an apex college at Cooper's Hill in England. This college was established in 1869–70 by the Secretary of State without consulting the Government of India; even contrary to its wishes.[105] Many of the officials in India did not like this superimposition of a 'superior' class of engineers. But the whole expense had to be borne by India without the advantage of any Indian benefitting from this education. The practical aspect of training at Cooper's Hill was found ineffective in Indian conditions and its syllabi too non-professional and academic. But the Home Government would not budge and the Government of India had to acquiesce. This college was abolished in 1903 after much hue and cry.[106] Its existence for more than thirty years nevertheless symbolized the supremacy of metropolitan institutions over colonial ones.[107] The higher engineering colleges in India offered meagre scientific and technical provisions and demonstrated little sensitivity to the specific, highly localized needs of the Indian economy.

The British interest remained with commerce, acclimatization, and the natural history enterprise,[108] and Raj policy did not erect institutions which could provide a significant cadre of skilled workers for service in either Indian or Western industrial enterprise. Furthermore, general socio-economic policy had reduced the ability of progressive indigenous groups to compensate for their loss of traditional systems of instruction.[109] At most, as far as technical instruction was concerned, the British believed only in the educational function of successful industrial projects. The government was not blind to the importance of technical education for training the requisite number of technicians for industrial employment, but its economic policies did not help the flow of capital leading to active industrial establishments which could, in turn, employ technicians. The reason of the ultimate failure of the Raj as a transfer mechanism for Western technologies may be found in a government resolution of 1888:

> ... the extension of railways, the introduction of mills and factories, the exploration of mineral and other products, the external trade, and the enlarged intercourse with foreign markets, ought in time to lead to the same results in India as in other countries, and create a demand for skilled labour and for educated foremen, supervisors and managers. It may be conceded that the effect of these various influences on an Asiatic people is very gradual, and that it would be premature to establish technical schools on such a scale as in European countries, and thereby aggravate the present difficulties by adding to the educated unemployed a new class of professional men for whom there is no commercial demand.[110]

Raj industrial policy did not, in fact, lead to either an increased demand for skilled Indian labour or the generation of educational servicing institutions.[111] Furthermore, several aspects of project development under British rule combined to severely reduce the overall developmental impact. The transplantation of techniques within enclavist projects[112] was not an effective means of transfer of technology into the Indian economy. Engineering and technical education thus had to remain confined to lower forms of instruction geared only to produce overseers, surveyors and mechanics of various hues, just as literary education produced clerks and pleaders.

TECHNICAL EDUCATION AND THE BENGALI *BHADRALOK*

In colonial India the acquisition of modern scientific knowledge was not purely a question of diffusion. The transmission of science was certainly one component in the process of political and logistic domination, in which it was necessary 'to convince the colonized that knowledge, whether in the sphere of culture, science or technology, could be acquired only through the mediation of the colonial rulers.'[113] It is a situation in which 'A knows B more than B either knows himself or A, and in which A tells B what he is or ought to be.'[114] The colonial discourse thus presents distinct categories and powerful hierarchies. Guns and sails could win territories but the empire could be sustained only by emphasizing differences and operating from a pedestal.

Western science and technology, viewed as a cultural import, were actively redefined by the recipient culture. A close contact with a vibrant, though alien, culture could not have failed to produce ripples in the minds of the local people. The continued display of new and improved technology by the British, though aimed at the consolidation of their power and an increase in productive resources, evoked a considerable amount of interest among the Indians. Their response to the scientific and technical education testifies to their awareness of the new phenomenon. The *bhadralok* of Bengal had become aware of the role of scientific and technical knowledge in transforming Indian society. As the reputed journal of the day, *Tattobodhini Patrika* observed:

> The founders of the Hindu College were interested to incorporate technical education in the curriculum. This was certainly a great proposal. If the government officials followed the path, then it would definitely help the larger student community. Recently many students after passing out from the college find it very difficult to get employment. Very few of them get government jobs and mediocre students mostly suffer. If technical education would form part of the college curriculum, students could live respectable lives. It is very necessary to commence technical education at the Hindu College. The college authority should consider the matter.[115]

The intelligentsia started showing its concern for technical education. The lead was taken by Dwarkanath Tagore (1794–1846). Although famous for his contribution to the promotion of Western medical knowledge among local youth,[116] his efforts to promote engineering education are less well known. Dwarkanath wrote a letter to the Secretary to the Council of Education on 1844:

> ... instruction is required upon no subjects in this country more than upon Civil Engineering and architecture I am anxious to be of some use to an institution in which I have ever taken the highest interest and for this purpose beg to place at the disposal of the Council of Education a sum of Co.'s, Rs.150 per mensem upon the following conditions, viz., that a chair of Civil Engineering be established in the Hindu College. . . .[117]

Ten years after his death, Dwarkanath's dream came true. The Calcutta College of Civil Engineering was established in November 1856.

The most important characteristic of the nineteenth-century Indian thinking was an unprecedented emphasis on cultural synthesis. Almost all the interlocutors of Victorian India talked of a cultural synthesis for the simple reason that it gave them the best of the both worlds. It enabled them to react to a strange culture and also promised a possible opportunity to transcend the barriers imposed by colonialism.[118] The assimilation of modern science naturally commences at the level of pedagogy. The standard tale informs us of the replacement of traditional pedagogy and curricula by new ones under the pressure of imperial dispensation. In reality science teachers had to contend with local cultural conceptions and knowledge forms as well as the need to mobilize the teachers of modern schools.[119] These contingent pressures opened up gateways for dialogue between modern science and the existing knowledge systems, a dialogue that generated interesting experiments both in pedagogy and in science and was to enrich both.

A new regime of technology was introduced as part of the instrumentalization of the programme of empire. For the Indian workmen, technology transfer under colonial relations offered very little scope for such a development. In fact, almost all the machinery came packed from outside, often along with a technician to handle it.

Opportunities for Indians to advance in the colonial educational and scientific services were limited. Indians were appointed to positions in the provincial and subordinate services, while the prestigious imperial services were reserved for Europeans. Whatever information Indians gathered regarding the making of some new technology was, therefore, a result of their quest for it.[120] *Grambarta Prakashika* a well-circulated Bengali journal in the *mofussil* areas, observed:

> We came to know that Babu Krishna Chand Bandopadhyay stood first in the final examination of the Roorkee College. He is the first person among Bengali students to achieve this distinction. Babu Umesh Chandra Mukhopadhyay who went to England to study medicine, secured the first place at the Glasgow College among two hundred British students. These are the proof that Bengalis can master European science and technology. But our government is still sceptical about the intellect of the Bengali students. The common argument is that due to caste prejudice, the Bengali people cannot perform well in the arena of Western science and technology. But after the achievements of these students, the government is now saying that Bengali people are not efficient in various higher level jobs. Passing an examination does not lead to success in professional life where one has to deal with various kinds of responsibility. These are actually excuses on the part of the government to exclude Bengalis from the higher level jobs.[121]

Even in an unfavourable atmosphere, in the field of medical and engineering education Bengal's performance on the whole was impressive. The response was perhaps better in the field of engineering. Even high-caste youths were not unwilling to study practical engineering and undertake mechanical work.[122] But the prospects were hardly lucrative. R.E. Fife considered the PWD 'singularly inimical to the native civil engineer'.[123] Native subordinates, however, intelligent they may be in engineering matters, had little chance of rising above the subordinate grades.

Bengali resentment of the preferential treatment Europeans received had grown since the second half of the nineteenth century.

This resentment was fostered by many highly publicized instances of transparent discrimination in appointments to the governmental services.[124] The resentment generated by this preferential treatment had twin effects. On the one hand, it led to demands for greater self-sufficiency in scientific and technological training and research; and on the other, it provoked the growing resentment among educated Bengalis towards British rule and hence helped the cause of Indian nationalism.[125] The government was only too acutely aware of this growing restlessness and sought to defuse it by clearing the lower decks for natives.

In the growing atmosphere of nationalism in the last quarter of nineteenth century, Dr. Mahendra Lal Sircar's concept of self-help in the matter of scientific education and research was a landmark in the history of modern India. He realized that science would never strike a deep root in this country under the tutelage of a foreign imperial power. What was needed was an institution for the generation of mass interest in science and for the training of scientists and cultivation of science by the Indians themselves under their own management.[126] Hence he wanted to establish an institution which would combine the character, scope and object of the Royal Institution and the British Association for the Advancement of Science (BAAS) of Great Britain. On 15 January 1876 Mahendra Lal established the Indian Association for the Cultivation of Science (IACS) with twin objectives. One was the cultivation of and research in science by Indians, the other the popularization of science.[127] Sircar thus set out his nationalist agenda: to build a culture of science in India through its practice and popularization.

This duality is an important aspect of modern science. Science has articulated itself in the modern world primarily in two diverse yet complementary modes.[128] One was the growing hegemony of science in the popular imagination. An unprecedented popular consciousness about, and participation in, the discourses of science marked the nineteenth and the early twentieth centuries. As a result, science was analysed, debated and re-analysed in astoundingly diverse ways. It was through this larger debate that science re-defined,

সমাচার দর্পণ

ON SCIENCE.—No. VII

Plate 1: *Samachar Darpan* was published by the Serampore Missionaries (23 May 1818) and lasted for a quarter of a century. J.C. Marshman was the editor. The journal was published in both Bengali and English from 1829 onwards.

One of the objects of this journal was to reproduce in Bengali articles about new discoveries and industrial developments published in books in Europe. As a result, many articles on science and technology appeared in *Darpan*.

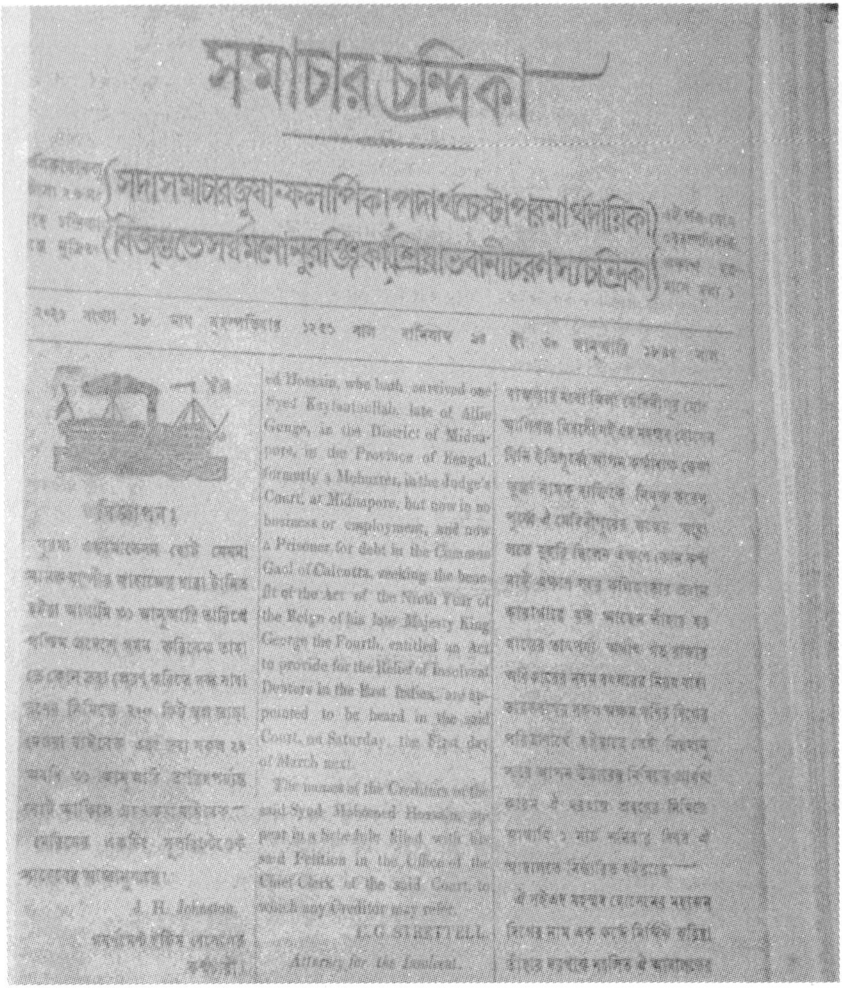

সমাচার চন্দ্রিকা

Plate 2: *Samachar Chandrika* was published in 1822 and Bhabani Charan Bandopadhyay was the editor. The journal represented the conservative section of the Hindu community. It opposed widow-marriage, female education, and the abolition of sati. However, contemporary scientific and technological innovations appeared regularly in the pages of *Chandrika*.

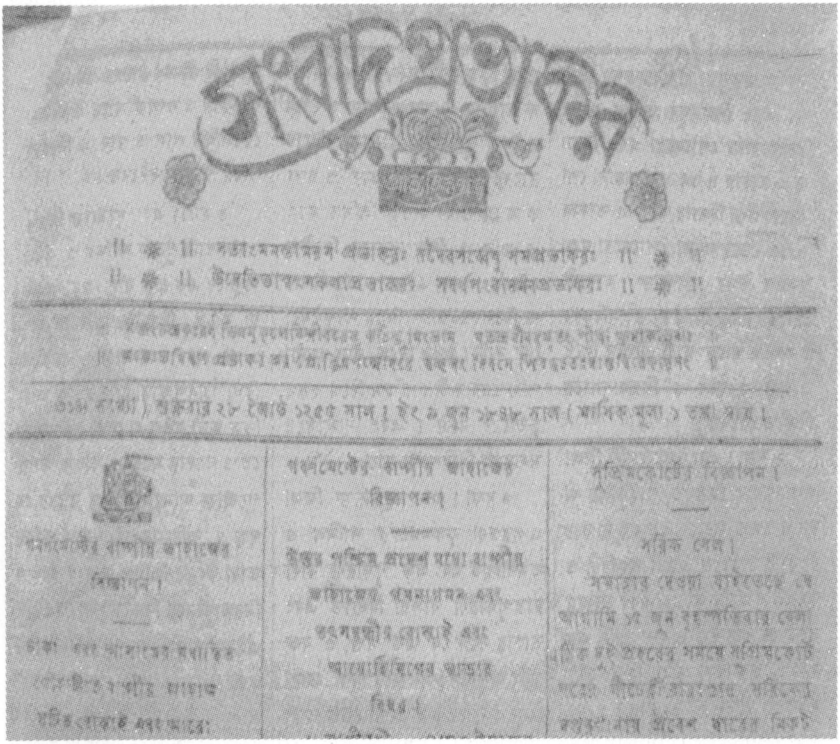

Plate 3: *Sambad Prabhakar* acquired an important place in nineteenth-century Bengal. It appeared as a weekly on 28 January 1831. Iswar Chandra Gupta, known as a conservative poet, was the editor. He was in favour of introducing modern technology in agriculture and advocated the development of factories and technical instruction in Bengal. *Prabhakar* asserted that the introduction of railways might be considered as a revolutionary event ushering in a new age (1849).

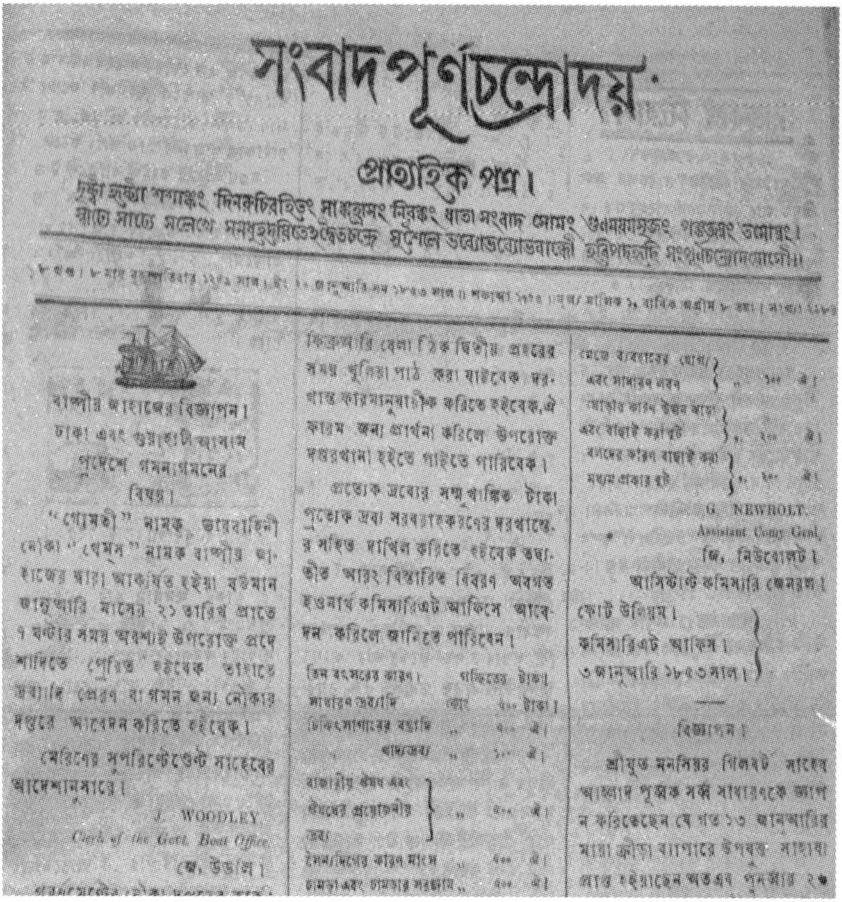

সংবাদপূর্ণচন্দ্রোদয়

প্রাত্যহিক পত্র।

বাষ্পীয় জাহাজের বিজ্ঞাপন।

J. WOODLEY

Clerk of the Govt. Boat Office

G. NEWBOLT.

Assistant Comy Genl,

বিজ্ঞাপন।

Plate 4: *Sambad Purnochandradaya* appeared as a monthly journal in 1835 and the editor was Harachandra Bandopadhyay. It was an excellent journal of the nineteenth century and circulated for almost 73 years. The various technological inventions of the day, steamships, electric telegraph, railways, etc., regularly appeared in the pages of *Purnochandradaya*.

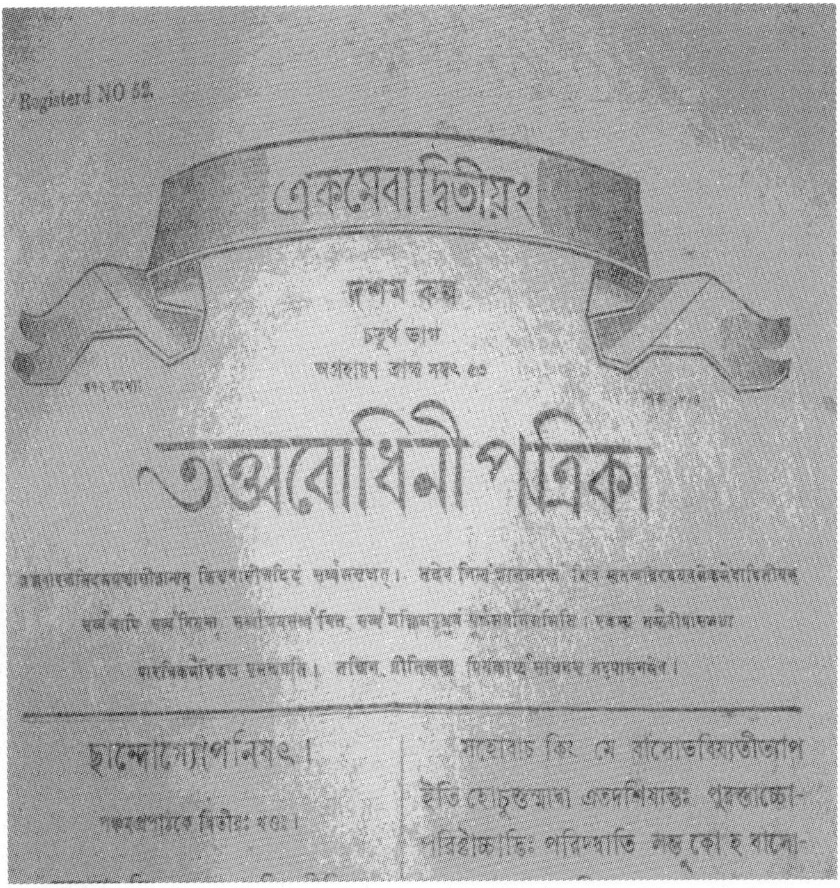

Registerd NO 52.

একমেবাদ্বিতীয়ং

তত্ত্ববোধিনী পত্রিকা

ছান্দোগ্যোপনিষৎ।

Plate 5: *Tattobodhini Patrika* appeared as a monthly journal in August 1843 and remained a crucial agent in the evolution of Bengali society almost throughout the nineteenth century. Although religious discussion was high on the agenda, many articles on science, technical knowledge, economy, etc., appeared in the journal. Akshay Kumar Dutta was the editor of *Tattobodhini* for twelve years (1843–55). Under his editorship it became the best journal of the day.

Plate 6: *Vividhartha Samgraha* (1851) was published with financial assistance from the 'Banga Bhasanubadok Samaj'. It declared itself as a monthly journal, with beautiful line engraved pictures, and was edited by Rajendralal Mitra. The variety of subjects, styles of presentation and illustration worthy of note, all contributed to the journal's ability to win over readers. During the tenure of Rajendralal (1851–9), many technological innovations appeared in *Vividhartha*.

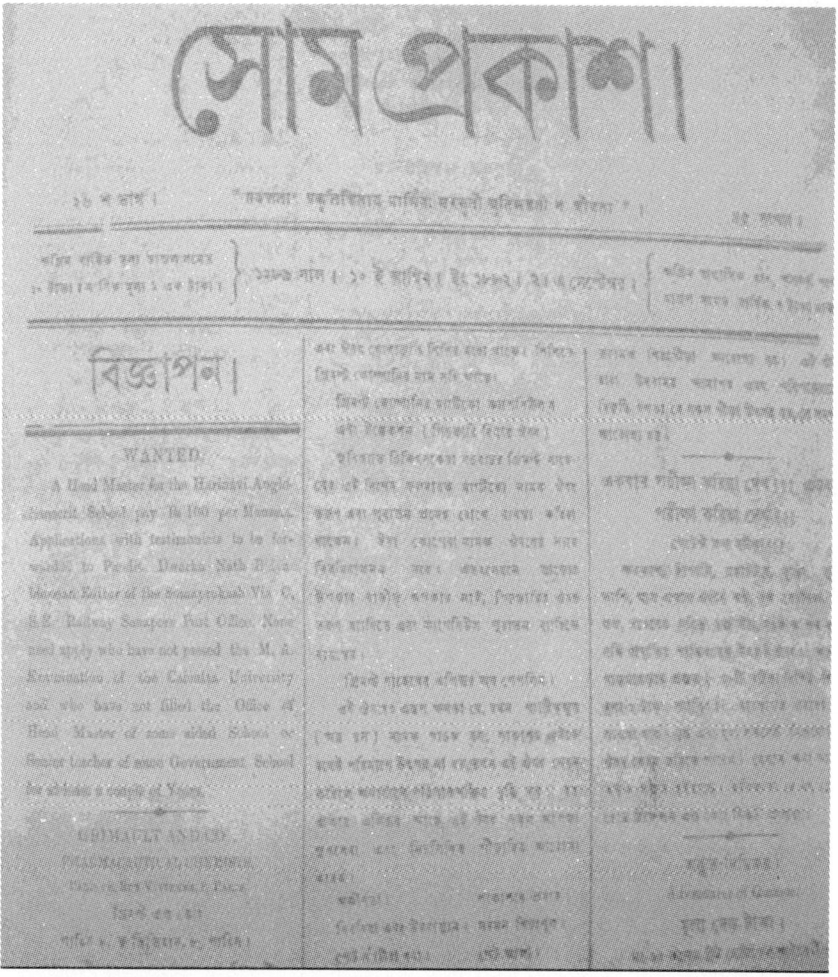

সোমপ্রকাশ।

বিজ্ঞাপন।

WANTED.

Plate 7: *Somprakash* was published on 15 November 1858 and was popular from the beginning. Dwarakanath Vidyabhusan was the editor. Pundit Iswar Chandra Vidyasagar was closely associated with *Somprakash*. The journal realized the importance of technical knowledge and industrialization. The demand for higher level of technical education occasionally appeared in *Somprakash*, along with the appeal to establish indigenous enterprise.

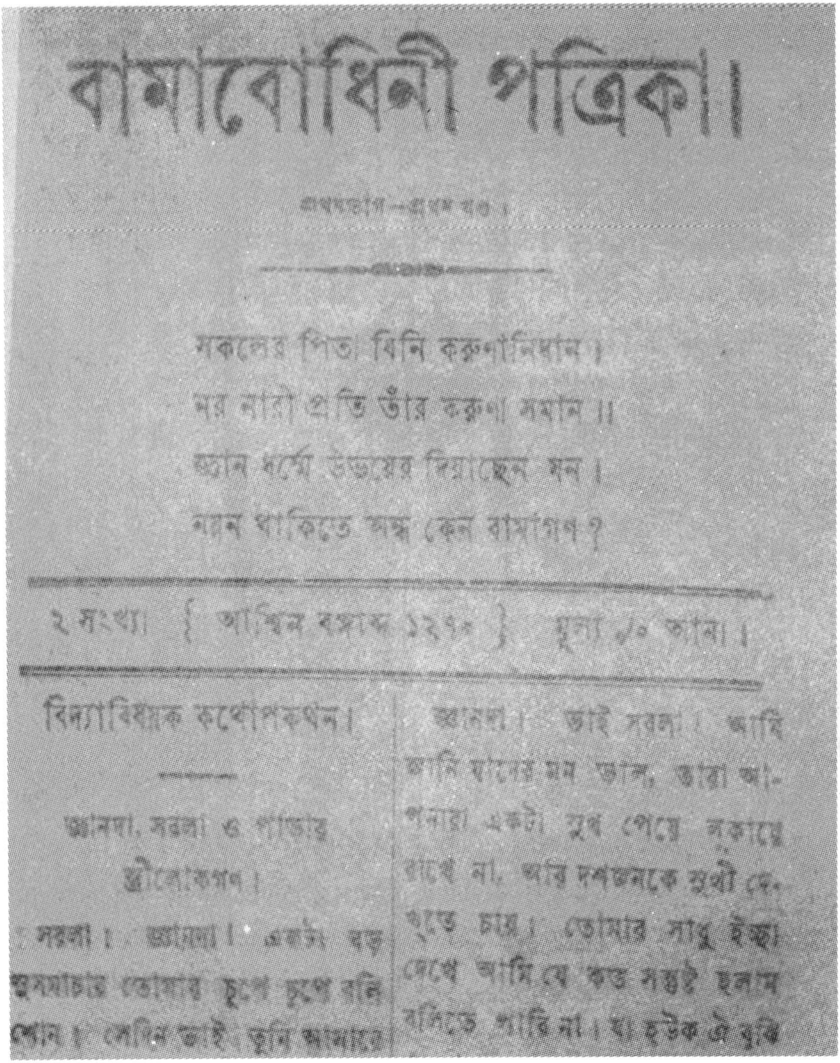

বামাবোধিনী পত্রিকা।

প্রথমভাগ—প্রথম খণ্ড।

সকলের পিতা যিনি করুণানিধান।
নর নারী প্রতি তাঁর করুণা সমান॥
জ্ঞান ধর্ম্মে উভয়ের দিয়াছেন মন।
নয়ন থাকিতে অন্ধ কেন বামাগণ?

২ সংখ্যা। { আশ্বিন বঙ্গাব্দ ১২৭০ } মূল্য ৵০ আনা।

বিদ্যাবিষয়ক কথোপকথন।

জ্ঞানদা, সরলা ও পাড়ার স্ত্রীলোকগণ।

সরলা। জ্ঞানদা! একটী বড় সুসমাচার তোমায় চুপে চুপে বলি শোন। সেদিন ভাই, তুমি আমারে

জ্ঞানদা। ভাই সরলা! আমি জানি যাদের মন ভাল, তারা আপনারা একটা সুখ পেয়ে লুকায়ে রাখে না, আর দশজনকে সুখী দেখতে চায়। তোমার সাধু ইচ্ছা দেখে আমি যে কত সন্তুষ্ট হলাম বলিতে পারি না। যা হউক ঐ বুঝি

Plate 8: *Bamabodhini Patrika* appeared in August 1863 under the editorship of Umesh Chandra Dutta. It was an initiative by the Brahmos to improve the position of women in the society. Here for the first time the Bengali women started writing about their own problems. The journal supported female education. Some articles on science of elementary nature were published in *Bamabodhini*.

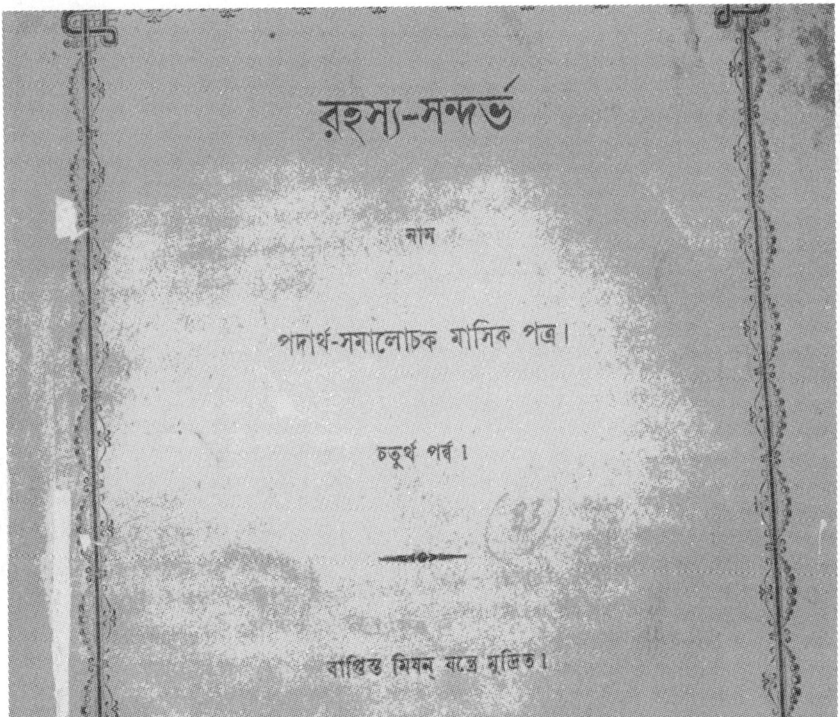

রহস্য-সন্দর্ভ

নাম

পদার্থ-সমালোচক মাসিক পত্র।

চতুর্থ পর্ব।

বাপ্তিস্ত মিষন্ যন্ত্রে মুদ্রিত।

Plate 9: *Rahasya-Sandarbha* was published with the financial assistance of the 'Calcutta School Book Society' and 'Vernacular Literary Society' in January 1863. Rajendralal Mitra was the editor. *Sandarbha* was a very popular journal of nineteenth century.

Plate 10: Cultivation of knowledge, both indigenous and Western, in Bengali was the objective of *Bharati* (1877). Dwijendranath Tagore was the editor. After him, Swarnokumari Debi, Hiranmoy Debi, Sarala Debi, and Rabindranath served the journal as editors. Contemporary eminent litterateurs of Bengal wrote for *Bharati*.

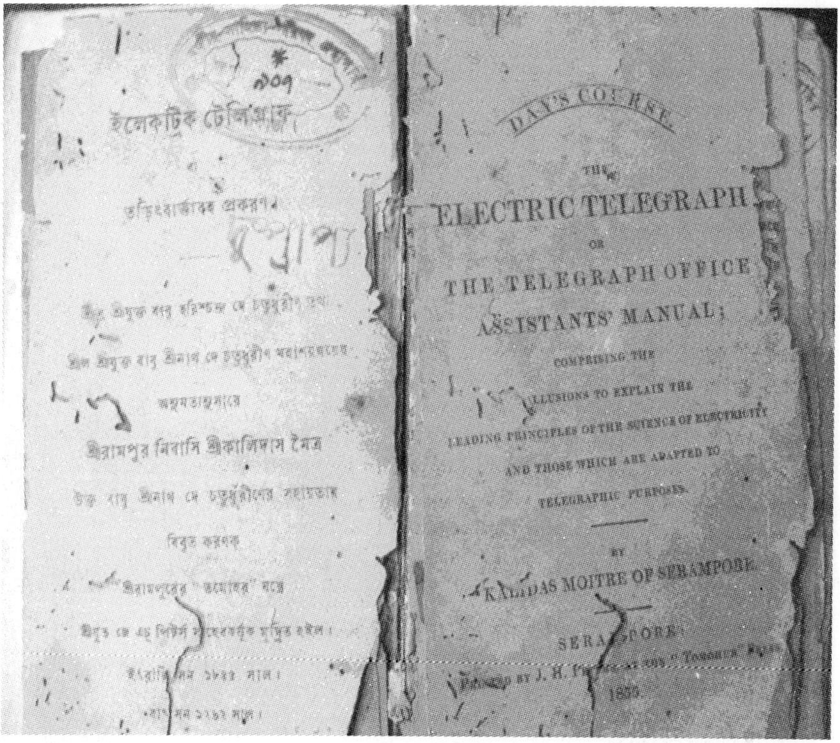

ইলেকট্রিক টেলিগ্রাফ

DAY'S COURSE.

THE ELECTRIC TELEGRAPH OR THE TELEGRAPH OFFICE ASSISTANTS' MANUAL; COMPRISING THE ILLUSTRATIONS TO EXPLAIN THE LEADING PRINCIPLES OF THE SCIENCE OF ELECTRICITY AND THOSE WHICH ARE ADAPTED TO TELEGRAPHIC PURPOSES.

BY KALIDAS MOITRE OF SERAMPORE.

SERAMPORE:

Plate 11: The year 1855 saw the publication of the first treatise of the electric telegraph in Bengali by Kalidas Moitra of Serampore. The author had first-hand knowledge of the progress of telegraph in India. The book contains a chart illustrating the Bengali keyboard as an alternative arrangement. He proposed sending messages in Bengali. Moitra ably described the functioning of electric telegraph in his book.

Plate 12: This engine was brought to India at around 1840 by M/S Steam Tug Association for running their tug repairing workshop at Kidderpur Dockyard. The managing agent of this company was M/S Carr, Tagore & Co. with Dwarkanath Tagore as one of the partners.

During 1844–5 the assets of the 'Steam Tug Association' including this engine was sold to a new company, 'India General Steam Navigation Co. Ltd.', for a sum of Rs. 58,000 only. This company employed this engine as its workshop prime mover at Garden Reach from 1846 till 1880. It was brought to a new site at Raja Bagan Dockyard in 1880 and did its duty till 1897 after which it kept as a relic in the premises of M/S Central Inland Water Transport Corporation Ltd. After July 1981 the company donated the engine to BITM, Kolkata.

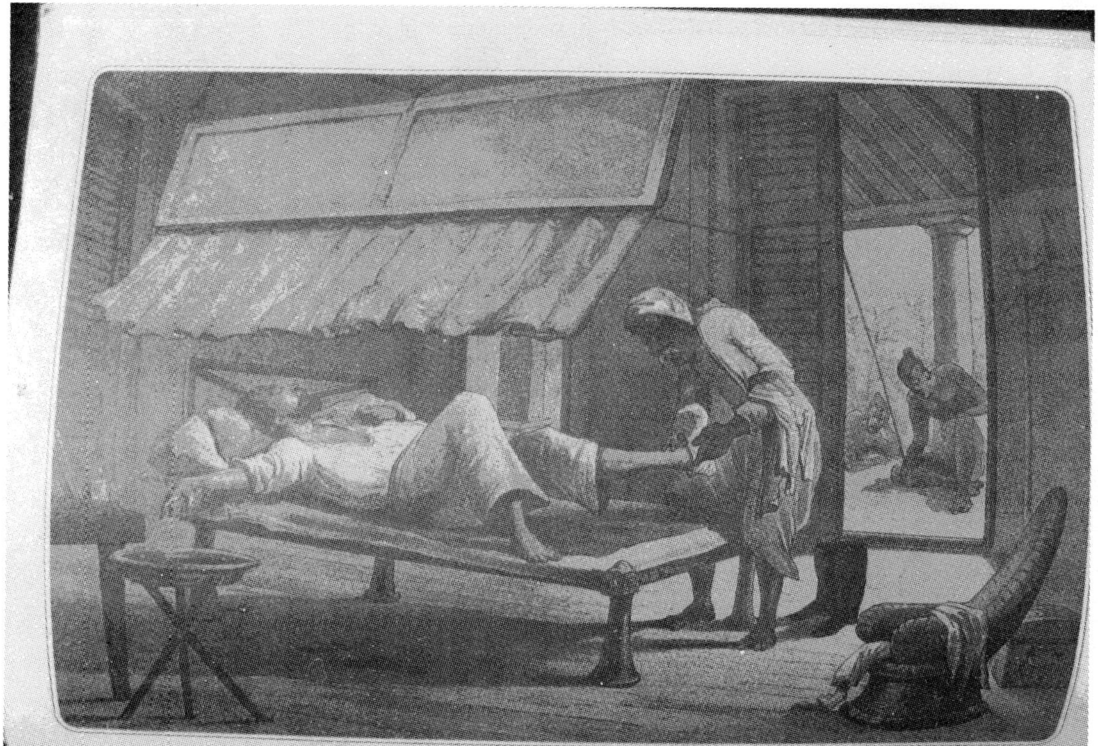

The 'Punkhah' — comfort before electricity

Plate 13: The *Punkhah*: Comfort before Electricity

Plate 14: *Electricity:* The Modern Wizard

কলিকাতা, বেনারস, খুলনা প্রভৃতি স্থানের ইণ্ডাষ্ট্রীয়াল একজিবিন্ হইতে ৮ খানি গোল্ড মেডেল প্রাপ্ত ও সর্ব্বজন সমাদৃত ও প্রশংসিত।

পি, এম, বাক্‌চী এণ্ড কোম্পানীর

এসেন্স পারফিউমারী।

সদ্য প্রস্ফুটিত পুষ্পের সারাংশ অভিনব উপায়ে বাহির করিয়া এই সকল উপাদেয় এসেন্স প্রস্তুত হইয়াছে। সৌরভ দীর্ঘকাল স্থায়ী, একফোঁটা রুমালে দিলে সৌরভে মনপ্রাণ বিমোহিত হয়।

১। কাশ্মীরকুসুম—ভূঃস্বর্গ কাশ্মীর পুষ্পের জন্য চিরপ্রসিদ্ধ তাই কাশ্মীরে চিরবসন্ত, তদ্দেশীয় সর্ব্বোৎকৃষ্ট ও সুমিষ্ট পুষ্পের দ্বারা ইহা প্রস্তুত। মূল্য ৸০ বার আনা মাত্র।

২। ভুলনা আমায়—(Forget me not.) ইহার গন্ধ সুমিষ্ট ও বহুদিন স্থায়ী। মূল্য ২৲ দুইটাকা।

৩। মনের মতন। (As you like it,) এমন প্রাণ মতোয়ারা সর্ব্বজন বাঞ্ছিত সুমিষ্ট গন্ধ আর নাই। মূল্য ১।০ পাঁচসিকা।

৪। জেসমিন্—সদ্য প্রস্ফুটিত জুঁইফুলের গন্ধ অতিশয় সুমিষ্ট ও বহু দিন স্থায়ী। ইহা অতিশয় তৃপ্তিজনক। মূল্য ॥০ আনা।

৫। রজনীগন্ধা।—এরূপ সুমিষ্ট ও তৃপ্তিজনক গন্ধ আর নাই। সদ্য প্রস্ফুটিত "রজনীগন্ধের" ন্যায় গন্ধ অথচ বহুদিন স্থায়ী মূল্য ৸০ বার আনা।

৬। গন্ধরাজ—পুষ্পের রাজা বলিয়াই ইহার নাম গন্ধরাজ সদ্য প্রস্ফুটিত গন্ধরাজ পুষ্পের তৃপ্তিকর সৌরভ চিরদিন স্থায়ী। মূল্য বার আনা মাত্র।

৭। বকুল—এরূপ সুমিষ্ট ও দীর্ঘকাল স্থায়ী অথচ হৃদয়ানন্দকারী প্রাণ মাতোয়ারা গন্ধ আর নাই বলিলেও অত্যুক্তি হয় না। মূল্য বড় শিশি গ্লাস্ ষ্টপার ৸০ কর্ক ষ্টপার ॥৵০ ছোট ।৵০ আনা।

স্পিরিটের ডিউটি অধিক হওয়ায় আমাদের প্রত্যেক এসেন্সের উক্ত নির্দ্দিষ্ট মূল্যের উপর /০ এক আনা অধিক বৃদ্ধি হইয়াছে।

কারখানা—৩৮, ৩৮।১নং মসজিদবাড়ী ষ্ট্রীট দর্জ্জিপাড়া কলিকাতা।

Plate 15: An advertisement of 'P.M. Bagchi & Co.'
Proprietor Kishori Mohan Bagchi, a prominent entrepreneure of late nineteenth-century Bengal, pursued a policy of self-reliance in the technological field and took particular care to promote research relating to swadeshi industries.

re-formulated, and ultimately affirmed itself. The other development was in the opposite direction. It was through the increasing specialization and professionalization of science that its cognitive language and symbols became refined and distinct. The growing institutionalization and specialization of science contributed to its esoteric and elitist status.

The Indian nationalist involvement with science demonstrates the manifestation of these trends. Science stirred the imagination of almost every nineteenth-century Indian intellectual, even one whose primary concern was not science. This was facilitated by the fact that science had established itself as the pinnacle of nineteenth-century European thought. Thus, science was debated within a wide spectrum of nationalist discourse.

The IACS was the first attempt at an institutional articulation of the relationship between nationalism and scientific research in colonial India. Mahendra Lal faced various oppositions at the moment of establishment of his brain child the IACS. Apart from funds, there were other more formidable hurdles. The Lieutenant-Governor, Richard Temple, was inclined more towards technical education than original scientific research. This made the big zamindars reluctant to contribute to Sircar's scheme liberally. The India League, founded by Motilal and Sisir Ghosh, came out with a rival proposal, of establishing a technical institute to be named after Prince Albert, consort of Queen Victoria who was then visiting India.[129] After realizing Temple's obsession with technical education, the zamindars of the India League hastened to call for the establishment of a big technical institute in Calcutta on the occasion of the royal visit.

At the request of the League and the Director of Public Instruction, Dinanath Sen, great educationalist and Headmaster of Dacca Normal School, prepared a proposal for the school of Industry or Practical Science.[130] Dinanath vividly described the necessity for such an institution, its objectives, mode of instruction in his proposal. According to him the reasons behind the backwardness of India in the industrial sector were 'the high pay necessary for employing European Engineers or Superintendents, the cost and risk of importing European made machinery, and the difficulty of having machines, when out of order, cheaply and expeditiously repaired on the spot'.[131] Dinanath's prescription was to create a local class of well-trained mechanical engineers and skilled workmen who could discover cheap and suitable indigenous raw materials and chemical agents for manufacturing operations. The existence of such a class of men would give a great impetus to the introduction of scientific methods in manufactures and agriculture.[132] He was interested mainly in mechanical engineering, as for civil engineering there was already Bengal Engineering College.

After few days of publication of Dinanath's 'A Scheme for the School of Industry or Practical Science', Pratap Chandra Ghosh strongly protested against it. He raised his objection in the *Hindu Patriot*: that the urgent need of the country was not a Western-educated engineering class but educating the native artisan class.[133]

Dinanath replied through his letter published in the same journal.[134] According to him the skill of the native artisan class was acquired by a very long course of training as apprentice under the elders of their families. So their artisanal skill was the result of hereditary aptitude generated by the same occupations being followed by the same families from generation to generation. No school could teach them such skills. He rightly said unless we could avail ourselves the two great advantages of European manufactures, first the extensive application of science to practical industry and second the adoption of the large system of production, and completely remodel our arts and manufactures on the European plan, there was no hope for the productive industry of this country.[135]

Dinanath lamented that native workmen were familiar with only portions of any branch of study; being devoid of any knowledge of theoretical principles, they did not know to proceed further. Our great want therefore, was of educated engineers able to take charge of mills, manufactories, and workshops and run them with the aid of country workmen and artisans. So the India League wanted to establish a 'European system of mechanical engineering and manufactures'.[136]

Such a great plan remained unheeded. The government did not want to spread technical knowledge beyond what was required for existing industries. It was more interested in the nuts-and-bolts aspect than in developing a higher level of scientific and technological education and research.

Mahendra Lal wanted 'pure-science learning and science teaching, with reference to the practical applications of science so far only as are naturally and necessarily inferable while carrying on experimental investigations. The object is not to drill men in the arts which constitute the manual and the mechanical industries.'[137] This was diametrically opposed to what Temple and the League had in mind.

Mahendra Lal Sircar received spirited support from Father Lafont of the St. Xavier's College. To quote Lafont: 'The other association wants to transform the Hindus into a number of mechanics, requiring forever European supervision, whereas Dr. Sircar's object is to emancipate, in the long run, his countrymen from this humiliating bondage.'[138]

The Association symbolized the search for a distinct Indian identity in the world of science. It encouraged Indians to engage in fundamental research in science and to develop their own hypothesis, and arguments, there by establishing themselves as citizens of modern scientific nation. For Sircar, science was the metaphor of nationalism. He stressed that political nationalism had no meaning without science as its guiding spirit.[139] Thus reported *Somprakash*:

> We are sorry to say that all the initiatives of the government to impart education are confined mainly in the field of literary education. Science and technical education remain the step-child of the government's educational policy. The only effort for advanced level of science education has been taken by Dr. Mahendra Lal Sircar. After him nobody is interested in this regard. For advancement in the field of science, rigorous scientific research is necessary. But unfortunately there is no such scientific research conducted in this country.[140]

It was easier for the government to shelve or refuse a proposal coming from an individual or a small group of persons. A big and organized forum could have exerted more pressure. The various landholders associations were basically spineless and happy to merely toe the official line. The scientific societies at Aligarh[141] and Muzaffarpur[142] did well, considering the constraints under which they worked. After their exit, Mahendra Lal Sircar's movement did try to fill the void. A decade later the Indian National Congress (INC) was to provide the most organized and the widest possible forum to ventilate grievances and raise demands.[143] The very third session in 1887 took up the question of technical education, and since then every subsequent session pondered over it. K.T. Telang and B.N. Seal pointed out how in the name of technical education the government was imparting merely lower forms of practical training.[144] They reeled out data in support of their criticism and looked to Germany and Japan as ideals. For D.E. Wacha, technical education signified higher education, especially of the sciences. Delivering the presidential address in 1901, he remarked:

> It is idle to talk of mere small industries in carpentry and brick-making and so forth. If there is to be an industrial revival of a practical character which shall change the entire surface of this country, you will have first to lay the foundation of teaching in the Applied Sciences. You cannot have the cart before the horse. Higher education must precede industrial development.[145]

Thus Congress was fast emerging as the most zealous vanguard of Indian interests. Whether it be education, agriculture or mining, Congress touched several problems in its wide sweep. The search for identity had found a sound and solid expression.

By 1900, Bengali intellectuals had developed a vigorous critique of the colonial discourse on scientific and technical education. In many cases, however, their criticisms were based on a number of equally restrictive assumptions, mirror images of the official ones. Thus the nationalists saw educational deficiencies as a problem of demand, rather than supply, brought about largely by the policies of racial exclusion imposed by the colonial state and its allies in the expatriate business sector.[146] The deliberate policy of training PWD officials in Britain, the limited colonial agenda for tertiary education, and the problems of getting Indian labour hired by expatriate capital were all important here. Furthermore, most Bengali enthusiasts for technical education linked the issue directly to the larger one of India's industrial backwardness.

Another, very limited, experiment in providing technical higher education was initiated at the 1901 education conference at Shimla, which led to the establishment of an Indian government scholarship scheme, especially for technical education, to enable ten students a year to undertake study at British universities.[147] It was agreed between Calcutta and London that the scheme should concentrate on the textile and mining industries.

A more ambitious scheme was launched in March 1904 with the formation of an Association for the Advancement of Scientific and Industrial Educations of Indians. Its primary object was to raise funds for the purpose of enabling properly qualified students to visit Europe, America and Japan to study science-based industries. The man behind this, Jogesh Chandra Ghosh, received donations from a large number of leading citizens of Bengal, including Europeans.[148] In 1905, 16 students were sent and gradually the number was increasing. An Industrial Conference sponsored by some Indian industrialists and the INC was held at Benares in 1905. The Conference recommended that a national polytechnic institute be established as well as at least one technical college in each province.[149] Regarding the first proposal, a person named Biharilal Ghosh submitted a memo on the necessity of establishing a polytechnic near Calcutta in 1897, eight years before the Industrial Conference.[150]

In Britain, the Industrial Revolution saw the emergence of the millwright from the tradition of village carpenters, blacksmiths and wheelwright. In fact, the millwright was the representative of the transitional stage between the traditional crafts and modern engineering. Such giants as Watt, Trevithick or the senior Stephenson and many others began their career as self-taught highly skilled artisans.[151]

A similar pattern, however, reduced in scale be it, does emerge from a study of the Indian pioneers working in an atmosphere not at all congenial, like Goluk Chunder, the first Indian 'engineer', Shiv Chunder Nundy of electric telegraph fame, etc.[152] But the introduction of engineering education did in no way help the Indians as it did their counterparts in England. In fact, the system of engineering education, which was primarily designed for manning the PWD, created a gulf between the illiterate *mistry* and the *babu* engineer. While the *mistry* with the traditional skill was denied the education, the engineer sought a profession tailor-made for the Raj and smugly got into an employment slot.[153] There was hardly any scope for creative application for the Indian engineer. Not only British imperialism but also the class-conscious and stratified Indian society was responsible for underrating the illiterate 'biswakarmas' in favour of Western-educated *babu* engineers. Thus the introduction of engineering education in Bengal had nothing to do with the people with talent and skill.

A few notable exceptions like Nilmony Mitra (1825–94),[154] the first Bengali engineer with a degree, pursued their trade independently. It is worth quoting in full the obituary published in the *Indian Mirror* after his death on 24 August 1894:

> During his college career, his extraordinary attainment in Mathematics, induced the Rev. Dr. Duff to exert all his influence with Sir Henry Lawrence, the then Lieutenant-Governor of the North-Western Provinces, to allow this first Bengali gentleman to enter Thomason Civil Engineering College in 1851 in Rurkee, and he more than justified Dr. Duff's expectations by heading the list in every examination and carrying off all the highest prizes. Specially recommended by Major Oldfield, the then Principal, he joined the public service at Calcutta and after five or six years of distinguished career, he retired from the service, determined, as he said, to open an independent line for men of his profession in Bengal, and he succeeded. Simple and unostentatious, strong in his principles and an upright and conscientious man, loved and respected by all, he rose to be one of the most distinguished men of Calcutta. He was an authority in his line, and was often consulted not only by Municipal Corporations, but sometimes by government officials. He had an unparalleled genius for Indian architecture, and devoted his life to its development, and many noble buildings, in and out Calcutta, are his living monuments. Thus, through

his exertion and personal sacrifices, Madhupur has risen to be the beautiful sanatorium it now is. Besides his professional duties, had to discharge others, no less arduous, as a respected citizen; and he discharged them all, conscientiously and to the satisfaction of all. He was a fellow of the Calcutta University, and Honorary Magistrate of the 24-Parganas and Dum Dum and also for some years a Commissioner of the Calcutta Corporation.[155]

The impressive list of Mitra's creations includes Pashupati Bose's house in Baghbazar, and renovation of the 'Belgachia Villa' along with the addition of a *zenana mahal*. Belgachia School building, the house of Metropolitan Institution established by Vidyasagar, the first building of the Cultivation of Science at Bowbazar Street, the palace of Jatindramohan Tagore, and 'Emerald Bower', were his. The plan for the Sadharan Brahma Samaj Temple was also drawn by him though he never embraced the Brahmo order. He was the first to build public bathing houses for men and women at Shyam Square in 1883.[156]

On 26 January 1895, Alfred Croft, Vice-Chancellor of Calcutta University, in his convocation address paying homage to Nilmony Mitra said,

> To the residents of Calcutta, it may be said *si monumentum requires, circumspice* (if you seek his monument look around you). The mansions of many of the wealthy inhabitants of Calcutta and other important buildings of public character, bear witness to the originality and success of his ideas.[157]

Yet, during the last years of the nineteenth century and early years of the twentieth century, a scientific and technical education was still conceived with a 'moral agenda'. Despite the increasing claims of science and materialistic philosophy, the education department clung to the notion that its goal was 'character formation'. A recent critic noticed an interesting ambivalence on the part of the British. While on the one hand, they complained that the Indians were too speculative, on the other they admitted that one virtue of having a contemplative, dreamy-eyed set of subjects was that it kept them from the pursuit of gain, allowing the British to step into the field.[158] While criticizing the British educational policy, one should remember that British Raj was not a philanthropic institution; they came not to rule like their predecessors, but to extract wealth for Great Britain. Their education policy revolved round that.

An interesting feature of the colonial education system was that it produced political leaders, professional men, and intellectuals, not just office clerks. No simple model or statement will help us understand why colonial education had the kinds of effects it had. It socialized many into colonial values but at the same time, it turned many of its products against those values. The rejection of colonial education may not have been sustained for long periods, but the broader rejection of colonial rule was sustained and we cannot ignore the role of education in inspiring this rejection.[159]

EDUCATION FOR INDUSTRIALIZATION

> The people of our country are more or less conscious about education. In a civilized society education deserves special attention. But the job-oriented education remains neglected so far. Through technical education the problem of unemployment can be solved. Technical education leads to industrialization which in turn maximizes the wealth of the country. But unfortunately the *bhadralok* community is unable to overcome its aversion towards technical education so far.[160]

In locating the history of the engagement of science, technical education and industrialization, Dhruv Raina and S. Irfan Habib introduce three significant conceptual dimensions. First was based on an ethical critique of the Western sciences and industrialization. Second comprised a pedagogical programme, accompanying the systematization of traditional systems of knowledge. Third acknowledged the importance of modern science and technology in effecting social transformation, but rejected the Western model of industrialization in favour of the Indian alternative.[161] There was a connection between industrialization, economic prosperity, and the growth of scientific and technical knowledge rooted amongst the Indian intelligentsia by the first half of the nineteenth century.[162] Later, however, several intellectual responses surfaced, of which the most important were revivalism, Westernization and revitalization.[163]

Revivalism and revitalization were not easily differentiable in the colonial setting. The intelligentsia arose for revitalization in the sciences, dangerously treading close to a revitalist edge in matters of culture.[164] This trend was very much present among the Indian positivists. Jogendra Chandra Ghosh felt that positivism and Western science and technology would liberate India from 'perpetual backwardness' without being enslaved by the 'Western juggernaut' and 'oriental exclusiveness and obliteration'.[165]

A large section of the Indian intelligentsia had awoken to the optimism that scientific knowledge brought wealth.[166] A missing connection between science and industry was being diagnosed. The search for identity intensified during the swadeshi movement. Perhaps the movement itself was an outcome of this search. 'The ideas of 1905' symbolized the determination of the people in two fields: (1) the promotion of education along 'national lines and under national control' with special reference to the exact sciences and technology, and (2) the industrialization of the country and advancement of materialism.[167]

Pramatha Nath Bose, one of the first Indians to be recruited to the Civil Service, superintendent of the prestigious Geological Survey of India, and later associated with the founding of Tata Iron and Steel Works, was probably the first to talk about science-based industries and the need to remodel the university curriculum accordingly. In 1886 he published a pamphlet on technical and scientific education in Bengal which attracted very wide notice and is said to have inaugurated the movement for technical education in Bengal.[168] He asked for the introduction of science at the intermediate level (FA). He found the B.Sc. course to be 'some sort of a compromise between the literary and the scientific courses' and which had proved a failure. He wanted science subjects to be taught with an eye to their application to industry. He was worried about the exploitation of Indian resources exclusively by Western enterprise. So he called for some sort of higher technical education to enable Indians to also measure up. An Indian Industries Association was formed in 1891.[169] Its principal members were P. N. Bose and Trailokya Nath Mukherjee. They arranged a series of popular lectures and experimented with indigenous raw-materials but without much success.

It was felt that scientific and technical education was a necessary precondition to industrial growth. Technical institutes were visualized as providing skilled workmen who would become the agents of technological progress. The task was to initiate an 'industrial regeneration of India' by educating the 'Indian artificer' with the skills of modern science and technology.[170] Effective strategy of industrialization could only be premised upon a system of technical education that was sensitive to the demands of real contexts. Industrialization required expansion of the system of technical education so as to provide an army of technologists and technicians.

Somprakash opined on 30 July 1883:

THE INDUSTRIAL DEVELOPMENT OF INDIA

Why is a high level of technological innovations like steam engine not produced in this country? Why we are still depending on others for advanced technology? The common answer is that our country is still underdeveloped. But we think you are not trying to upgrade yourself, blaming the country is very easy. Many artisans of our country are making beautiful products. So why we are still importing bulk of such products from foreign country? We are confident, if proper encouragement and capital are provided to the artisans, they would definitely excel in their field. Locomotives can also be produced here. But due to lack of encouragement in the part of our countrymen that the situation will gradually worsen. Our students are getting academic degrees like the M.A. and B.A. But if they study technical education, then nobody can stop us.

Many artisans of India are very promising. The artisans of Burdwan and Bhawanipur are making various industrial goods imitating foreign products. Their attempts are very satisfactory. There are some iron factories in Calcutta also; some brilliant workers are working there. But they are not properly trained in their field. If they get sufficient technical education, the outcome would be far better.

More and more people are interested in education now. What should be the aim of education in this context? The aim should be self-reliance. Printing products, good quality ink, paper, etc., should be prepared here. The environment should also be protective. The higher levels of industrial projects require huge investment which is outside the capacity of middle-class people. So the rich people should come with these ventures. We are requesting the British Indian Association to think on this and to not confine them in matters like rent bill only.

The members of the associations should consider the condition of the iron factories of Calcutta. We came to know a member of Indian Association has sent a student to appear in the civil service examination in England. Such kind of patronization is very necessary in the field of technical education. We are again requesting the members of the association to call technicians from Britain to train the artisan class of this country. If machines like steam engine are produced here at a low cost, then it would certainly stimulate various industries. The moulding of iron has started in this country. But due to lack of expertise, few faults are hampering the process. If we bring the experts of the iron industry from England to instruct our artisans, then the out-products would be faultless.[171]

In Bengal the first decade of twentieth century proved critical for science and technology where the political topography was radically altered by two events. Firstly, the Bengali *bhadralok* formed a large intellectual proletariat, who turned unemployed in the prevalent dispensation and this became a reproductive ground for agitation and political militancy.[172] Secondly, the self-esteem of the newly emerging class was crushed by the partition of Bengal in 1905.[173] The nationalist movement was strengthened by the rising unemployment and the partition of Bengal.

The Dawn Society, established in 1902 by Satish Chandra Mukherjee, was thinking in terms of a 'national' education in literary, scientific and technical subjects, and in the wake of the political stimulus provided by the partition of Bengal, it was transformed into the National Council of Education (NCE) in November 1905. As the IACS was mainly concerned with pure and popular science, technology remained an uncharted terrain till the end of the nineteenth century. At last the Dawn Society took the charge and the cultivation of science and technology were automatically transformed into the agenda of the swadeshi movement.[174]

Although the Dawn Society was established in 1902, its mouthpiece, *The Dawn Magazine*, had been started in 1897. In 1904 it was renamed *The Dawn and the Dawn Society's Magazine.* Although the Dawn Society merged with the NCE in 1905, the magazine lasted till 1913.[175] The reflection of the intellectual climate of the period and the thinking on science and technical education was evident in the pages of *The Dawn.*

The NCE had the support of the cream of the intelligentsia and the most prominent Bengalis of the time. The Council was intended to be a National University, free of European control and aid, and aimed at a fusion between the best of the East and West. It formulated an ambitious scheme touching upon all aspects of education, literary, scientific and technical.[176] This clearly pointed to the lack of access to much coveted educational and career opportunities within the government or even in Calcutta University. But cracks soon began to appear. Influential persons like Taraknath Palit, Neelratan Sarkar and P.N. Bose wanted the Council to confine itself to scientific and technical education. This was not acceded to by the majority of council members, so on the very day the NCE was officially registered, a second organization, its rival, was ushered into existence. This was the Society for the Promotion of Technical Education (SPTE).[177] The SPTE went on in 1906 to set-up the Bengal Technical Institute (BTI), and while the NCE established the Bengal National College and School two weeks later.

The aim of the BTI as announced was to impart scientific and technical education to the 'Indian people to further their industrial progress'.[178] The division within the *bhadralok* was based on the place of science and technology in a 'liberal education' and the nature of technical education best suited to the Indian environment.[179] The Bengal National College (BNC) hoped to grow into a 'poly-facultied university', competent in replacing the Calcutta University gradually.[180] But the BTI did not intend to interrupt the process culturally perceiving itself as a body for the instruction of industrial education which had been ignored by the Calcutta University and the Directorate of Public Instruction (DPI) so far.[181] J.C. Bose, P.N. Bose, P.C. Ray, B.N. Seal served the BTI while the BNC had the support of Rabindranath Tagore, Gurudas Banerjee, Ramendra Trivedi, Aurobindo Ghose, Benoy Sarkar and many others. Modern industrialization was perceived as a final solution of their problem caused by widespread education and growth of population. A new educational philosophy, different from the traditional apprenticeship, was required for the proposed modernization of the industrial system. The new pedagogy of the industrial era supposed to be 'instructional' and not 'commercial'; as manifested in *The Dawn*, 'The workshop should not be a shop or a factory but an educational classroom.'[182]

The modification of the curriculum of technical education was guided by two fundamental grounds: (i) need for a systematic reorganization of traditional knowledge against the setting of the modern scientific-technological system, and (ii) need for a new pedagogic vision of technical education, both theoretical and practical.[183] The core programme of technical education was confined to the dissemination of technical knowledge which did not provide the artisan with instruments to defend him in the industrial milieu. Technical education had to be supplemented by a more general education. The purpose of general education was the 'moral reawakening' of the worker and to sensitize him to commercial trends.[184] Seeing the technical schools as an 'important factor in modern industrial progress', P.N. Bose nevertheless held this to be pernicious unless complemented by a training in 'the mental and moral sciences'.[185]

The activities of this era had an important feature. Almost all the exponents of swadeshi looked to Japan as for inspiration.[186] Japan's emergence as a viable industrial power and its subsequent military victory over Russia in 1904–5 caught the imagination. The lesson was that 'if the rice-eating Japs could do it why not the rice-eating Bengalis'.

The *Education Gazette O Saptahik Bartabaho* commented on 25 January 1889:

> [M]achine-made products are cheap due to the blessings of technology. Here physical force is replaced by mechanical force and the products become cheap due to low labour cost. It is a totally wrong conception that many labours of our country would be jobless due to rapid industrialization like the West. Most of the population of our country depends on agriculture. Naturally the pressure is huge on the agricultural sector. Through industrialization this gigantic pressure can be transferred to the industrial sector from agriculture. But unfortunately there is no sign of industrialization so far in our country.
>
> At present there are only 350 industries in India. Among these, 61 industries are situated in Bombay Presidency and 86 in Calcutta and its adjacent areas. Although Russia is mainly an agricultural country, it has more than 500 textile industries. The poor state of industry is the proof of India's backwardness in science and technology.
>
> Japan is learning European science and technology very fast. They visit the European countries and America in large numbers and learn the principles of various industrial arts. After returning home, they start their own industries with newly-acquired Western science and technology. Unless we follow the Japanese and learn technical education, India will remain backward in the industrial sector. To overcome this situation we have to acquaint with Western science and technology.[187]

Redefinition of the relationship of science, technical education and industrialization by the recipient culture had a functional link, referring in particular to the requirements of the industrial setting. The major emphasis was on developing 'science-based' industries[188] without generating evils of 'Western industrialism'. Addressing the industrialization of India, this concern articulated differences with the form of Western industrialization, voicing doubts, about the alienation of the industrial working class and consequent labour unrest. P.N. Bose felt that the miseries of the world were largely due to the uncontrolled and thoughtless application of natural science to industrialism. He believed that 'at the present state of our industrial development, I have always understood its function to be chiefly the revival of our own practically extinct industries on modern lines'.[189] He was fully conscious of the manifold evils of modern industrialism, but, to quote his words: 'If I had choice, I would go back to the old ways. But there is none, at least under present conditions.'[190] He repeatedly suggested that refusing participation in the project of modernization would only limit the growth of the Indian economy and will be harmful to the realization of sovereignty. Majority of the interlocutors felt that India could try to avoid the evils of industrialism of the West. But as marked by V.G. Kale, 'we cannot remain where we were or what we are. We must advance, we must imitate, we must assimilate'.[191]

Industrialize or Perish

The logic of the metropolis–colony relationship was not in favour of the latter getting anything like a higher form of scientific or technical education. What it got was some sort of a hybrid emerging out of a careless fusion between industrial and technical education. For the colonial administrators technical assistance from Indians was more important than Indian expertise. Proper scientific and technical education did not fit into the exigencies of the Raj. In Europe technical education was developed in order to facilitate the process of industrialization. In India there was no such imperative. The numerous English journals of the period also echoed the same official version regarding technical education and industrialization. As the *Calcutta Review* remarked, 'For the development of her natural resources, India's most crying need is not higher technical education, but private enterprise and private capital.'[192]

Discrimination, it has been seen, was a major plank on which the British policy rested. But with the passage of time Indians were not likely to accept this without protest. The ground had already been prepared as early as the 1840s[193] by the initiatives of the vernacular press. The Bengali journals of nineteenth century started demanding technical education for the Bengalis. The growing problem of educated unemployment among Bengalis gave rise to questions concerning the relationship between higher education and business as a career. In the latter half of the nineteenth century, Bengali journals demanded higher levels of technical education, instead of the current plan which was comprised of few technical skills to fill up the lower strata of various government jobs, specially the PWD. Realizing that higher technical education and industrialization were of the utmost necessity for India's salvation, journals like *Sambad Prabhakar*, *Sambad Purnochandradaya*, *Somprakash*, and *Tattobodhini Patrika* started propagating the new tenor among the Bengali people.[194]

Discrimination in scientific and technical education made Indians react strongly during the last quarter of the nineteenth century. M.L. Sircar, P.N. Bose, J.C. Bose, P.C. Ray, etc., were the first rays of the new dawn. In the early 1880s P.N. Bose emerged as a link between India's demand for higher level of technical education and its fulfilment through the works of the BTI's students of the second decade of twentieth century, who came to be referred to as the Jadavpur engineers and technologists. The British model was inadequate. The new icons were Japan and Germany, and the new watchword was science-based technology. The nationalists were largely instrumental in ushering in the modern capitalist era in Bengal in the first half of the twentieth century, based on higher levels of techno-scientific education.

Delivering the presidential address at the Bengal Industrial Conference in 1891, P.N. Bose stated:

> The condition of the middle class is no better than that of the mass of the people; probably it is worse. The government services can offer only a few drops of water amongst thirsty millions; can afford relief only to an insignificant fraction of our distressed population. The only remedy that is likely to be of very wide application, that is likely to afford substantial relief to all classes of our people, is the development of our industries. It is industries alone that can relieve the distress of the mass of the people by lightening the pressure upon land; it is industries alone that can relieve the distress of our middle classes by affording them openings other than clerkships.[195]

Nothing could describe the call of the time better than this.

NOTES

1. S. Ambirajan, 'Science and Technology Education in South India', in Roy Macleod and Deepak Kumar (eds.), *Technology and the Raj: Western Technology and Technical Transfers to India 1700-1947*, Sage, New Delhi, 1995, p. 112.
2. See, for instance, George Basalla, 'The Spread of Western Science', *Science*, vol. 156, no. 5, 1967, pp. 611–22.
3. Referred to somewhat loosely as technical education in the colonial records.
4. See J.C. Cumming, *Technical and Industrial Instruction in Bengal, 1880–1908* (part I of special report), Office of the Superintendent Government Printing, Calcutta, 1908.
5. Ibid.
6. E.W. Collin, *Report on the Existing Arts and Industries in Bengal*, Bengal Secretariat Press, Calcutta, 1890, pp. 14–15.
7. P.N. Bose, 'Technical and Scientific Education in Bengal', Pamphlet, 1886, *Essays and Lectures on the Industrial Development of India*, Newman & Co., Calcutta, 1906, p. 59.
8. Deepak Kumar, *Science and the Raj: A Study of British India*, 2nd edn., Oxford University Press, New Delhi, 1995, p. 113.
9. Gauri Viswanathan, *Masks of Conquest: Literary Study and British Rule in India*, Columbia University Press, New York, 1989.
10. T.E. Colebrooke, *Life of the Hon'ble M. Elphinstone*, vol. II, Parker, Son & Brown, London, 1884, p. 149.
11. *A Treatise on Popular Education in India*, by a civil servant, Calcutta, 1841, pp. 122–3; quoted in Satpal Sangwan, 'Science Education in India under Colonial Constraints, 1792-1857', *Oxford Review of Education*, vol. 16, no. 1, 1990, pp. 81–95.
12. B.B. Misra, *The Indian Middle Class: Their Growth in Modern Times*, Oxford University Press, New Delhi, 1978, p. 152.
13. Sangwan, op. cit.
14. Daniel R. Headrick, *The Tentacles of Progress: Technology Transfer in the Age of Imperialism, 1850-1940*, Oxford University Press, New York, 1988, p. 306.
15. Ibid., p. 316.
16. B.V. Subbarayappa, 'Western Science in India up to the End of the Nineteenth Century A.D.', in D.M. Bose, S.N. Sen and B.V.

Subbarayappa (eds.), *A Concise History of Science in India*, Indian National Science Academy, New Delhi, 1971, pp. 548–51.

17. Susobhan Sarkar, *On the Bengal Renaissance*, Papyrus, Calcutta, 1979, p. 124.
18. Maitland latter recalled: 'there was a terrible dearth of practical men for the public service, and may account for the very expenditure of artillery carriages, carts and mechanics in the ordnance departments', quoted in Deepak Kumar, *Science and the Raj*, p. 54.
19. Deepak Kumar, 'Calcutta: The Emergence of a Science City (1784–1856)', *Indian Journal of History of Science*, vol. 29, no. 1, 1994, pp. 1–8.
20. B.V. Subbarayappa, 'Western Science in India up to the End of the Nineteenth Century A.D.', op. cit., p. 548.
21. S.N. Sen, *Scientific and Technical Education in India*, Indian National Science Academy, New Delhi, 1991, p. 156.
22. Rama Deb Roy, 'The Great Trigonometrical Survey of India in a Historical Perspective', *Indian Journal of History of Science*, vol. 21, no. 1, 1986, pp. 22–32.
23. The Committee wrote: 'As yet, surveying is taught in only two of our Institutions, the Hindu and Mahomedan Colleges at Calcutta, but we are very desirous that the study should be commenced at some of the others'; GRCPI, 1835, S.N. Sen, *Scientific and Technical Education in India*, p. 282.
24. Amitabha Ghosh, 'Colonial Constraints and Technology: Marginalized Indian Attainments', in Arun Kumar Biswas (ed.), *History, Science and Society in the Indian Context*, The Asiatic Society, Calcutta, 2001, p. 162.
25. A.K. Chakravarty, 'Three 19th Century Calcutta Astronomers', *Indian Journal of History of Science*, vol. 30, nos. 2–4, 1995, pp. 151–8.
26. Satpal Sangwan, *Science, Technology and Colonization: An Indian Experience 1757-1857*, Anamika Prakashan, Delhi, 1991, p. 59.
27. Russell Dionne and Roy Macleod, 'Science and Policy in British India, 1858-1914: Perspectives on a Persisting Belief', *Proceedings of the Sixth European Conference on Modern South Asian Studies*, Sevres, CNRS, Paris, 1979, pp. 55–68.

28. *The Friend of India*, 23 March 1854.
29. S.N. Sen, *Scientific and Technical Education in India 1781-1900*, p. 282.
30. *The Bengal Hurkaru*, 7 September 1854.
31. Satpal Sangwan, *Science, Technology and Colonization*, p. 60.
32. Arthur Cotton, *Report on the Mahanuddy River in Orissa*, Calcutta, 1858, p. 23. This is a report from Cotton, commandant of the Madras Engineers, to Richard Strachey, R.F., Secretary to the Government of India.
33. Despatch from the Court of Directors of the EIC to the Governor-General of India in Council, no. 49, 19 July 1854, para 41; quoted in Aparna Basu, *Essays in the History of Indian Education*, Concept Publishing Company, New Delhi, 1981, p. 39.
34. J.A. Richey (ed.), *Selections from Educational Records, 1840-1859*, part 2, Government Printing, Calcutta, 1922, p. 387.
35. *Sambad Prabhakar*, 13 September 1852.
36. *Sambad Purnochandradaya*, 24 September 1852.
37. Satpal Sangwan, *Science, Technology and Colonization*, p. 61.
38. Zaheer Baber, *The Science of Empire: Scientific Knowledge, Civilization, and Colonial Rule in India*, Oxford University Press, New Delhi, 1998, p. 208.
39. Minute by Lord Dalhousie, 25 August 1854, PWDP, 1 September 1854, no. 41; quoted in Satpal Sangwan, *Science, Technology and Colonization*, p. 61.
40. *Bengal Engineering College Centenary Souvenir*, Calcutta, 1956, p. 16.
41. S.P. Gupta, *Modern India and Progress in Science and Technology*, Vikas, New Delhi, 1979, p. 122.
42. *Somprakash*, 4 May 1863.
43. Ian Inkster, *Science and Technology in History: An Approach to Industrial Development*, Palgrave Macmillan, London, 1991, p. 214.
44. DPI Report, Bengal, 1862-63, p. 10; quoted in Deepak Kumar, *Science and the Raj*, p. 137.
45. K.V. Mital, *History of Thomason College of Engineering*, University of Roorkee, Roorkee, 1986, pp. 17, 30.
46. Bholanath Das argued that, 'It cannot be that the Bengalis are so slow in acquiring a scientific education that they would take

five years while the alumni of the sister college of NWP would take only two'; Francis, J.E. Spring, *Technical Education in Bengal*, Government Press, Calcutta, 1886, pp. 27–9.

47. *Sulav Samachar*, 7 February 1880.
48. Ibid., 13 April 1880.
49. *Bengal Engineering College Centenary Souvenir*, p. 22.
50. Deepak Kumar, *Science and the Raj*, p. 138.
51. First Quinquennial Review of Education in Bengal, 1892–6, p. 106, n. 34. To meet the expenses of electric installation, students were levied Re. 1 each for ten months of the year.
52. S.P. Gupta, *Modern India and Progress in Science and Technology*, p. 117.
53. *Sambad Prabhakar*, 8 June 1847.
54. S.N. Sen, *Scientific and Technical Education in India*, p. 298.
55. Jitendranath Ray, *Banglar Kalkarkhana O Karigari Bidyar Itihas*, Dey Publishing, Kolkata, 2004, p. 15.
56. *Sambad Prabhakar*, 9 May 1854.
57. *The Bengal Hurkaru*, 15 October 1854.
58. E.B. Havell, 'Technical Education in India', *Calcutta Review*, vol. 104, no. 208, 1897, pp. 223–46.
59. B.V. Subbarayappa, 'Western Science in India up to the End of the Nineteenth Century A.D.', p. 550.
60. Aparna Basu, *Essays in the History of Indian Education*, p. 40.
61. Sir Alfred Croft, *Review of Education in India in 1886*, Government Printing, Calcutta, 1886, p. 85.
62. Deepak Kumar, *Science and the Raj*, p. 139.
63. Report of the Committee appointed to enquire into the details of a scheme for the establishment of a School of Apprentices in Calcutta in connection with the Mint and other Government Establishments employing skilled mechanical labour, Calcutta, 1875; quoted in S.N. Sen, *Scientific and Technical Education in India*, p. 406.
64. Daniel R. Headrick, *The Tentacles of Progress*, pp. 323–4.
65. *Sulav Samachar*, 31 May 1879.
66. Zaheer Baber, *The Science of Empire*, p. 206.
67. *Report of the Public Works Reorganization Committee*, vol. I, Government Press, Calcutta, 1917, p. 4.
68. Col. Chesney, cited in Russell Dionne and Roy Macleod.

69. *Quinquennial Review on the Progress of Education in India, 1897-1902*, vol. I, Government Press, Calcutta, 1904, pp. 248–9, para 745.
70. J. Richey (ed.), *Selections from Educational Records, 1850–1859*, part II, Government Press, Calcutta, 1922, p. 339.
71. *Souvenir of 125th Anniversary of Bengal Engineering College*, Sibpur, 1981, p. 3. See also *Selections from the Educational Records of the Government of India, 1859-1871*, vol. I, National Archives of India, New Delhi, 1960, p. 26.
72. See Arun Kumar, 'Engineering Education and Public Works Department, 1906-1947', Ph.D thesis, University of Delhi, 1989.
73. *Report of the Public Service Commission, 1886-87*, Government Press, Calcutta, 1888, p. 7.
74. Arun Kumar, 'Colonial Requirements and Engineering Education: The Public Works Department, 1847-1947', in Roy Macleod and Deepak Kumar (eds.), *Technology and the Raj: Western Technology and Technical Transfers to India 1700-1947*, Sage, New Delhi, 1995, p. 227.
75. Margaret Gowing, 'Science, Technology and Education: England in 1870', *Oxford Review of Education*, vol. 4, no. 1, 1978, pp. 3–17.
76. Irfan Habib, 'Colonization of the Indian Economy, 1757-1900', *Social Scientist*, vol. 3, no. 8, 1975, pp. 23–53.
77. D.S.L. Cardwell, *The Organization of Science in England*, Heinemann, London, Chapter 3.
78. Margaret Gowing, op. cit.
79. Ibid.
80. G.W. Roderick and M.D. Stephens, *Scientific and Technical Education in 19th Century England*, David and Charles, London, 1972, p. 39.
81. Letter from B. Samuelson to Lord Montagu, 16 November 1867; Margaret Gowing, op. cit.
82. G.W. Roderick and M.D. Stephens, op. cit., p. 41.
83. J. Blanchet, 'Science, Craft and State, 1867-1906', Ph.D thesis, Oxford University, 1952, quoted in Margaret Gowing, op. cit.
84. G.W. Roderick and M.D. Stephens, op. cit.
85. J.A. Ewing, *The University Training of Engineers*, Cambridge University Press, Cambridge, 1891.

86. David S. Landes, *The Unbound Prometheus: Technological Change and Industrial Development in Western Europe from 1750 to the Present*, Cambridge University Press, Cambridge, 1969, pp. 331–2.
87. Margaret Gowing, op. cit.
88. K.V. Mital, *History of Thomason College of Engineering*, p. 17.
89. Ibid., p. 98.
90. Russell Dionne and Roy Macleod, op. cit.
91. Deepak Kumar, *Science and the Raj*, p. 150.
92. J.P.C. Roach, 'Victorian Universities and the National Intelligentsia', *Victorian Studies*, vol. 3, no. 2, 1959, pp. 131–50.
93. Deepak Kumar, op. cit.
94. Aparna Basu, *Essays in the History of Indian Education*, p. 39.
95. *Report of the Indian Education Commission*, Calcutta, 1882, pp. 121, 206, 207, 217, 218.
96. Government of India Resolution No. 10/399, 22 October 1884, para 21, quoted in Aparna Basu, op. cit., p. 40.
97. Sir A.P. MacDonnell, 'Note on Technical Education in India', in K.D. Bhargava (ed.), *Selections from the Educational Records of the Government of India*, vol. 4, Technical Education, Delhi, 1968.
98. Alfred Croft, *Review of Education in India*, p. 261.
99. Francis J.E. Spring, *Technical Education in Bengal*, p. 11.
100. E.W. Collin, *Report of the Existing Arts and Industries in Bengal*, p. 2.
101. Ibid., p. 28.
102. Ibid., pp. 31–2.
103. *Education Gazette O Saptahik Bartabaho*, 25 January 1889.
104. Daniel R. Headrick, *The Tentacles of Progress*, pp. 324–5.
105. Anil Kumar, 'Colonial Requirements and Engineering Education: The Public Works Department, 1847-1947', in Roy Macleod and Deepak Kumar (eds.), *Technology and the Raj*, p. 227.
106. *Royal Indian Engineering College Committee Report*, Simla, 1903, p. 13.
107. Deepak Kumar, *Science and the Raj*, p. 140.
108. Ian Inkster, 'Science, Technology, and Imperialism in India', in S. Irfan Habib and Dhruv Raina (eds.), *Social History of Science in Colonial India*, Oxford University Press, New Delhi, 2007, p. 214.

109. For socio-economic policy of the Raj see Sekhar Bandopadhyay, *From Plassey to Partition: A History of Modern India*, Orient Longman, New Delhi, 2004.
110. Government of India Resolution No. 199, 18 June 1888, paras 22–5; quoted in B.V. Subbarayappa, op. cit., p. 551.
111. Ian Inkster, 'Science, Technology, and Imperialism in India', p. 215.
112. Tapan Raychaudhuri, 'A Re-Interpretation of Nineteenth Century Indian Economic History?', in M.D. Morris (ed.), *Indian Economy in the 19th Century: A Symposium*, Hindustan Publication, Delhi, 1969.
113. G.G. Joseph, V. Reddy, and M. Searle Chatterjee, 'Eurocentrism in the Social Sciences', *Race and Class*, vol. 31, no. 4, 1990, pp. 1–26.
114. T.O. Ranger, 'From Humanism to the Science of Man: Colonialism in Africa and the Understanding of Alien Societies', *Transactions of the Royal Historical Society*, 1976, vol. XXVI, p. 126.
115. *Tattobodhini Patrika*, vol. IV, no. 86, 1850.
116. *Samachar Chandrika*, 18 July 1844: 'Babu Dwarkanath Tagore offered to defray the entire expense of sending two students of the Calcutta Medical College. He conveyed his message to the principal of the College. We are not aware yet about the reaction of the college authority.'
117. Rabindra Bharati University Archive, mss., quoted in Siddhartha Ghosh, *Kaler Sahar Kolkata* (in Bengali), Ananda Publishers, Calcutta, 1991, pp. 71, 219.
118. Deepak Kumar, 'Science and Society in Colonial India: Exploring an Agenda', *Social Scientist*, vol. 28, nos. 5/6, 2000, pp. 24–46.
119. S. Irfan Habib and Dhruv Raina (eds.), 'Introduction', *Social History of Science in Colonial India*, p. xxxi.
120. Satpal Sangwan, 'Indian Response to European Science and Technology 1757-1857', *The British Journal for the History of Science*, vol. 21, no. 2, 1988, pp. 211–32.
121. *Grambarta Prakashika*, 9 September 1876.
122. Administrative Report, Bengal, 1879-80, p. 54; quoted in Deepak Kumar, *Science and the Raj*, p. 186.

123. R.E. Fife, *The Civil Engineering Profession in India*, London, 1879, p. 8.
124. Deepak Kumar, 'Racial Discrimination and Science in Nineteenth Century India', *Indian Economic and Social History Review*, vol. XIX, 1983, pp. 63–82.
125. Aparna Basu, 'The Indian Response to Scientific and Technical Education in the Colonial Era, 1820-1920', in Deepak Kumar (ed.), *Science and Empire: Essays in the Indian Context*, Anamika Prakashan, New Delhi, 1991, p. 131.
126. Mahendra Lal Sircar, *On the Desirability of a National Institution for the Cultivation of the Sciences by the Natives of India*, Calcutta, 1869, pp. 3–6.
127. Mahendra Lal Sircar, *The Indian Association for the Cultivation of Science*, Calcutta, 1877, p. 29.
128. Pratik Chakraborty, 'Science, Morality, and Nationalism: The Multifaceted Project of Mahendra Lal Sircar', *Studies in History*, vol. 17, no. 2, 2001, pp. 245–74.
129. Chittabrata Palit, 'Mahendra Lal Sircar, 1833-1904: The Quest for National Science', in Deepak Kumar (ed.), *Science and Empire*, p. 156.
130. Dinanath Sen, *A Scheme for the School of Industry or Practical Science Proposed to be Established in Calcutta, from Funds Raised by the India League, with Government Aid, Drawn up, by the Order of the Director of Public Instruction*, Minerva Press, Calcutta, 1876.
131. Ibid.
132. Adinath Sen, *Sargiya Dinanath Sener Jiboni O Tatkalin Purbobanga*, vol. 2, Calcutta, 1948, pp. 141–9.
133. Siddhartha Ghosh, *Kaler Sahar Kolkata* p. 211.
134. *Hindu Patriot*, 6 March 1876.
135. Ibid.
136. Adinath Sen, op. cit., p. 145.
137. Pratik Chakraborty, *Western Science in Modern India: Metropolitan Methods, Colonial Practices,* Permanent Black, New Delhi, 2004, p. 159.
138. Mahendra Lal Sircar, *The Indian Association for Cultivation of Science*, p. 106, n. 89.
139. Samarendra Nath Sen, *Vijnanacharya Dr. Mahendra Lal Sircar*, Calcutta, 1985, p. 55.

140. *Somprakash*, 16 April 1883.
141. A.L. Azmi, 'The Aligarh Scientific Society', *Proceedings of the Indian History Congress*, Varanasi, 1969.
142. V.A. Narain, 'The Role of Bihar Scientific Association in the Spread of Western Education in Bihar', *Proceedings of the Indian History Congress*, Varanasi, 1969.
143. Jagadish N. Sinha, 'Science and the Indian National Congress', in Deepak Kumar (ed.), *Science and Empire*, pp. 161–81.
144. INC sessions of 1888 and 1892; A.M. Zaidi (ed.), *The Encyclopaedia of the Indian National Congress*, vol. II, Indian Institute of Applied Political Research, New Delhi, 1978, p. 163, n. 108.
145. Ibid., vol. IV, p. 251.
146. B.R. Tomlinson, 'Colonial Constructs and Technical Education in India, 1880-1914', paper presented at the *20th Conference of International Association of Historians of Asia*, JNU, New Delhi, 14–17 November 2008.
147. J.C. Cumming, *Technical and Industrial Instruction in Bengal, 1880-1908*, p. 27.
148. Deepak Kumar, *Science and the Raj*, p. 210.
149. Aparna Basu, 'Indian Response to Scientific and Technical Education in the Colonial Era, 1820-1920', in Deepak Kumar (ed.), *Science and Empire*, p. 133.
150. Home, Education, nos. 14–88, October 1897; quoted in Deepak Kumar, *Science and the Raj*, p. 206.
151. J.D. Bernal, *Science in History*, Watts, London, 1954, p. 389.
152. See Chapter 2 for elaborate discussion. For more information, Siddhartha Ghosh, *Karigari Kalpana O Bangali Udyog*, Dey's Publishing, Calcutta, 1988, pp. 17–56.
153. Amitabha Ghosh, 'Colonial Constraints and Technology: Marginalized Indian Attainments', in Arun Kumar Biswas (ed.). *History, Science and Society in the Indian Context*, p. 165.
154. Subodh Chandra Sengupta (ed.), *Sansad Bangali Charitabidhan*, Sahitya Sansad, Kolkata, 1976, p. 273.
155. *The Indian Mirror*, 26 August 1894.
156. Jnanendramohan Das, '*Sarvapratham Bangali Engineer Nilmony* Mitra', *Pravasi*, Aswin 1332 (1925).
157. Amitabha Ghosh, 'Some Eminent Indian Pioneers in the field of Technology', *Indian Journal of History of Science*, vol. 29, no. 1, 1994, pp. 63–75.

158. Gauri Viswanathan, *Masks of Conquest: Literary Study and British Rule in India*, p. 161.
159. Krishna Kumar, 'Colonial Citizen as an Educational Ideal', *Economic and Political Weekly*, 28 January 1989, pp. 45–51.
160. *Sambad Purnochandradaya*, 13 January 1853.
161. Dhruv Raina and S. Irfan Habib, 'The Unfolding of an Engagement: The Dawn of Science, Technical Education and Industrialization in India, 1896–1912', *Studies in History*, vol. 9, no. 1, 1993, pp. 87–117.
162. Sumit Sarkar, 'Rammohun Roy and the Break with the Past', in V.C. Joshi (ed.), *Rammohun Roy and the Process of Modernization in India*, Vikas, New Delhi, 1975, pp. 46–68.
163. The revivalists were those who considered the knowledge contained in the Vedas and the Quran to be enough for the needs of the Indian subcontinent. The Westernizers found tradition to be outdated and stood for an unqualified adoption of Western ways and forms of knowledge. The revitalists had respect for the traditional knowledge system, but they felt there was much to be learned from the West. See David Kopf, 'The Brahmo Samaj Intelligentsia and the Bengali Renaissance: A Study of Revitalization and Modernization in 19th Century Bengal', in R.I. Carne (ed.), *Transition in South Asia*, Duke University Press, Durham, 1970, pp. 7–48.
164. S. Irfan Habib, 'Science, Technical Education and Industrialization: Contours of a Bhadralok Debate, 1890–1915', in Roy Macleod and Deepak Kumar (eds.), *Technology and the Raj*, p. 237.
165. G.E. Forbes, *Positivism in Bengal: A Case Study in the Transmission and Assimilation of an Ideology*, Minerva Associates, Calcutta, 1975, p. 78.
166. Dhruv Raina and S. Irfan Habib, 'Copernicus, Columbus, Colonialism and the Role of Science in the 19th Century India', *Social Scientist*, vol. 17, nos. 3-4, 1989, pp. 51–66.
167. Sumit Sarkar, *The Swadeshi Movement in Bengal*, People's Publishing House, New Delhi, 1975, p. 33.
168. P.N. Bose, 'Technical and Scientific Education in Bengal', Pamphlet, 1886, *Essays and Lectures on the Industrial Development of India*, Newman & Co., Calcutta, 1906, pp. 59–74.
169. Deepak Kumar, *Science and the Raj*, p. 210.

170. G. Subramanya Iyer, 'Our Artisans and Mechanics: or Indian Arts and Crafts', *The Dawn*, vol. VII, no. 9, April 1904, p. 272.
171. *Somprakash*, 30 July 1883.
172. S. Irfan Habib and Dhruv Raina, 'Bhadralok Perceptions of Science, Technology and Cultural Nationalism', *Indian Economic and Social History Review*, vol. 32, no. 1, 1995, pp. 95–117.
173. The term, as Sumit Sarkar points out, was first used in the 'Bengal District Administration Report, 1913-14'; see Sumit Sarkar, *The Swadeshi Movement in Bengal*, p. 150.
174. Chittabrata Palit and Subrata Pahari, *Satish Chandra Mukherjee, the Dawn Society and National Science*, Readers Service, Kolkata, 2002, p. 11.
175. Haridas Mukherjee, *Satish Chandra Mukherjee and the Dawn Magazine*, Calcutta, 1953, p. 5.
176. Benoy Kumar Sarkar, *Education for Industrialization: An Analysis of Forty Years of Jadavpur College of Engineering and Technology, 1905-45*, Chuckervertty, Chatterjee and Co., Calcutta, 1946, p. 73.
177. Since the NCE was heavily loaded with personalities committed to the programme of cultural nationalism, its commitment to science also being a cultural one, some of those present at the November 1905 conference went on to found the Society for the Promotion of Technical Education (SPTE) on 1 June 1906.
178. R.K. Dasgupta, 'National Education', in *Concept of National Education in India, National Council of Education, Bengal*, National Council of Education, Calcutta, 1970, p. 13.
179. S. Irfan Habib and Dhruv Raina, 'Bhadralok Perceptions of Science, Technology and Cultural Nationalism', *Indian Economic and Social History Review*, op. cit.
180. Dhruv Raina and S. Irfan Habib, 'Technical Content and Social Context: Locating Technical Institutes', in Patrick Petitjean, C. Jami and Anne Marie Moulin (eds.), *Science and Empires*, Kluwer Academic Publishers, Dordrecht, 1992, pp. 121–36.
181. Benoy Kumar Sarkar, *Education for Industrialization*, p. 94.
182. 'The Indian System of Training Workmen for the Manual Industries', *The Dawn*, November 1904, p. 37.
183. Benoy Kumar Sarkar, 'Education for Industrialization', p. 107.
184. 'The Indian System of Training Workmen for the Manual Industries', *The Dawn*, September 1904, p. 27.

185. J.C. Bagal, *Pramatha Nath Bose*, P.N. Bose Centenary Committee, Calcutta, 1955, p. 97.
186. Deepak Kumar, *Science and the Raj*, p. 212.
187. *Education Gazette O Saptahik Bartabaho*, 25 January 1889.
188. While industries that relied heavily on the steam-related technologies were referred to as mechanical industries, science-based industries were those requiring processes that drew upon developments in synthetic organic chemistry. See J.D. Bernal, *Science and Industry in the Nineteenth Century*, Oxford University Press, London, 1953.
189. P.N. Bose, *Essays and Lectures on the Industrial Development of India*, p. 68, 69.
190. Ibid., p. 68.
191. V.G. Kale, 'The Present Economic Condition of India', *The Indian Review*, XI(5), May 1910, p. 346.
192. *Calcutta Review*, 104 (1897) 238. It sums up succinctly the colonizer's point of view.
193. For instance, see *Sambad Prabhakar*, 22 July 1847.
194. For example, see *Somprakash*, 30 July 1883; *Education Gazette O Saptahik Bartabaho*, 25 January 1889.
195. P.N. Bose, *Essays and Lectures on the Industrial Development of India*, p. 7.

CHAPTER 4

Indigenous Enterprises

> Foreigners come here and in a short time earn enough to live in comfort back home, and our country is being pumped dry in the process. Perhaps things will now change. Downtrodden Hindustan will now compete with other trading countries. Many others follow the path shown by Tagore (Dwarkanath) and engage in similar ventures, which are beneficial and bold and deserve praise, and thus help remove the bad name of the Hindus as idle and ignorant.
>
> *Jnananeshan*,[1] August 1834

> When I founded the BCPW I had not only the idea of wiping out the reproach that the Bengalees were good for nothing in business affairs, but also of making it a model institution.
>
> P.C. Ray to a colleague at BCPW (1897?)[2]

The nineteenth century was a century of arrested development for indigenous business enterprises in Bengal. This has engaged the attention of scholars for long and no single agreed explanation exists to account for it. The standard trope informs us that Indians as a nation were indifferent to business, lacking enterprise and acumen, averse to toil beyond raising enough crop to sustain them. Yet there were many Bengalis who started their own business enterprises. How they emerged is certainly a very important area of historical research. By the end of the nineteenth century, especially during the swadeshi movement (1903–8), the number of Bengali enterprises arose with moderate success. After the First World War (1914) some Indian enterprises, exclusively mercantile, small scale, family firms, transformed themselves into pioneers of advanced and heavy industry. What role, then, did the Bengali entrepreneurs of the nineteenth century play in the 're-industrialization' of Bengal?

Technical education is but one way in which the culture of technology spreads. Another way is through enterprises and experience. While European enterprise and the government restricted non-Europeans to the lower jobs (until they were forced to do otherwise by political pressures at the very end of the colonial era), enterprises owned by the Indians, had every incentive to use their own people, for reasons of ethnic solidarity as well as economy.[3]

But entrepreneurship alone does not lead to economic development. The kinds of enterprises that could have led to economic development required other elements: information about foreign machines, technical processes, and business practices, information which was not forthcoming from the educational system.[4]

India was once a manufacturing nation whose industrial products supplied, for centuries, the needs of vast Asian and European markets; spinning and weaving and other handicrafts had provided whole-time or part-time employment to millions of men and women. But all these had gradually disappeared with the advent of the British. One of the most momentous consequences of the establishment of British supremacy was the disruption of the centuries' old union between agriculture and manufacturing as a result of the progressive decline and destruction of the Indian town handicrafts and village artisan industries.[5] Thus British rule brought the destruction of traditional handicrafts along with their technical know-how, drainage of wealth through direct plunder and revenue extraction, and the transplantation of Western type industrial capitalism in India.[6] The fact that England underwent an industrial revolution while India could not stage one gave England the superiority she deserved. Superior manufacturing methods based on steam power and improved machinery enabled British manufacturers to undersell Indian artisans in their own country. The mechanization of industries, the growth of capital, the institution of the joint-stock company and managing agency, and the monopolization of colonial markets for finished goods, enabled England to score a complete victory.[7] Contemporary Bengali journals were vocal about the necessity of indigenous enterprise to strengthen the economy throughout the nineteenth century. *Samachar Darpan* reported:

> Europeans properly utilized capital and achieved a distinct place in world civilization by their business skills. We are advising our fellow countrymen to give up their laziness and follow the European path of business. They should learn from the people of western India how to start business ventures successfully.
>
> The Bengali people prefer to lend money with interest to Europeans. Here the irony is the poor Europeans become rich by properly utilizing the loans in various business ventures and the rich Bengalis become poor. So the affluent class of our society should start their own business and stop flattering the Europeans. Then only Bengal can start her journey towards the road of prosperity.[8]

Modern business activities developed by the European agency houses in the early part of the century had a substantial element of Indian partnership before new developments drew a clearer line between the black and white spaces. The agency houses[9] were originally the carriers of private European trade in Asian waters. These agency houses built ships, employed them in the trade of the Indian Ocean, and by a natural extension went into the promotion of insurance companies and banks. In Calcutta they promoted industrial ventures inland: they financed the indigo planters, they sank money into silk filature, and even came to manage some indigo concerns themselves. The history of the agency houses falls into three periods.[10] From 1783 to 1813 the houses were few in number and their partners closely associated with company officials who were also their constituents. The second phase began after the opening of India to private trade in 1813, when a large number of new houses were formed by adventurers from Britain. The third phase of agency-house history began in 1834 and lasted until the commercial crisis of 1847. In the second phase, although there were moderate participation of the Bengali businessmen, in the third phase they emerged as an active partners of various managing agency houses.[11]

Closely associated with the agency houses were their brokers. Their function was to bring in and guarantee contracts for the supply of exportable produce from inland merchants. The brokers were called Banians in Calcutta.[12] Sometimes they could even be important merchants conducting business on their own. Raghuram Gosain, the Bengali banian of Palmer & Co., was a rich merchant in his own right. The model early nineteenth-century banian was Ramdulal Dey, who acquired a fortune as a factor for the American traders. The banians were English-speaking Bengalis from Brahmin, Kayastha, and Banik castes, frequently financiers of their European principals. Motilal Seal, a Bengali shipowner and merchant magnate, lent money while acting as broker to Oswald Seal & Co. Dwarkanath Tagore was in his own unique way the pioneer entrepreneur of the mid-nineteenth century. An individual study of few of these Bengali entrepreneurs would give us a better understanding about the indigenous enterprises of nineteenth century.

Ramdulal Dey (1752-1825): In the late eighteenth and early nineteenth century, a number of Bengali businessmen made their mark in shipping and other commercial activities. The most important of them was Ramdulal Dey.[13] Born in a very poor family, he became an orphan early in life. He took shelter in the house of Madan Dutt, the Dewan of the Export Warehouse. There he got the post of a Bill Sircar (who keeps the accounts of a firm) at a salary of Rs. 5. Gradually he saved Rs. 100 from his salary and invested it in a timber depot at Bagbazar. However, his real fortune came when he bought a wrecked ship for Rs. 14,000 and sold it after some time to a European at a profit of Rs. 1 lakh.[14] This capital became the keystone of his fortune, on which was piled colossal wealth that became the wonder and envy of his contemporaries. The *Sambad Prabhakar* reported:

Among the residents of Calcutta, Ramdulal Dey was the richest businessmen. In early life he was very poor, later on he achieved an immense wealth by business. It was told that he was owner of one crore of rupees. Ramdulal had close relationship with the American and British businessmen. He mostly dealt with the Americans. One such businessman of Philadelphia gifted a statue of Washington to Ramdulal which shows the close tie between them.[15]

So great was the confidence of the Americans in Ramdulal that for the first time in the history of Indian commerce, American merchants dispensed with European agents in Bengal altogether, transacted direct with this indigenous house, sent ships to its consignment and drafts to its credit for buying Indian products. Thus Ramdulal acted not only as an intermediary to the Americans, but also became the real pioneer of American commerce in Bengal.

Along with American trade, Ramdulal directed his energies to expand trade relations with England and China. He undertook the banianship of Fairle Fergusson & Co., the then largest English house in Calcutta.[16] The great houses of Palmer & Co., Alexander & Co., Mackintosh & Co. were dwarfs before Ramdulal Dey. His four ships, viz., *Ramdulal Dey*, *Bemola*, *David Clarke* and another, carried goods to England, America, China, and Malta.

Ramdulal died in 1825. His sons Asutosh Dey and Pramathanath Dey were two of the richest men in Calcutta in the second quarter of the nineteenth century. They carried on their father's business with the same American connections as *Ashutosh Dey & Nephews.* However, the avarice and mismanagement of Ramdulal's heirs reduced the capital to only a few lakhs of rupees.[17]

Dwarkanath Tagore (1794–1846): Dwarkanath,[18] a Western-educated Bengali Brahmin, was acknowledged civic leader of Calcutta during the 1830s and 1840s. Though a brilliant entrepreneur, he subordinated his business activities to political and social ends. Tagore envisioned a future India that was Westernized and industrialized and whose inhabitants enjoyed, without discrimination, the rights and liberties of Englishmen.

Carr, Tagore & Co. was the first equal partnership between European and Indian businessmen and the initiator of the managing agency system in India. Dwarkanath launched the firm in 1834 with the partnership of William Carr, a respected indigo trader of Calcutta. Tagore not only provided the firm's capital, but selected the partners, directed the investment strategy, and throughout his lifetime, actively guided the house. Carr, Tagore & Co. was, in fact, more a patriarchy than a partnership. The incident drew the attention of the Bengali press, as is revealed by a notice in the *Samachar Darpan*:

CARR, TAGORE & CO.

The new firm of Carr, Tagore & Co. is announced today. The second member of this firm is Baboo Dwarkanath Tagore, some time Dewan of the Salt Board, which office he vacated about six weeks ago for the purpose of commencing the career of a general merchant and agent. The circumstance is worthy of notice since it is the first instance of a Hindoo adopting European habits of business in Calcutta, and entering into the field of agency and foreign commerce on European principles.... [19]

When the Calcutta Chamber of Commerce was set-up in 1834 Dwarkanath became one of its members,[20] along with Rustomji Cowasji.[21] Tagore's fortune had been founded on landholding and moneylending, and among his business interests were the import and export trade, indigo and silk manufacture, sugar refining, ocean shipping, docking, newspapers, insurance and banking.

In the Indian community, as in government circles, the climate of opinion was ripe for Dwarkanath's move. Ever since the commercial crisis of 1830, the idea of Bengalis launching modern business firms had been under discussion in the Bengali press. The conservative *Samachar Chandrika* urged zamindars to purchase and operate the European-owned indigo factories left idle by the crisis, and forestall the colonization of the countryside by Europeans.[22] The moderate *Reformer* called on the Bengalis to 'compete with the nations of Europe and America, not only in English literature, but in fine arts, sciences and commerce'; Hindus could no longer blame their religion for entrepreneurial backwardness because there were now 'enough enlightened Hindoos who can lead the way.'[23] Radical Young Bengal, voicing their opinions in the journal

Jnananeshan, urged their countrymen to cast off their 'natural idleness and lethargy, and armed with the weapons of business, commerce and industry, triumph over the enemies of their prosperity'.[24] When Dwarkanath launched his firm, Young Bengal found a hero.[25]

On 2 January 1836, Tagore made the most momentous investment of his entire career. He purchased for Rs. 70,000 India's largest coal mine, the Raniganj Colliery, in Burdwan.[26] To further the sale of coal, Tagore prompted during the next decade a series of coal utilizing enterprises and was responsible, more than any other individual outside of government service, for leading India into the age of the steam engine. Between 1836 and 1846 Dwarkanath promoted six joint stock companies: the Calcutta Steam Tug Association (1836), the Bengal Salt Company (1838), the Calcutta Steam Ferry Bridge Company (1839), the Bengal Tea Association (1839), the Bengal Coal Company (1844) and the India General Steam Navigation Company (1844).[27] He was also one of the doyens of the modern system of banking in India. The Union Bank, of which he was a director,[28] contributed to the development of native trade and commerce by extending commercial credit. Rowland Macdonald Stephenson, the pioneer of the Indian railways, came to India to survey the route and to urge support for his plan in 1844. Dwarkanath realized the importance of railways for the upliftment of the economy and extended his support. His friend William Theobald wrote to Stephenson that Tagore 'is very desirous to have a Railway to the Collieries (Raniganj), and would raise one-third of the capital for this portion of the line, if undertaken immediately'.[29] Towards the end of his life, he joined in the promotion of the Great Western of Bengal Railway Company.[30]

One of Tagore's goals was to carry over the commercial partnerships and other organizational forms of the mercantile age into the industrial age. A second goal was to import the industrial revolution into India and to adapt the steam engine to commercial use. While launching Carr, Tagore & Co. he rightly said his house would be an instrument of national regeneration and a model to be emulated by his countrymen.

Motilal Seal (1792-1854): Motilal Seal, began his business career after having acquired working knowledge of English. Initially a trader in corks and bottles, he was destined to be a big entrepreneur.[31] As was customary in those days he became very soon a banian to European firms. He was the banker and banian of the Oswall Seal & Co. He associated with Strand Flour Mill, Messrs. Leech, Ketlewell, Mehowd, Fagan & Co., Chapman & Co., Kelsall & Co., etc., as a banian.[32]

Motilal realized that he was in a better position than Europeans to speculate in indigo, silk, sugar, salt, etc., and resolved to export them to foreign markets. Exports and imports became his chief occupation and gave him fabulous fortune.[33] He was also a notable ship-owner and zamindar. He was not interested in investing in Company papers or securities, but in the circulation of capital. The field where he invested was shipping. He owned about twelve ships of different sizes running to China and Europe. *Raj-Rani* and *Banian* were the names given to two of his ships.[34] He was one of the first few to introduce tug steamers in coastal steamers.

In an essay on Motilal Seal, Kissory Chand Mitra admonished Bengali youth for considering government employment the pinnacle of all careers; he encouraged them to emulate the great merchant of the 1840s. Kissory Chand asked why it was that 'this most fertile province has been sunk, till late, in poverty and intellectual torpor? It is chiefly because industrial activity and commercial enterprise have not come to convert it into a garden.'[35] Motilal Seal was an enlightened philanthropist and patron of Western education.

Ram Gopal Ghosh (1815–1868): Ram Gopal[36] was educated at the Hindu College and took a prominent role in city politics. He owed his prosperity to Messrs Kelsall & Co. of which he was a banian. He was a rich merchant of Akyab, and owned a steam boat—the *Lotus*.[37]

Perhaps with Ram Gopal Ghosh and Motilal Seal in mind one observer noted that Europeans were employed 'as agents of native capital',[38] and another that the new banians had 'assumed airs which their more wealthy predecessors had never taken on themselves;

they treated their European connections not only with contemptuous disregard, but often with much insolence. The Hindoo star was in the ascendant, and these men made the most of it.'[39]

The careers of Digambar Mitra, Surya Kumar Tagore, Raghunath Goswami, Bholanath Chandra, etc., only illustrate that there was no dearth of entrepreneurial ability among Bengali people in the first half of nineteenth century. They successfully utilized the prevailing atmosphere in their favour and acquired a huge fortune. By 1840 it appeared that Calcutta and its hinterland were on the threshold of a small-scale industrial revolution. Despite the paucity of capital, the local business community embarked upon a broad range of steam-powered industries. In 1844 one observer noted that 'on approaching Calcutta, the smoke chimneys of steam-engines are now seen in every direction, on the either side of the river, presenting the gratifying appearance of a seat of numerous extensive manufactories, vying with many British cities'.[40] Then a series of commercial crises shook the Calcutta business community and by 1850 the momentum failed. If the dynamism of the 'age of enterprise' had been sustained, if the 'Industrial Revolution' of the 1840s had not been aborted, Bengal might have developed indigenous industries with its natural and human resources.

THE MOMENTUM THAT FAILED: *BHADRALOK* PERCEPTIONS

For a brief interlude at midpoint in the history of Bengal–the 1830s and 1840s–Bengalis were the most active associates of the British in the modern sector of the economy. The era of Bengali participation coincided with the growth of inter-racial civic institutions and local community spirit. It also witnessed the introduction of the steam engine on a commercial scale, the development of new industries such as tea, steam shipping, and coal mining; and the application of new forms of business organization: the joint stock company, the managing agency system, and commercial banking.

In the first half of the nineteenth century Calcutta's largest business institution was the Union Bank. But due to unsound exchange transactions with London and insecure advances in the falling indigo market, the Union Bank crashed in 1848,[41] bringing down with it various others. Indian enterprise in Calcutta, including the giant Carr, Tagore & Co., which had sprung up in partnership with Europeans, suffered a blow, from which it did not recover.[42]

After mid-century the international environment was no longer favourable to the growth of big Indian business in the country's ports and abroad. Between 1850 and 1880 a series of technological and organizational changes–the completion of the railways reaching far into the interior, the development of the steamship services through the Suez Canal, and the linking up of the inland telegraph and the overseas cables into one gigantic worldwide system of information at electrical speed[43]–decisively shifted the business balance of power away from smaller Indian firms to bigger European firms in India, and from India itself to the world centre of trade and finance located in the city of London. From the suppression of the Mutiny (1858) to the outbreak of the First World War (1914), private European enterprise, which had already established new forms of industry, enjoyed a position of unchallenged supremacy in the Indian economy.

The enterprises undertaken during the period from 1830 to 1850 were poorly managed and failed to make good use of modern technology. Although Dwarkanath tried to incorporate Western technology in his business ventures, many of his enterprises failed or nearly failed as a result of poor management. His fundamental error was to miscalculate the strength and to misread the nature of the British commitment to India.[44] Carr, Tagore & Co. was not truly a partnership of equals. Dwarkanath established the house and invited William Carr, William Prinsep, and other impecunious British merchants to join him in the use of his capital. They had nothing to lose and everything to gain by accepting his offer, and they left for home as soon as possible. Nor did the British reciprocate his bid for genuine social intercourse. It was at his home that they gathered to be lavishly entertained by–they did not return the invitation. If Dwarkanath wanted inter-racial cooperation, he had to provide the framework, whether it be a charitable society or a joint-stock company. Dwarkanath laboured in vain, for the British would not accept genuine partnership with an Indian.[45]

In the first half of the nineteenth century the European trading companies employed as compradors Brahmins and Kayasthas as well as members of the indigenous trading and artisan castes—Subarnabaniks, Gandhabaniks, Tantubaniks and Telis.[46] We have seen that from 1750 to 1850 the Bengali compradors or banians steadily rose to prominence in the economic life of the province. After 1850, those employed by these firms were gradually reduced to the status of petty clerks, then dismissed in favour of young Englishmen.[47] Thus the banians of Calcutta were eliminated from modern business as the economics of empire attained maturity.

Since the early nineteenth century spokesmen of the Bengali middle class have searched for the causes of entrepreneurial backwardness and for ways to stimulate business enterprise among Bengalis. Basically the problem of the Bengalis was one of conflicting values. There were deep-seated social and cultural factors. Power over land, not mercantile or industrial enterprise, was the economic hallmark of social status. Trade was associated with low ranking castes; Brahmins and Kayasthas considered only the intellectual and administrative professions as proper occupations. Thus the indigenous Bengali elite turned its back on business and left modern industry and international commerce in Calcutta to Europeans.[48]

The Permanent Settlement, Regulation VII of 1799 and regulation V of 1812 ensured security of landed property to zamindars.[49] The Bengali mind could now think only about land. Under the circumstances moneyed men considered investment in zamindari as safe, prestigious and profitable.

Throughout the British period, the timidity of Bengali entrepreneurs was a recurrent topic of Bengali writers. The campaign was begun as early as the 1830s by the spokesmen of Young Bengal.[50] They criticized those banians, who instead of launching their own commercial ventures, supplied British merchants with capital.[51] In the 1840s and 1850s, the chauvinistic Iswar Chandra Gupta, editor of the *Sambad Prabhakar*, became the chief advocate of independent mercantile enterprise. One Tarini Charan Chaudhury, school student of Medinipur, voiced his anger over the idleness of Bengalis regarding business and enterprise in *Prabhakar*.[52] On this the editor of the journal observed:

> We have published the letter of Babu Tarini Charan Chaudhury of Medinipur on the condition of our country in the Student's Column of today's *Prabhakar*. We are happy that Tarini Babu requested his fellow countrymen to start their own business enterprise. We have written on the subject on several occasions, but unfortunately all in vain. The people of Bengal are against any kind of hard work. They prefer to spend their time at home with no energetic work. From the condition of such countrymen, we can easily assume the reason behind the miserable condition of the country. Forget about foreign trade, they are not interested in inland business either, not even within Bengal. Those with wealth prefer to lend money to the Europeans for the sake of 'tension free' income from interests. Only if the affluent Bengalis start their own business enterprise, can they bring back the prosperity of our country.[53]

On another occasion the journal wrote:

> The improvement of the material condition of our people is a major concern of all. Our government has closed the door of various prestigious jobs to Bengali people. So there is little hope of employment in the government sector for them. There are many obstacles in the field of independent business also. Bengalis are not acquainted with business skills, especially in foreign trade. Due to religious taboo they cannot cross the ocean. The traditional business classes have a very low status in our society. So for the upper castes (Brahmins and Kayasthas) to involve in trade is a shameful matter.
>
> Many suggest that the rich people should engage in business enterprise like Englishmen, so that others can be inspired by their initiatives. This is very much true. But the irony is they don't have the necessary courage to start such ventures. They prefer to nourish the business of the Europeans by sponsoring them and acted as banian in the European firms.
>
> So the prospect for Bengal is not very bright. The lower clerical

> posts are the only hope. Unless the government removes the ban on recruiting Indians to higher governmental jobs and the Bengali people start their own business enterprise, there is no sign of hope.[54]

The usual explanations for the backwardness in industrial entrepreneurship in Bengal were generally that: (a) the Bengali middle classes were averse to trade and industry and preferred the liberal professions; (b) the Bengali businessmen in general were interested only in trade and would not enter industry because it did not promise a quick return; (c) the big merchants of eastern India had been eliminated by the Permanent Settlement and eastern India had been converted into 'a landlord paradise' so that investment in land was much more attractive than other types of investment.

The *Sambad Purnochandradaya* observed:

> If our countrymen start their own business enterprise, then they can live an independent life. Few of our brothers understood this and started their own business ventures. But the general trend is not very encouraging. Actually in business, the entire risk relies on the investor. So our Bengali friends are afraid to take such risks. They hand over their wealth to the Europeans and secure the head clerkship in those European firms. Although a few people have sufficient money to start their own business enterprise, due to lack of stamina they are unable to take such steps.[55]

The journal *Sambad Prabhakar* maintained a conservative stand on various social reform movements. It vehemently opposed the Westernization of Bengali society and supported traditional Indian culture. But in the field of trade and commerce, it was a follower of the Western system of business enterprise. The editors criticized the Bengali people for not entering trade and commerce like their English counterparts. Once they reported:

> The prospect of a country depends on trade and business. The Bengali people like to do slavery. When a child gets a little education, his father takes him to his European master for a clerical job. Due to this trend, our country is suffering a lot. Many intelligent students are forced to join clerical jobs, abandoning their study.

In the developed countries, students after getting proper education, start their own business enterprises. By following this line, countries like England, France, America became so prosperous. But the picture is entirely different in our country. The rich Bengalis prefer to depend on 'interest' from their wealth. So the independent business culture becomes very rare in Bengal. Unless they start their own business enterprise in large numbers, there is no hope for our country.[56]

The urban industry of India, at the beginning of the nineteenth century, was mainly handicrafts, producing fine textiles or other luxury products for the aristocracy. There is little doubt that in these handicrafts Indian urban industry had reached a highwater-mark of excellence. The products of Indian industry enjoyed a worldwide reputation. Among these the cotton industry was easily the first. But the nexus of colonialism destroyed the Indian textile industry. India became the chief exporter of raw cotton and the biggest importer of Manchester clothes. The textile industry became extinct and there was no initiative to revive the once most flourishing industry of India. Observing that, well circulated journal *Somprakash* wrote:

PROMOTION OF INDIGENOUS ENTERPRISE

Recently the Russians adopted a policy to promote their trade and industry. They have taken an oath not to wear anything except Russian clothes. Almost a hundred years ago the Americans were entirely dependent on Britain for clothes like us. During the American freedom movement, the people of that country opposed the English made clothes and started building their own textile industry. Today American clothes are the biggest competitor of Manchester.

In many European countries there is no business of Russian clothes. On the other hand many Russians love to wear foreign made clothes. But in spite of that they determined to wear only Russian clothes. Their government also started encouraging cotton cultivation. Combining these two, we hope the Russian textile industry will flourish very soon.

Now let's turn to India. The whole of Europe depends on Indian cotton and its cultivation is increasing day by day. But we should think of the long-term prospects. If Manchester gets cheaper cotton from other places, then what would be the condition of several cotton cultivators of India? If we really bother for our country, then we should devote ourselves to start textile industry in our country. Every year India imports huge amounts of clothes from England. So we are requesting our countrymen to not sit idle and do something to promote the textile industry.[57]

The upper-caste Bengalis were partial to administrative, professional, and intellectual occupations. As the expansion of British rule increased, young Bengalis flocked to the colleges to prepare themselves for careers in administration, law, medicine, journalism, and education. In Dwarkanath's day, business was still a possible component of the *bhadralok* lifestyle, but after the middle of the nineteenth century, training for a profession was usually substituted for entering business. Not only were there more opportunities in the professions, but these careers were more in accord with the *bhadralok* value system.

Entrepreneurship was a recurrent theme in the editorials of the *Tattobodhini Patrika*, a leading journal of the 1870s. 'Our young men excel in all other spheres', wrote the editor, 'but in business they were apathetic'. He urged the orthodox to defy the injunction against crossing the oceans and to take up international commerce. And he called on those who had flaunted the taboo and were studying in Britain to train in business instead of the liberal arts and upon their return to establish schools of commerce in Bengal.[58]

The *Amrita Bazar Patrika* observed,

Our country is developing very fast. So the people of this country should start various business enterprises considering the current economy. If they try hard, they will definitely be successful. Honesty and punctuality are the two requirements for successful business ventures. Why is America so prosperous? What are the reasons behind the advancement of Britain and other European countries? The only answer is trade and industry.[59]

Somprakash wholeheartedly wanted modern industry to be

established in Bengal. Tirelessly it campaigned for the cause. Once the journal observed:

THE DEVELOPMENT OF INDIAN INDUSTRY

India has been ruled by Englishmen for more than a hundred years. We have observed many changes during this tenure. But there is no sign of industrialization in India. Why did we not learn industrial education during these hundred years?

The answer to this question lies in three facts. Obviously there are other reasons also, but these three, according to us, are the prime cause. Firstly the development of modern industries in Europe; secondly India lost its sovereignty to England; and third is the lack of business skills among Indians.[60]

Such an assessment only proved the maturity of the Bengali journals of nineteenth century. Gradually they started realizing that not only Bengali character, but the subordination of India by a foreign country was also responsible for India's industrial backwardness.

Somprakash frequently dwelt on the growing problem of educated unemployment. For example, the journal once wrote in its editorial, 'They (i.e. the job-seekers) don't have the means to get hold of capital for taking up business or industry. . . . Students of Civil Engineering can look for no improvements; the Medical Department has no vacancy to absorb even one more person. . . .'[61]

Sadharani,[62] another important and popular journal of nineteenth century, shared the concern of *Somprakash* for the promotion of Bengali business and industry and was sharper in its opposition to the existing scheme of things. To cite a few examples, it once remarked that rich Bengalis were invariably accustomed to making wealth from government bonds, house-rent, rack-renting and seizure of revenue free lands;[63] it also had a clear recognition that 'the real wealth of the country lay in the fertility of its soil and in the labour and enterprise of its people'.[64] Again, in its disavowal of the allurement of government service, *Sadharani* wrote that a resort to free enterprise in agriculture or business would save people from the daily ignominy of being called 'savage niggers' by their foreign masters.[65]

In the second half of the nineteenth century great private wealth was rare and concentrated mainly among big landlords who in their aptitude for conspicuous consumption, were oriented neither to industrial investment nor enterprise. Bengali merchants showed little inclination to turn into industrial entrepreneurs. The fact of uneven competition with British manufactures ruled out the scope of entrepreneurial efforts on the part of men of moderate means.

Thus we have seen the nineteenth-century Bengali journals were vocal on the lack of business enterprise and industry in the province. Most of them were of the view that one of the important causes of Bengal's industrial backwardness was the insufficiency of the spirit of initiative and enterprise among its people. It was the existing social institutions, customs, and traditions of the land which were largely responsible for her industrial backwardness in general and for the lack of the spirit of enterprise amongst Bengalis in particular.

SWADESHI ENTERPRISE

When we speak of swadeshi we generally think of the period which was directly linked with the partition of Bengal (1905). In a broader sense, however, it embraces a larger period, started in the 1870s and continued till 1947. The period of late nineteenth and early twentieth century was one of the most happening periods in the history of modern India. During that period, swadeshi ideas of different strands took shape, handicraft industries showed signs of revival, modern industries were set up, and technical education was disseminated through the newly-constructed technical institutions. In the following pages we survey the nature of swadeshi economic thinking and entrepreneurial activities on the part of the few Bengali people during that period.

The country had no state of its own; it was a subject of the British Empire. Patterns of change sponsored and executed by such a system of power did not make for the emergence of an advanced mode of production, informed with its own intellectual and moral equipment. The pace and content of transformation was subservient to the more primary object of colonialism to generate wealth in India and use it for the advancement of Britain's own social order. This was inherent in all the twists and turns of imperial statecraft, however, masked such exercises were in the ideologies of Orientalism, Evangelism, or Liberalism.[66] Official economic policy in the nineteenth century cannot really be explained in terms of an abstract creed of *laissez faire*,[67] and government expenditure on the railway, military and PWD did encourage certain types of industries;[68] yet the crucial point is that the benefits of such state patronage went overwhelmingly to Europeans. In Bengal the age of great Calcutta merchants and entrepreneurs (Ramdulal Dey, Dwarkanath Tagore, Digambar Mitra, etc.), collaborating and competing on equal terms with the British was definitely over by the 1850s. The Bengali business community by the late nineteenth century consisted of socially not-too respectable 'second-hand merchants and commission traders doing small scale business'[69] and even here Bengali traders were being squeezed out by Marwaris.[70]

Recently a scholar has raised his voice against the inadequate importance given to the small and middle bourgeoisie by the economic historians of India.[71] The small and middle bourgeoisie, unlike the big bourgeoisie, were neither brokers nor intermediaries of foreign capital. They were self-reliant in capital, management, and marketing. Although they depended to some extent on foreign machinery, there were many examples of self-reliance in this field too. Despite their limitations, they sought to be self-reliant in the field of technology.[72] In the study of indigenous enterprise in the swadeshi era, the small and middle bourgeoisie deserve special importance.

In Bengal the idea of swadeshi may be traced back to the efforts of Nabogopal Mitra, who, in 1867, organized the annual Hindu Mela which regularly met for nearly fourteen years. One of the major functions of the Mela, apart from its other nation building activities, was the promotion of indigenous manufactures. Nabogopal Mitra was inspired and supported by Rajnarain Bose, who was also among the first nationalist leaders to encourage the use of indigenous cloth and other articles to the exclusion of foreign products.[73] Dwijendranath and Ganendranath Tagore helped Nabogopal Mitra in starting the Mela.[74]

Swadeshi enthusiastis like Chandranath Bose[75] and Bholanath Chandra[76] also raised their voices for the cause. Bengali journals played a vital role in championing the cause of swadeshi among common people. *Grambarta Prakashika* appealed:

> Foreign clothes are cheaper than Indian clothes. So people buy foreign made clothes. But if we think logically, our clothes are more durable than those. So in long run Indian clothes are more useful. Due to the development of the textile industry, Europeans produce cheaper machine made clothes. If our countrymen would try to develop the textile industry in India, then we can defeat Manchester. But it will take time. We are requesting our countrymen to kindly consider the miserable condition of the people attached to handicrafts and for the sake of these people buy Indian clothes.[77]

Some articles which appeared in these journals were very encouraging. *Bharati*, run entirely by the Tagore family, was optimistic in emphasizing the role of indigenous enterprise:

> In spite of loss of sovereignty, that the Bengali people have not lost their determination is really a good sign. They are learning agriculture in Scotland, achieving distinct positions in England in various branches of science, studying the principles of mathematics, getting professorship at Russian university, fighting to unite India politically, denying obeying the social taboos and raising their voices against the misrule of the government.
>
> It is not far away that Bengali youth would learn marine science, mechanical engineering, etc. There is very limited scope in the government jobs. So in near future they would go abroad to acquire technical education and business skills. Gradually they would become interested in trade and business.
>
> We are very hopeful that independent business enterprise would flourish in Bengal. If the government does not create an adverse environment, then our trade and business would definitely shine. The people of the other parts of India are very much interested in business.

They are facing many adversities due to absence of proper education. But educated and intelligent Bengalis would definitely overcome these obstacles and earn immense wealth through trade and business. So these two are the most important catalysts for the development of our country.[78]

The employment creating potential of industrialization formed a major theme of swadeshi propaganda. Many started believing that a faulty system of education combined with lack of industrial development had led to the services and professions being overcrowded. In the latter half of nineteenth century, few Bengalis with great entrepreneurial abilities, started their own business ventures. Hemendramohan Bose, Kishori Mohan Bagchi, etc., were ideal examples of this period.

Hemendramohan Bose, better known as H. Bose, was the first commercially successful perfumer of India. Kuntalin, a hair oil, the perfume Delkhos, many kinds of fruit syrups, and hair wash, all of his products won a big market. Tambulin in a way was years ahead of the present-day Pan-parag.[79] In promoting consumer products, Bose was the first Indian to exploit the art of advertisement.[80] He employed an Indian artist named P.C. Ghosh who was the first to depict Indian women to illustrate the advertisements. The copywriting was done by Bose himself. In fact, it is the unique style of Bose's advertisements which constitutes the source material for recording and interpreting his entrepreneurship. One such example:

> For the hair you have Kuntalin
> For chewing betel take Tambulin
> In the handkerchief use Delkhos
> Thanks says H. Bose[81]

Bose was choosy about selecting avenues to promote his wares. He preferred *The Bengalee* and *Amrita Bazar Patrika*, under Indian ownership, to *The Statesman* which was the leading newspaper of the day.

Hemendramohan was also the first to turnout indigenous voice recordings on a commercial scale in India. He founded the phonographic business in 1905. 'The Talking Machine Hall', as it was named, was situated in Marble House at 41, Dharmatala Street. In early 1906, at the peak of the anti-partition agitation in Bengal, the first batch of phonographic records (so-called cylinder records) were offered for sale.[82] Labelled as H. Bose's Records, all of them were of patriotic songs and sung by Rabindranath Tagore, Dwijendralal Roy, etc. In the domain of the history of technology Bose will be well remembered for his endeavour to produce sound-recordings. He was awarded a gold medal at the Industrial Exhibition of Calcutta, 1905–6, for these on the recommendation of Prof. J.C. Bose, the judge.[83] With the advent of the disc record, H. Bose felt the need to switch from the cumbersome cylinders. He got into a partnership with the famous French firm of Pathe and got many of his cylinders transferred into discs bearing the label, *Pathe–H. Bose's Record.* One such record, containing the recitation of 'Sonar Tari' on one side and the song *Bande Mataram* on the other, is the oldest existing voice recording of Rabindranath.[84]

Another prominent entrepreneur of late nineteenth century was Kishori Mohan Bagchi. He set-up 'P.M. Bagchi & Co.' in a rented house in north Calcutta in 1883. It was initially called 'Durjeepara Chemical Works', then renamed 'Durjeepara Chemicals and Rubber Stamp Works'. After three years it was known as 'P.M. Bagchi & Co.'.[85] Its first product was ink. Advertisements declared: 'Aniline ink was first invented in Germany in 1879, after four years in 1883 it was manufactured in the Eastern world by PMB.'[86] They manufactured many different types of ink, which required not only individual initiative but also sufficient knowledge about chemistry.

The principle of self-reliance adopted by the firm was reflected not only in the purchase of raw materials for ink, but also in other essential goods, e.g. dyes, pots, bottles of different sizes, tin-boxes, etc. In the last quarter of the nineteenth century a large number of swadeshi companies manufacturing glass articles sprang up in many areas of Calcutta: the Indian Glass Works Ltd., Calcutta Glass Works, Bengal Glass Works, etc.[87] The Indian Glass Works was such a swadeshi company which supplied glass articles to PMB.

Essence and perfumery constituted the second major branch of the firm. Another major department was the Rubber Stamp Department. Of the technological fields in which they excelled, the manufacture of wooden blocks was one. The need for wooden blocks arose out of demands from the press. Wooden blocks were necessary for printing pictures in books and advertisements. These needed skilled artisans, settled in the Garanhata and Battala areas of north Calcutta. Their artistic skill and knowledge of printing was commendable and they brought line and half-tone-effects to books and advertisements. PMB is the only firm that produced such a wide variety of goods. It could be combine almanac and publication with ink, perfumes, type foundry, rubber stamp, first syrups and medicines.[88] PMB did not simply manufacture different commodities by mainly relying on indigenous sources; it also pursued a policy of self-reliance in the technological field, despite limitations. The small and middle Bengali entrepreneurs, like Kishori Mohan Bagchi and his firm, took particular care to promote research relating to swadeshi industries.

Among modern industries, the first and in many ways the most remarkable of all was the Bengal Chemical and Pharmaceutical Works (BCPW), founded by the great scientist and patriot Prafulla Chandra Ray in 1892.[89] Drugs produced from indigenous materials included Ayurvedic items as well as standard British pharmacopoeia preparations. Patriotic-minded distributors like Buttokristo Paul and doctors like Radhagobinda Kar and Nilratan Sircar helped popularize the drugs and acids manufactured by BCPW. The manufacture of laboratory apparatus and perfumes was also taken in hand. The BCPW did not use imported machinery; all the machines were designed and constructed in the workshop of the firm. In 1908 Cumming observed the enterprise as an 'object lesson to capitalists in this province'.[90]

Perhaps the last initiative by Bengali entrepreneurs in the nineteenth century was the formation of the Bengal Providential Railway Company. On the recommendation of the Famine Commission (1881), the railway line between Howrah and Tarakeswar was established in 1885. The local zamindars played a vital role in that venture. The motive behind their move was to connect the area with the market of Calcutta to strengthen the local economy. One alumnus of the Thomson Engineering College, Roorkee, Anandaprasad Roy with the help of Amritlal Roy, editor of the English journal *Hope*, prepared a plan to establish a railway connection between Tarakeswar and Mogra on swadeshi lines.[91] With the help of local zamindars and wealthy persons the Bengal Providential Railway Company was established in 1889. *Sambad Prabhakar* reported:

> We have been listening for long about the opening of railway communication between Tarakeswar and Mogra. Lastly we came to know from the *Calcutta Gazette* that Raja Pari Mohan Bandopadhyay, Babu Nandalal Goswami, Babu Chandicharan Sinha, Moulobi Ahmed Bux, Babu Ananda Prasad Roy, Babu Sri Ramchandra Basu and Babu Amritlal Roy took the initiative to establish the railway line. They were waiting for permission from the Bengal government. On January 13 the government gave the necessary permission to go ahead with the plan.
>
> They established a joint-stock company to raise money for the project. The name of the company is 'Bengal Providential Railway Company Ltd.' The line will start from Tarakeswar and after touching Gopinagar, Dasghara, Bonpur, Dhanekhali, Majinan, Gopalpur, Melki, Dwarbasini, Mahanad, Sultan Gacha, will reach Mogra. Two bridges of 40 feet length have to be build near Dasghara and Bonpur. The speed of the train on the proposed line would be 12 miles per hour. So it would take two and half hours from Tarakeswar to Mogra.[92]

In the primary stage, Anandaprasad was the chief engineer and later Dhanakrishna Basu took over charge. The first railway line built entirely on Indian initiative began running on 2 April 1895.[93] The Bengal Providential Railway Company was a true example of swadeshi capital and management.

Thus we have seen there was a positive atmosphere in Bengal by the end of the nineteenth century. Many indigenous enterprises came up during that period, but few of these were really successful. Examples of H. Bose, P.M. Bagchi & Co., the zamindars of rural Bengal to establish railway communication and above all Prafulla

Chandra Ray proved that there was no dearth of entrepreneurial abilities among the Bengali people at the turn of the nineteenth century. The Bengali journals continued their crusade to promote local industries. As *Education Gazette O Saptahik Bartabaho* reported:

> A few lawyers and rich people of Jessore decided to establish a joint-stock company namely 'Deshiyo Panna Samiti'. The aim of the company is the development of local industries. The capital of the company is twenty thousand and the price of each share is Rs. 10. In spite of small capital, if the company will stick to its principles and work hard, it will certainly help restore the condition of the local industries.[94]

THE SUITABLE MODEL OF INDIAN INDUSTRIALIZATION

There was a lively controversy by the end of the nineteenth century over the type of industrialization most suitable to India. It involved not only economic but also social and ideological issues. Indian intellectuals were becoming increasingly aware of the social evils produced by large-scale industry in the capitalist West—the two poles of wealth and misery, class conflict, the erosion of moral and aesthetic values in the rat-race for material success—and a search began for a peculiarly 'Indian' path which could preserve the virtues of traditional society even while solving the economic problems of the country.

Indians, noting the effects of both machine-made imports and Fort Gloster yarn on the rural weavers and spinners, were at first less certain of the efficacy of industrialization.[95] A Hindu traveller who visited Fort Gloster Mill in 1830 reported that the local people considered industrialization a mixed blessing. As consumers they benefited from cheaper cloth, but some, who had learned from English friends about the results of the industrial revolution in cities like Glasgow and Manchester, were fearful of the long-term effects of industrialization on human life.[96] Thus the proper path of industrialization became apparent in the pages of the Bengali journals during the early nineteenth century. By the turn of the century, it was one of the most debated issues. In 1892, the pioneer sociologist, Bhudev Mukhopadhyay, urged his countrymen to borrow modern technology and apply it to Indian industry, but to beware of borrowing any other aspect of Western culture.[97] From 1898 onwards, *The Dawn*[98] repeatedly warned against the uncritical transportation of Western industrialization. Satish Chandra Mukherjee referred to Engels' *The Condition of the Working Class in England* as evidence of the horrors caused by the industrial revolution in England.[99] He advocated a kind of 'dual economy', with capitalist organizations only where these were absolutely necessary (like railways, mines, chemicals, etc.), while small-scale organizations would be encouraged in other sectors of the economy.[100]

The moderate economists of India displayed an occasional nostalgia for the loss of handicrafts of India, but their vision of the future was firmly modernist, seeking the solution of the poverty problem of the country in the rapid development of large-scale factory industries.[101] But in Bengal the industrial impetus came from patriotic sentiment and fear of unemployment rather than any considerable accumulation of capital. Handicrafts of certain types could attract the educated *bhadralok* through their artistic qualities.[102] The great science enthusiast Pramathanath Bose was of the view that the handloom alone could not drive out foreign products and the need of the hour was to cast yourself into the whirl of Western industrialism.[103] The swadeshi movement (1903–8) took the form of a crusade to encourage business entrepreneurship. The movement promoted indigenous industry, both artisan and factory.[104]

LIMITATIONS OF ECONOMIC SWADESHI

A string of consumer goods industries of dubious stability, a few banks, trading and insurance firms—the sum total hardly amounted to the industrial rejuvenation dreamt of at the beginning of the movement; and the strongholds of British capital in jute, tea and coal remained entirely unaffected. One of the limitations of the economic swadeshi in Bengal was the meagre achievement in the vital field of engineering.[105] Since basic industries like steel or engineering depended for their markets mainly on government orders in those days, in Bengal indigenous entrepreneurs got little support from the government.

Lack of capital proved an even more serious limiting factor. Zamindars and established businessmen interested in industrial ventures were relatively few in number. During the swadeshi period most of the efforts came from the men of the middle class with no business experience. J.C. Cumming pointed out the weaknesses of economic swadeshi:

> . . . the capital for these new enterprises is not coming from the large capitalists, but from the savings of the middle class. It is the opinion of a leading native merchant that it is much easier to make money by an agency in imported goods than by investment in industrial enterprise. The large capitalist has still to be persuaded that he can get a good return for his money in manufacture, rather than in zamindari, or agency or moneylending.[106]

The Indian Industrial Commission Report (1918) attributed the failure of swadeshi industries in Bengal to the lack of enterprise and business sense among the Bengalis.[107] Contemporaries thus tended to attribute Bengal's lag in indigenous industrial development to the prospect of quick profits in trade and to the lure of land created by the permanent settlement.[108] Although the Bengalis agreed in part with these hypothesizes, they felt that these evaded a large issue: the role of the government in thwarting entrepreneurship in Bengal. In numerous writings they blamed the government for discrimination in employment, establishing the permanent settlement to divert Bengali capital from commerce to land, encouraging literary education to provide a pool of cheap clerical labour, and finally, favouring British over Indian merchants in tariff and purchasing policies.[109]

DE-INDUSTRIALIZATION TO 'RE-INDUSTRIALIZATION'

India was a rich prize and the British held on to her well beyond the age of imperialism, en route for her leadership of world capitalism. Although India was the first of the oriental countries to feel the import of industrialism, she never completed the transition, whereas Japan, starting later and with fewer resources, did.

Early colonialism deflated and depressed the Indian economy, and was accompanied from around 1830 by a deliberate policy of de-industrialization by means of discriminating duties against Indian artisan manufactures. The triumph of the free traders over the Company monopolists (by the successive Charter Acts of 1813 and 1833) had resulted in allowing free trade to England but without permitting the same freedom of trade to India. By the time internal duties were fully removed within India (on the recommendations of the Trevelyan Report of 1838) and a perfectly free two-away oceanic traffic established between the colony and the metropolitan country, India was already integrated into the capitalist world economy as a supplier of raw materials and market for its industrial products.[110] After 1857, various changes in company law, coinciding with the extension of the railways up the Gangetic valley, gave a marked impetus to the formation of companies under the typically European system of the managing agency. By the end of the 1870s the railway system was complete in all essential respects, and business corporations, came for the first time to occupy an important position in the country's economy.[111]

During the vital years when India became linked by the railways, the country missed the opportunity of rapid growth of iron and steel manufacture, coal production, and related engineering industries on the pattern of what took place in Russia and Japan around the same time. The railway system, which represented the greatest single injection of British capital into India, was built almost entirely by means of imported locomotives, rolling stock, track materials, technicians and managers.

The 'Buy British' policy, as Daniel Thorner has pointed out, withheld from India an impetus to industrial development that proved quite effective among other leading railway powers, particularly the United States, Russia and Germany, where the railway was the veritable dynamo of the Industrial Revolution.[112] India alone of these countries, remained unindustrialized, with her capacity for production of capital goods and her potential for the basic and heavy industries remaining almost entirely untapped. British manufacturers of locomotives had a monopoly of the Indian market, and several attempts at manufacturing locomotives in India by the railways themselves proved futile because of the lack of official support. However, when the necessity arose, the railway workshops successfully manufactured locomotives. The railways in India promoted lines of commercial and industrial activity in which European firms with strong links to Britain could easily overshadow Indian firms which had no such links.

A major factor influencing private investment in any country is the attitude of the government to industry and the operational content of government policy towards industry.[113] British rule over India was translated into gains for European businessmen in India. It is they who had an edge over Indians in all public affairs, including affairs connected with money making. The entry of the Indians into modern industry was barred by European control over foreign trade, wholesale trade and finance.

In specific instances in which government patronage to industry was important, Europeans far outdistanced Indians in the enjoyment of such patronage. One such industry was the engineering industry. Large government contracts for construction and engineering were rarely given to Indian firms. Since engineering firms in a poor economy with little industry had to depend mainly on contracts placed by public authorities, there were practically no large Indian firms.[114]

Sir Rajendra Nath Mookerjee made a name for himself in the construction of waterworks for the Calcutta Corporation. But he found that, as 'T.C. Mookerjee and Company', his firms could not obtain contracts for the construction of waterworks in the United Provinces, though theirs were the lowest tenders. He then had to join forces with Acquin Martin and adopt the name of 'Martin and Company' in order to obtain contracts. Such a great entrepreneur as Rajendra Nath who had dared to establish an engineering firm, had to join a British engineer to survive. His major dream was the industrialization of India.[115]

European businessmen had established organizations and institutions for building up their advantages and protecting them against intruders all over India. They were organized in Chambers of Commerce to which very few Indians were admitted. In Bengal the jute industry was almost entirely in European hands[116] and they were organized into associations whose general interests were looked after by the Bengal Chamber of Commerce. Thus, in most fields, European businessmen were well organized, maintaining something approaching collective monopoly. The situation was supplemented and buttressed by European control of the organized money market.[117]

The standard trope behind the economic stagnation in India during the British rule highlights the caste restrictions or the other-worldly features of Indian value systems, along with the Permanent Settlement which was responsible for the relative lack of Indian enterprise in the field of industry. A few portray the Europeans or the Parsis as inherently more dynamic by virtue of either race, or superior social customs, or some sort of protestant religious-cultural ethos.[118] Had a 'Protestant ethic' been the only factor, the progressive-minded English-educated Bengalis, after the success of their initial ventures in collaboration with the Europeans, would not have faded out after 1848.

The caste system as a pattern of stratification into endogamous groups survived intact through nineteenth century and definitely put some restrictions on entering into trade and business ventures. But at the turn of the century in Bengal, particularly in Calcutta, many castes—particularly the upper ones—had been divorced from their traditional occupation. This liberalizing tendency did not, however, throw up new entrepreneurial groups of any major significance from among the Bengalis. Even more ironically, many of the new trading and banking groups which emerged into industrial entrepreneurship (the Chettiars, the Jains, and the Hindu banians) were much given to building temples, *dharmashalas*, etc.[119] So it is difficult to locate any direct connection between caste prejudice, Westernization, and success in making money in a big away.

It would also be misleading to suggest that landlords were immune to the lure of profit or that they stuck to their semi-feudal privileges so steadfastly as to ignore the changes going on around them. In Bengal there were landlords starting industrial enterprises and successful traders buying up land.[120] Amiya Kumar Bagchi denies that the land tenure system only or even mainly affected industrial development through the restriction of investment in industry by wealthy Bengalis.[121]

Daniel Thorner, a highly critical analyst of foreign investment in India, made this reflective observation:

> Had the British never come to India, the great likelihood is not that India would by now have transformed itself into a leading economic power, but rather that there would have been an even slighter degree of industrialization. As things did happen, India's development under the British has been strangely lopsided. Amidst a general landscape characterized by backwardness and perhaps even retrogression, there stand out a few substantial economic achievements.[122]

This is a balanced judgement which can hardly be faulted. British rule brought about the transformation of the country from a feudal into a colonial and semi-feudal one and the conversion of the Indian economy into a material-supplying appendage to metropolitan Britain.

The dominance of modern industry by European business houses before the First World War was supported and reinforced by a whole set of administrative, political, and financial arrangements within India. British paramountcy was very much in evidence in 1900. The unchallenged political supremacy of the British favoured, among other things, the exercise of economic power by the Europeans in India who derived special advantages from linguistic and racial identification with the rulers of India. The entry into modern industry was barred by European control over foreign trade, inland trade, and finance. It required a loosening of this grip—facilitated both by the First World War and the greater importance of internal trade in relation to external trade which came about in the 1920s and 1930s–before Indian businessmen could effectively challenge the Europeans in the industrial field.

After the First World War, and much more clearly after the coming of protection,[123] Indian entrepreneurs took the lead in the development of industries such as cement, paper, and sugar. Indian entrepreneurs came from groups with connections in trade; very few professional, Westernized Indians emerged as big industrialists.

The major reasons for the triumph of indigenous entrepreneurs in the inter-war period were probably: (i) political uncertainty connected with the gathering strength of the nationalist movement and the concessions made to it by the British government; (ii) the greater attractiveness of investment in the Far East; and (iii) the difficulties faced by the British economy, which led to a massive repatriation of British capital, mainly public, in the early 1930s.[124]

Thus the emergence of Indian entrepreneurship in Bengal was systematically discouraged by the political, administrative, and financial arrangements maintained by the British. In the few cases before 1914 in which Bengali entrepreneurship had emerged, it was no less enterprising or interested in industry than the British businessmen in India. Bengali entrepreneurs showed a greater degree of courage, since they did not have many of the tangible advantages that British businessmen enjoyed because of their birth.

The Indian industries that grew up under the umbrella of tariff protection were confined to the production of consumption goods such as cotton cloth, sugar, and matches. But the development of the capital goods industries was meagre. Moreover, the newly emerged Indian entrepreneurs depended mostly on Western countries for their techniques of production.[125] Whatever the developments that took place, they were in the context of a borrowed technology and a very narrow base of technical personnel. There were very few technical improvements pioneered in India and applied to the solution of industrial problems.

THE QUEST FOR TECHNICAL KNOWLEDGE

One of the important factors hampering the growth of industry in Bengal was the dearth of adequately trained technicians. Consequently, one of the important and oft-repeated demands of the Bengali leadership was for new technical schools, colleges, and institutes in order to spread technical knowledge far and wide.

The Bengali intellectuals pointed out that one of the reasons why youth did not show enthusiasm for technical education was the lack of employment opportunities, because of the industrial backwardness of the country. The government was urged to encourage recipients of technical education by providing them with jobs, and in particular to throw open to Indians the higher posts in the PWD, telegraph department, and railways.

Lack of technical education had been used as a justification for the exclusion of Indians from responsible posts in industry and government through the nineteenth century. While stressing the responsibility of the government, the Bengali leadership laid a great deal of emphasis on self-help. The scientist Prafulla Chandra Ray appreciated and tapped the advantages of industrialization. He was inspired by the close coordination of the West between industry and science to enrich each other. Ray endeavoured to make his science directly relevant to the immediate needs of his society. He started the BCPW to put scientific knowledge to immediate industrial use, to encourage the idea of self-sufficiency, and to provide employment to many science graduates. According to him technological education was of great importance, considering the stunted industrial development of India. Sir Asutosh Mookerjee, the vice-chancellor of Calcutta University during 1906–14 and 1921–3, laid increasing stress on industry-institution alliances.[126]

The nature of technical education to be imparted in the technical institutions also drew the attention of Bengali leaders. They took strong exception to, and trenchantly criticized the official policy of confining technical education mostly to the improvement of the style of work of carpenters, smiths, and other handicraftsmen. They pointed out that Bengal already had enough trained artisans. What the province needed was modern engineers. The main goal of technical education had to be not the revival of the extinct and dying industries but the establishment of new large-scale industries which would produce goods which were at that moment being imported. So the Bengali intellectuals vigorously pressed for the opening of high-level institutions where the most advanced technical education would be provided. The popular journal *Sulav Samachar* rightly said:

> If consumer goods are prepared in this country and the government encourages such industries, the poverty of India can be eradicated. The wealth of our country would remain here if such industries would develop. But the Bengali people are not interested in this. They are basically talkative in nature. They always blame the government for unemployment and write long articles in the journals. Our suggestion to them is to learn technical education and start their own industrial enterprises. By these two measures, all problems can be solved.[127]

NOTES

1. *Jnananeshan* was the mouthpiece of the Young Bengal. This weekly journal appeared on 18 June 1831 and Dakkhinaranjan Mukhopadhyay was the editor. The journal found a model Bengali entrepreneur in the enterprising Dwarakanath Tagore who started his own commercial house in full partnership with Englishmen. See Bajendranath Bandopadhyay, *Bangla Samayik Patra*, vol. 1, Bangiya Sahitya Parishad, Calcutta, 1935, p. 39.
2. Bengal Chemical and Pharmaceutical Works Ltd. (BCPW) was founded by P.C. Ray in 1892. He strongly held that the Bengalis should cease to take clerical jobs and turn to business and industry. *Acharya Prafulla Ray Birth Centenary Volume*, Calcutta University, Calcutta, 1962, p. 299.
3. 'Engraji Muldhon Biniyoge Bharater Upokar Ki?', *Somprakash*, 18 Baishak 1290 (April 1883).
4. *Sambad Prabhakar*, 22 July 1847.
5. D.R. Gadgil, *The Industrial Evolution of India in Recent Times 1860-1939*, Oxford University Press, New Delhi, 1924, see chapters III and XII.

6. Sakharam Ganesh Deuskar, *Desher Katha*, Calcutta, 1904.
7. Chittabrata Palit, 'Indigenous Business Enterprise in Bengal: 1780-1880', *New Viewpoints on Nineteenth Century Bengal*, 2nd edn., Progressive Publishers, Kolkata, 2006, p. 49.
8. *Samachar Darpan*, 21 April 1838.
9. The *modus operandi* of an agency house is described thus by R.M. Martin in 1832: 'A large mercantile house is established at Calcutta, with a branch in London; the partnership formed of various individuals–one a retired civil servant of the Company, another a military man, a third a doctor, and fourth a London merchant. They possess no real capital, but establish an agency and banking business, receive as deposits the accumulating fortunes of the East India Company's servants and trade on these deposits'. Quoted in Rajat Kanta Ray (ed.), 'Introduction', *Entrepreneurship and Industry in India, 1800-1947*, Oxford University Press, Delhi, 1992, p. 19.
10. Blair B. Kling, *Partner in Empire: Dwarkanath Tagore and the Age of Enterprise in Eastern India*, University of California Press, Berkeley, 1976, pp. 55–6.
11. In essence, a managing agency involves the vesting of the management of a joint-stock company in the hands of a firm of professional managers. In practice, the managing agent is responsible for the initial promotion, financing, underwriting, and organizing of the joint-stock company. See S.K. Basu, *The Managing Agency System*, Government of India, Publication Division, New Delhi, 1957.
12. A banian is a person by whom all purchases and all sales of goods, merchandise and produce are made and through whom all shipments are made on account and on behalf of the merchants or mercantile firm in whose establishment he is a banian. See Narendra Krishna Sinha, 'Indian Business Enterprise: Its Failure in Calcutta (1800-1848)', *Bengal Past and Present*, Diamond Jubilee number, July–December 1967, pp. 121–48.
13. The earliest available biography is by Girish Chandra Ghosh, *Ramdoolal Dey: The Bengalee Millionaire*, Calcutta, 1868.
14. Amit Bhattacharya, *Swadeshi Enterprise in Bengal 1900-1920*, Readers Service, Calcutta, 1986, p. 141.
15. *Sambad Prabhakar*, 21 October 1856.

16. Narendra Krishna Sinha, 'Indian Business Enterprise: Its Failure in Calcutta (1800–1848)', op. cit.
17. N.K. Sinha, *The Economic History of Bengal 1793-1848*, vol. 3, K.L. Mukhopadhyay, Calcutta, 1970, p. 111.
18. Kissory Chand Mittra, *Memoir of Dwarkanath Tagore*, Thacker, Spink & Co., Calcutta, 1870.
19. *Samachar Darpan*, 4 October 1834.
20. Ibid., 18 April 1835.
21. This celebrated Parsi had the unique credit of being the first Indian to challenge European monopolies in the fields of insurance and banking. Rustomji, Turner & Co. was his singular attempt at a joint stock company with foreign collaboration (1827). He owned a fleet of 40 ships which sailed regularly to the Far East, Australia and Southern Coast of India. In 1837 he started a Docking Company and bought up Kidderpore and Salkia Docks. Many ships were built here. He had the far sight to plan a regular steamer service in the rivers of Bengal. For the purpose, the Indian General Steam Navigation Company (1844) was founded, of which Rustomji was the only director. He launched the Bengal Salt Company in the Sunderbans area. See Chittabrata Palit, 'Indigenous Business Enterprise in Bengal: 1780-1880', op. cit.
22. *Samachar Chandrika*, 9 February 1833.
23. *Reformer*, 18 March 1833. This was published by Prasanna Kumar Tagore and representing views close to those of Dwarkanath.
24. *Jnananeshan*, 14 December 1833.
25. Ibid., 9 August 1834.
26. *Samachar Darpan*, 9 January 1836.
27. For more information see, Blair B. Kling, *Partner of Empire: Dwarkanath Tagore and the Age of Enterprise in Eastern India*.
28. *Samachar Darpan*, 1 July 1835.
29. Dipesh Chakrabarty, 'The Colonial Context of the Bengal Renaissance: A Note on Early Railway-Thinking in Bengal', *Indian Economic and Social History Review*, vol. 11, no. 1, March 1974, pp. 107–11.
30. *Samachar Chandrika*, 22 September 1845: 'We came to know from Englishmen that Babu Dwarkanath Tagore, now in Lon-

don, has agreed to help the Company which was formed to establish a railway-line in the north-western part of Bengal.'

31. 'Sargiyo Motilal Seal', *Rahasya Sandarbha*, vol. I, no. 6, 1280 (1873).
32. Amit Bhattacharya, *Swadeshi Enterprise in Bengal*, p. 143.
33. N.K. Sinha, *The Economic History of Bengal 1793–1848*, vol. 3, p. 121.
34. Birendranath Ghosh, 'Sargiyo Motilal Seal', *Bharatbarsha*, Jyaistha, 1338 (1931), pp. 994–5.
35. Kissory Chand Mitra, *Mutty Lal Seal*, Calcutta, 1869, p. 41.
36. For biographical sketches of Ghosh, see Nirmal Sinha (ed.), *Freedom Movement in Bengal, 1818-1904; Who's Who*, Education Department, Government of West Bengal, Calcutta, 1968, p. 107.
37. Amit Bhattacharya, op. cit., p. 145.
38. George Campbell, *Modern India: A Sketch of the System of Civil Government*, J. Murray, London, 1852, p. 204.
39. John Capper, *The Three Presidencies of India: A History of the Rise and Progress of the British Indian Possessions*, Ingram, Cooke & Co., London, 1853, pp. 381–2.
40. J.H. Stocqueler, *The Handbook of India*, 2nd edn., Wm. H. Allen, London, 1845, p. 348.
41. Rajat Kanta Ray (ed.), 'Introduction', *Entrepreneurship and Industry in India*, p. 24.
42. *Sambad Prabhakar*, 4 April 1848, reported the sad demise of Carr, Tagore & Co.
43. For more information in this regard see Daniel R. Headrick, *The Tentacles of Progress: Technology Transfer in the Age of Imperialism, 1850-1940*, Oxford University Press, New York, 1988.
44. Binay Ghose, *Banglar Samajik Itihaser Dhara 1800-1900*, Bengal Publishers Pvt. Ltd., Kolkata, 1968, pp. 110–13.
45. Blair B. Kling, *Partner in Empire*, pp. 251–3.
46. D.R. Gadgil, *Origins of the Modern Indian Business Class*, Institute of Pacific Relations, New York, 1959, pp. 18–19.
47. Girish Chandra Ghosh, *Ramdulal Dey, The Bengali Millionaire*, pp. 57–8.
48. Blair B. Kling, 'Entrepreneurship and Regional Identity in Bengal', in David Kopf (ed.), *Bengal Regional Identity*, Michigan State University, Michigan, 1969, p. 25.

49. Narendra Krishna Sinha, 'Indian Business Enterprise: Its failure in Calcutta (1800-1848)'.
50. Young Bengal was a group of Western-educated graduates of Hindu College given to measuring their countrymen by the yardstick of British achievement.
51. *Jnananeshan*, 14 December 1833.
52. *Sambad Prabhakar*, 22 June 1847. Tarini Charan wrote, '. . . if we were courageous and laborious like the Englishmen, then nobody could snatch the wealth of our country. England becomes the richest country of the world by utilizing the wealth of our country. They collect the raw materials from India and convert them into various finished products in their industries. Then we are compelled to buy these goods in a higher price. If our countrymen become interested in technical education like the British and start their own industrial enterprise, the misery of our country would certainly come to an end.'
53. *Sambad Prabhakar*, 22 June 1847.
54. Ibid., 23 November 1853.
55. *Sambad Purnochandradaya*, 1 February 1853.
56. *Sambad Prabhakar*, 17 August 1854.
57. *Somprakash*, 13 July 1863.
58. *Tattobodhini Patrika*, vol. 321, 1870, quoted in Binay Ghose (ed.), *Samayik Patre Banglar Samajchitra*, vol. 2, Bengal Publishers Pvt. Ltd., Kolkata, 1963, p. 250.
59. *Amrita Bazar Patrika*, 6 January 1869. The title of the article is very interesting, '*Chakuri Kukuri*'.
60. *Somprakash*, 6 August 1883.
61. Ibid., 23 March 1886.
62. *Sadharani* was a weekly published on 11 Kartik 1280 B.S. (1873) from Chuchura. Akshay Chandra Sarkar was the editor. Writers like Bankim Chandra Chattopadhyay and Jogesh Chandra Basu used to write for it frequently. *Sadharani* was in circulation till 1889. Bajendranath Bandopadhyay, *Bangla Samayik Patra*, vol. II, Bangiyo Sahitya Parishad, Kolkata, 1951, p. 12.
63. *Sadharani*, 28 December 1873.
64. Ibid., 21 June 1874.
65. Ibid., 5 September 1875.
66. Asok Sen, *Iswar Chandra Vidyasagar and His Elusive Milestones*, Riddhi-India, Calcutta, 1977, p. 95.

67. Sabyasachi Bhattacharya, 'Laissez Faire in India', *Indian Economic and Social History Review*, vol. II, no. 1, January 1965, pp. 1–22.
68. Sunil Kumar Sen, *Studies in Industrial Policy and Development of India*, Calcutta, 1964, pp. 3–4.
69. Sumit Sarkar, *The Swadeshi Movement in Bengal 1903-1908*, People's Publishing House, New Delhi, 1973, p. 94.
70. 'About this time (1891-92) another matter began seriously to occupy my thoughts . . . the adventurous non-Bengalis, notably the Marwaris from the barren deserts of Rajputana, were swarming not only in Calcutta but also in the interior of Bengal and capturing all key-points of the export and import business . . . ', Prafulla Chandra Ray, *Life and Experiences of a Bengali Chemist*, vol. 1, Chuckervertty, Chatterjee & Co., Calcutta, 1932, pp. 89–90.
71. Amit Bhattacharya, 'Heterogeneity of the Indian Bourgeoisie in Colonial India: A Comparative Study', *Business, Politics and Technology*, Readers Service, Kolkata, 2005, pp. 90–110.
72. P.M. Bagchi & Co. was one of such companies belonged to this category. Kishori Mohan Bagchi set-up the company in 1883. See Amit Bhattacharya, 'Swadeshi Industry and Technology: P.M. Bagchi & Co. (1883-1947)', in Chittabrata Palit and Amit Bhattacharya (eds.), *Science, Technology, Medicine and Environment in India: Historical Perspectives*, Bibhasa, Kolkata, 1998, pp. 108–27.
73. Bipan Chandra, *The Rise and Growth of Economic Nationalism in India*, Anamika Publishers, New Delhi, 1966, p. 64.
74. The fifth session (1871) of the Mela was memorable from the point of view of technological innovation. Here Sitanath Ghosh of Jessore demonstrated for the first time the cotton spindle he had invented, by which yarn was produced and twisted mechanically. See *Sadharani*, 27 February 1876. Sitanath Ghosh also organized an annual agricultural and educational fair in Roygram. From the river front to the fair site, he set-up telegraph lines for dignitaries to speak to the office from the ferry ghat for their reception. See Anjali Basu (ed.), *Sansad Bangali Charitabidhan*, Kolkata, 1996, p. 366.
75. 'She (India) is yet only the hewer of wood and drawer of water of English civilization in the East. But once let manufactures be

established in Bengal, let Bengal once know that cloth which she wears, the paper on which she writes will be no longer prepared for her by England.... Then will England herself form with her a friendship more close, more intellectual than subsists at present.' Chandranath Bose while addressing at the Social Science Association in 1869; B.B. Majumdar, *History of Indian Social and Political Ideas*, Firma KLM, Calcutta, 1967, pp. 278–9.

76. 'To strip naked the disguised truth, the English want to reduce us all to the condition of agriculturists... let us receive a commercial and industrial education. Allow us a share in the administration and to frame our own tariff and with perhaps at starting a bit of patriotism to buy foreign goods, the children of India will prove to the world whether providence has willed them to be mere agriculturists or whether they cannot dethrone king cotton of Manchester and once more establish their sway in the cotton world', Bholanath Chandra, 'A Voice for the Commerce and Manufactures of India', *Mukherjee's Magazine*, 1873–6.
77. *Grambarta Prakashika*, 22 July 1876.
78. *Bharati*, vol. I, 1799 Saka (Magh 1284), January 1877.
79. Siddhartha Ghosh, *Karigari Kalpana O Bangali Udyog*, Dey's Publishing, Kolkata, 1988, p. 195.
80. The small and medium swadeshi entrepreneurs used advertisements in journals, almanacs, propaganda literature, and as handbills. These ads became one of the major sources of information on the industrial development of Bengal along swadeshi lines. For more information see Amit Bhattacharya, 'Swadeshi Industries in Colonial Bengal: Advertisement as a Source of Information', in *Business, Politics & Technology*, pp. 30–51.
81. Siddhartha Ghosh, op. cit., p. 199.
82. *Amrita Bazar Patrika*, 19 March 1906.
83. *Indian Industrial Exhibition* (a Hand Book), Calcutta, 1906.
84. Amitabha Ghosh, 'Colonial Constraints and Technology: Marginalized Indian Attainments', Arun Kumar Biswas (ed.), *History, Science and Society in the Indian Context*, The Asiatic Society, Calcutta, 2001, p. 175.
85. Arabinda Bhattacharya (ed.), *Satabarsha-purti Smarak Patrika P.M. Bagchi & Co. 1883-1983*, Calcutta, 1983, p. 9.

86. Quoted in Amit Bhattacharya, 'Swadeshi Industry and Technology: P.M. Bagchi & Co.', op. cit., p. 111.
87. Amit Bhattacharya, 'More About Swadeshi Enterprise', *Journal of History*, Jadavpur University, vol. 7, 1986–7, pp. 70–3.
88. PMB's policy of self-reliance was manifested also in the medicine department. It had two branches: one, Kabiraji Siddhasram (Ayurvedic section) and the other was the allopathic section. The first was set-up in 1907 and the second in 1941. The allopathic department was significant for original research and invention. The company manufactured a number of patent medicines for the treatment of fever, dysentery, colitis, etc.
89. 'Our educated young men, the moment they came out of their colleges, were on the look out for a situation or a soft job under the Government . . . or failing that in a European mercantile firm. The professions were becoming overcrowded. A few came out of Engineering College, but they too were helpless seekers after jobs. . . . What to do with all these young men? . . . How to bring bread to the mouths of the ill-fed, famished young men of the middle classes?' Thus Ray explains the motives behind his setting-up of BCPW. P.C. Ray, op. cit., pp. 89–92.
90. J.C. Cumming, *Review of the Industrial Position and Prospects in Bengal in 1908–with Special Reference to the Industrial Survey of 1890*, Government Press, Calcutta, 1908, p. 31.
91. Subhas Sen, 'Bengal Providential Rail Company: Hooghly-r Zamidarbarger Akti Swadeshi Udyog (1890-1906)', *Itihas Anusandhan* 7, K.P. Bagchi & Co., Kolkata, 1993, pp. 341–53.
92. *Sambad Prabhakar*, 25 January 1892.
93. *Sahachar*, 3 April 1895. The journal was published in 1873 and inspired by Somprakash. Biprodas Bandopadhyay was the editor. Bajendranath Bandopadhyay, *Bangla Samayik Patra*, vol. II, p. 11.
94. *Education Gazette O Saptahik Bartabaho*, 9 August 1889.
95. *Reformer*, 3 April 1835.
96. *Samachar Darpan*, 8 May 1830.
97. Pramathanath Bishee (ed.), *Bhudev Rachana Sambhar*, 2nd edn., Calcutta, 1962, p. 66.
98. Though the *Dawn Society* was established in 1902, the mouthpiece of the society *The Dawn Magazine* was started in 1897.

Satish Chandra Mukherjee (1868–1945) was the founder of the journal and later the society.

99. 'One has to cast only a passing glance at the reports of the various commissions and blue books which investigated the state of industrial life in the factories, mines and workshops between 1833 to 1842; or to read the passages of Engels's State of the Working Classes in England in 1844 to convince himself of the truth of the total degradation and suffering of the English working-classes brought on by the Industrial Revolution.', Satish Chandra Mukherjee, 'The Indian Economic Problem', *Dawn*, vol. III, March–June 1900, p. 263.
100. Ibid., pp. 264–5.
101. R.C. Dutt, in his presidential address at the first Indian Industrial Conference, stated that a shift in emphasis from cottage crafts to urban industries was inevitable; *Report of the Indian Industrial Conference*, Benares, 1905, quoted in Sumit Sarkar, op. cit., p. 100.
102. *Bharati*, Aswin 1312 (1905); 'Boycott abong Swadeshikata', an article written by Pramathanath Chaudhury, states that down to 1905, swadeshi had meant essentially the use of costly but artistic hand-made goods by the educated minority.
103. J.C. Bagal, *Pramatha Nath Bose*, P.N. Bose Centenary Committee, Calcutta, 1955, pp. 93–5.
104. For details see Sumit Sarkar, op. cit., pp. 92–148, Sarkar identified five aspects of the swadeshi economic activity of the period between 1890 and 1910: the organization of technical education and something like industrial research; the promotion of swadeshi sales through exhibitions, shops and cost-price hawking by volunteers; the fostering and revival of the traditional indigenous craft; the starting of new industries based on modern techniques; and the floating of swadeshi banks, insurance companies and inland shipping concerns; also see Amit Bhattacharya, *Swadeshi Enterprise in Bengal 1900-1920*, passim.
105. The Sibpur Iron Works, Das and Co. of Chitpur, Arya Factory of Mechhuabazar, are a few examples. But for raw materials and machineries they had to depend on England.
106. J.C. Cumming, op. cit., p. 4.
107. *Report of Indian Industrial Commission of 1916-1918*, Government Press, Calcutta, 1918, pp. 73–4.

108. *Bengalee*, 2 August 1906.
109. Blair B. Kling, 'Entrepreneurship and Regional Identity in Bengal', p. 34.
110. Rajat Kanta Ray (ed.), 'Introduction', *Entrepreneurship and Industry in India*, p. 65.
111. R.S. Rungta, *The Rise of Business Corporations in India 1851-1900*, Cambridge University Press, Cambridge, 1970, p. 119.
112. Daniel Thorner, 'The Pattern of Railway Development in India', *Far Eastern Quarterly*, vol. XIV, no. 2, 1955, pp. 201–6.
113. Amiya Kumar Bagchi, *Private Investment in India 1900-1939*, Cambridge University Press, Cambridge, 1972, p. 5; the operational content of government policy in an economy embarking on industrialization under the auspices of private industry is largely determined by the tariff policy of the government.
114. Amiya Kumar Bagchi, 'European and Indian Entrepreneurship in India, 1900-30', Rajat Kanta Ray (ed.), *Entrepreneurship and Industry in India*, p. 161.
115. 'Our political friends are busy translating their aspirations into terms of constitutions and are thinking about majorities, electorates and votes. I . . . picture an India of busy workshops, smoky factories, sanitary dwellings for the work-people and eager money-getters.', Quoted in Kailash Chandra Mahindra, *Sir Rajendra Nath Mookerjee*, Calcutta, 1933, pp. 236–7.
116. *Somprakash*, 26 Jaistha 1287 (1880). The title of the article was 'Chater Babosa'.
117. Jyotirindranath Tagore's business venture was shattered by unfair competition on the part of the British company backed by the government. He launched a major venture with his Inland River Steam Navigation Service in 1884. Five ships were bought at enormous cost, to carry passengers between Khulna and Barisal and cargo up to Calcutta; but soon Jyotirindranath had to face cut-throat competition from the Flotilla Company, a British-owned concern. Barisal students took up the cause of the swadeshi company with great enthusiasm, composing songs in its honour and recruiting passengers for it. But the rate-war between the two companies led to passengers enjoying virtually free rides. An accident at the Howrah Bridge proved the final blow, and Jyotirindranath's shipping concern was ruined. Raja Peary Mukherjee of Uttarpara bought the ships as agent for the Flo-

tilla Company. Thus events proved that patriotic sentiment among the people was no substitute for solid capital resources. See Sumit Sarkar, *Swadeshi Movement in Bengal*, pp. 109–10.

118. R.E. Kennedy, 'The Protestant Ethic and the Parsis', *American Journal of Sociology*, vol. 68, 1962, pp. 16–20.
119. Amiya Kumar Bagchi, 'European and Indian Entrepreneurship in India', pp. 194–5.
120. For example, Maharaja Manindra Chandra Nundy of Cossimbazar started the Calcutta Pottery Works in collaboration with Baikunthanath Sen, another landlord; the Raja of Baneli started the Kirtyanand Iron and Steel Works Ltd., which manufactured iron and steel castings; the Maharajas of Durbhanga and Burdwan invested in modern industry on a large scale. See Henry Hemantakumar Ghosh, *The Advancement of Industry*, R. Cambray & Co., Calcutta, 1910.
121. Amiya Kumar Bagchi, op. cit., pp. 189–92.
122. Daniel Thorner, 'Pattern of Railway Development in India', op. cit.
123. In 1823 the government adopted the policy of discriminating tariff protection towards Indian industries. It clearly marked the end of the era of free trade and the beginning of the growth of industry under tariff protection.
124. Amiya Kumar Bagchi, *Private Investment in India*, p. 216.
125. Ibid., p. 442.
126. 'Industry and education will march forward more and more, hand in hand for this is pre-eminently a time to awaken industry and education alike. Industry in its many-sided interest will look to education for enlightenment and support and out of the laboratories of the University will emanate in an ever-increasing measure the influences that make for economic and industrial improvement and contribute to the betterment of human living and to the good of mankind.' Asutosh Mookerjee, Calcutta University Convocation Address, 26 December 1913, quoted in J. Lourdusamy, *Science and National Consciousness in Bengal (1870-1930)*, Orient Longman, New Delhi, 2004, p. 223.
127. *Sulav Samachar*, 30 August 1879.

CHAPTER 5

Conclusion

> In the Bengal Engineering College at Shibpore the teaching of Chemistry, Physics, Geology, Metallurgy and Mining, on which the Science Industries are dependent is subservient to the requirements of a Civil Engineer, and is of a highly elementary character. All of these subjects are there taught by one and the same teacher—an arrangement of questionable efficiency even as regards the requirements of an ordinary Engineer. For the successful industrial application of the sciences, however, the instruction must be far more advanced.
>
> P.N. Bose, *Technical and Scientific Education in Bengal*, Pamphlet, 1886.[1]

In the larger project of science, technology, medicine and environment (HISTEM),[2] the recipient culture's perception of modern science and technology and its response towards it is very important. Another important question is how the recipient culture situated modern technical knowledge within the framework of the social transformation of its own society. An enquiry into the dissemination of modern science and technology in nineteenth-century Bengal reveals a close connection between science, technology, politics, and culture.

The Bengali intelligentsia was the first Asian social group of any size whose mental world was transformed through its interaction with the West. In 1817, Bengal's social leaders took the initiative to establish the first institution of Western higher education in Asia. By then, through trade and colonial government, Bengalis had more than six decades of close contact with a European nation. The change in their mental world was part of a process described by two expressions, although unsatisfactorily, 'modernization' and 'Westernization'.[3] The basic determinant of the change was that in the close contact between two different cultures, one was perceived as dominant.

Colonization had brought forth a massive cultural collision which influenced profoundly the cognitive and material existence of both the colonizer and colonized.[4] This encounter was initially disturbing, even agonizing. Gradually relations stabilized and the recipients started examining what was living and what was dead in their system, and under the new dispensation, what to accept and what to reject. The encounter also comprised the question of attitudes toward the other, an uneasy acceptance, a quest for identity and finally, the seeds of decolonization. The question of identity was important for a colonized society.[5] The most important characteristic of the nineteenth-century Indian thinking was an unprecedented emphasis on cultural synthesis. A number of cultural interlocutors from Rammohun Roy to Vivekananda worked for it. Akshay Kumar Dutt (1820–86) worked to 'Indianize Western science'.[6] Numerous Bengali journals of the period, like *Sambad Prabhakar*, *Tattobodhini Patrika*, *Vividhartha Samgraha*, claimed the same objective. The idea of cultural synthesis gave them the best of both worlds.[7]

Journals are the blessings of printing technology. Before the invention of the printing press, there were hand-written books. The first known journal in any language after the introduction of the printing press was *Journal des Scavans* (later renamed *Journal des Savants*) (1665–1791) published in France. In English, the first journal was *Gentleman's Magazine* (1731–1868).[8]

The vernacular journals were steeped in the local culture. For a clear conception about contemporary Bengali literature, culture and thinking, one has to depend heavily on Bengali journals. The period under study was marked by constant tussle between two cultures, which re-shaped modern Bengali thinking. One of the outcomes of that was the literary expression on the part of the Bengali intelligentsia. Here Bengali journals played the most crucial part.

The Bengali mind was wonderstuck by the marvel of the Western science and technology in the first half of nineteenth century. However, after absorbing the initial shock, it gradually internalized and mastered modern science and technology. The Bengali journals of that period are reliable testimony to this entire transformation.

The essence of modern technology, Martin Heidegger wrote, is a form of revealing, an 'unconcealment' that occurs as technology 'sets upon' and challenges nature to yield energy, to be available as a 'standing-reserve'.[9] He says the truth of modern technology resides in an 'enframing' that not only encloses nature but also gathers human beings in the ordering and challenging of all beings as resources.[10] Human beings form part of the enframing and work into the system of revealing and challenging that renders all natural, human, and technical forces into resources, always available and completely manipulable. This is not technological determinism; it is not a claim that power and social hierarchies are reducible to the autonomous logic of technology, but rather that the rendering of the human and natural world as resources contains political imperatives.[11] In British India, the political imperative unleashed by this 'setting upon' nature and the gathering together of human beings can be identified at the level of the state, which, after the mid-nineteenth century, acted as the primary instrument of India's technological reorganization. Forging India into a productive, interlocking network of irrigation works, railways, telegraphs, mines, and manufacturing, the colonial state introduced and oversaw the establishment of modern technics. In an important sense, however, technology was not only the instrument but also the substance of state power.

Another important point is that colonized people were not mere objects at the hands of the colonizers. The introduction of the steam vessel, steam railways, electric telegraph, printing technologies and a host of other inventions began to arrest the attention of the indigenous population. The continued display of new and improved technology by the British aimed at the consolidation of their power in India and to increase its productive resources, but it also evoked a considerable amount of interest among Bengalis.

The Western invasion created new desires among indigenous people. Railways and telegraphs built by the Europeans for their own benefit were soon flooded with Indian customers. Along with the demand for technical devices has arisen a parallel demand for technological knowledge. Western technology flowed to India, first pushed by the Europeans and later pulled by the awakening demands of the Indian people.[12] One of the primary means of dissemination of Western scientific and technological knowledge were the Bengali journals of the nineteenth century.[13] These journals were vocal throughout the century for better implementation of various technological projects like telegraphs, railways, etc.[14]

Amidst its social and cultural responsibilities, a state pursues various objectives through its educational policy. However, in the Indian context the expansion and consolidation of the British Empire necessitated the training of native Indians in selected branches of Sciences. As a result, building and expanding infrastructure led to creation of a continuous demand for cheap but well-trained workers *inter alia* overseers, assistant engineers and surveyors. Country wide expansion of public works generated interest regarding development of schools and colleges, exclusively for engineering and technical education.[15] Since its inception the PWD (1854) influenced the growth of engineering education. Civil engineering remained the favoured subject as the prime aim of the technical education in British India was to meet the immediate requirements of the PWD.[16]

Although the British government repeatedly announced as policy level its intention to educate Indians in Western science and technology, they remained hesitant to do so, throughout its rule. This gave rise to a discriminatory policy in the recruitment of Indians for government jobs.[17] Thus, confining engineering and technical education to lower forms of instruction geared to produce cheap semi-skilled technicians.

Realizing the vital link between technical education and economic development, the Indian intelligentsia became restless and disappointed with the British educational policy. Hence, they started asking for advanced level of instruction. Technical education was one of the themes of struggle between the British authority and an awakening Indian intelligentsia by the turn of the nineteenth century. For the government technical education was only to meet the existing demands and anything more was perceived as flooding the labour market with unemployed graduates. However, Indians held an optimistic view of technical education. Many nineteenth-century educationalists argued that the educational system must develop a technical-scientific orientation for the industrial development of the country.[18] In India, the push for economic independence (swadeshi) even preceded the struggle for political independence (swaraj). To nationalists, technical education would prepare the future by training Indians to replace the Europeans and create a new economy.

Nineteenth century was the period of controlled and restricted growth for the indigenous Bengali business enterprises. Throughout the nineteenth century, many Bengalis started their own business enterprises, even though the conditions were not feasible for them. The number of Bengali enterprises arose with moderate success by the end of the century, especially during the swadeshi movement (1903–8). Remarkably, after the First World War (1914), some of the Indian entrepreneurs transformed into pioneers of advanced heavy industry.

Before the new developments from mid-nineteenth century closed doors for the indigenous entrepreneurs, modern commercial activities developed by the European agency houses during early part of the century included a significant proportion of Indian partnership. The agency houses were originally the carriers of private European trade in Asian waters. In Calcutta, 'Banians' were closely associated with these agency houses as brokers. Sometimes they might be important merchants conducting business of their own. The model early nineteenth-century banian was Ramdulal Dey. Raghunath Gosain, Digambar Mitra, Motilal Seal, Ramgopal Ghosh, etc., represented the prominent Bengali business community of that period. However, marking a niche, Dwarkanath Tagore became the pioneer modern entrepreneur of mid-nineteenth century, while many others made huge fortunes for themselves. Their lives dispel the myth of dearth of entrepreneurial abilities among Bengali people in the first half of nineteenth century as they successfully utilized the prevailing atmosphere in their favour. Calcutta and its adjoining areas were on the verge of an Industrial Revolution on a small-scale by 1840. Despite the paucity of capital, the local business community started a broad range of steam-powered industries. Unfortunately, a series of commercial crises shattered the Calcutta business community and by 1850, the momentum failed.[19]

Spokesmen of the Bengali middle class were introspecting the causes of entrepreneurial backwardness from the early nineteenth century, and for ways to stimulate business enterprise among them. Basically the problem with Bengalis was one of conflicting values while deep-seated social and cultural factors also existed. The economic hallmark of social status was power over land and not mercantile or industrial enterprise. Trade was associated with low rank castes and Brahmins and Kayasthas considered only intellectual or administrative professions as proper occupations.[20] Thus the indigenous Bengali elite turned its back on business and left modern industry and international commerce in Calcutta to Europeans.

From 1870s onwards few Bengali entrepreneurs emerged and successfully carried on various industrial ventures. Examples of H. Bose, P.M. Bagchi & Co., the Bengal Providential Railway Company and above all P.C. Ray and his BCPM further drive the point that there was no dearth of entrepreneurial ability among Bengalis at the turn of the twentieth century. We have, besides, also gone into the European organizations and institutions for building advantage and protection against competition all over India. Europeans were organized in Chambers of Commerce to which very few Indians were admitted. The situation was supplemented and buttressed by British control of the organized money market.

Recent researches deny that the caste system or land tenure system affected industrial development through the restriction of investment in industry by wealthy Bengalis.[21] Scholars have identified British rule as the sole cause for industrial backwardness. British rule brought about the transformation of the country from a feudal into a colonial and semi-feudal one and the conversion of the Indian economy into a material supplying appendage to metropolitan Britain. The emergence of indigenous entrepreneurship in Bengal was systematically discouraged by the political, administrative and financial arrangements maintained by the British rulers.

Indian entrepreneurs led the development of industries such as cement, paper and sugar after the First World War (1914). Thereafter, the nationalists and indigenous entrepreneurs began influencing various policies *inter alia* industrial, trade and commerce. Very few Indian entrepreneurs who were professionals and Westernized emerged as big industrialists, most of them came from groups with connections in trade.[22]

Bengali intellectuals developed a vigorous critique of the colonial discourse on science and technical education by the end of the nineteenth century. Inspired by the Baconian episteme, a large section among them, were optimistic that scientific knowledge brings wealth and they tried to connect science and technical education with industrialization. During the swadeshi movement this was intensified. The ideas of 1905 symbolized that the people were determined in two fields: (i) promoting education along 'national lines and under national control' with special reference to the exact sciences and technology, and (ii) industrializing the country and advancing materialism.[23] Bengali luminaries felt that scientific and technical education was a precondition for industrial development. Technical institutes were the birth place of a desired skilled workforce to usher in the technological progress of the country. The task was to educate Bengali artificers in modern science and technology so that they could take part in the industrial regeneration of Bengal. Bengali journals of nineteenth century were the chief promoter of Western scientific and technical education. In the last two or three decades of the nineteenth century they were tirelessly engaged in raising awareness among the Bengali people for technical education.[24]

British educational experiments were severely criticized by Bengali intellectuals. Education was no doubt an important part of the colonial enterprise and was designed to strengthen it. Viswanathan calls it as 'mask of conquest',[25] and Goonatilake considers it as a tool for 'cultural blanketing'.[26] Ambirajan believes that chance, more than foresight, determined the colonial educational policies.[27] Here we should not forget that British Raj was not a philanthropic institution; so it ensured the primacy of colonial requirements. For the colonial administrators it was technical assistance from Indians that was important, not expertise. They required a number of subordinates, overseers, and technicians to assist them in various departments. So some sort of technical education for Indians came on the agenda. Engineering colleges were made for the PWD. The nature and pattern of engineering education in India differed from that in England where it evolved from below and gradually became part of the university curriculum. In India engineering education was organized from above. Whereas in Europe engineering education was developed to facilitate the process of industrialization, in India there was no such imperative. Here the focus was not on material development, but on moral upliftment. In fact, the whole aim of colonial education was 'moral development' and 'character formation'. The native character was considered defective, immoral and superstitious. The 'modern' form of education armed with Western rationality was supposed to correct it.[28] But a PWD-oriented education was unable to achieve this.

During the latter half of the nineteenth century, a period of consolidation and institution-building, knowledge was 'imported', imparted and to some extent generated in Bengal. The 'new' knowledge was not diffused only through class rooms; practical demonstration of new tools and technologies were more effective. For example, railways and telegraph were the technological manifestation of cutting-edge knowledge. But these also worked under colonial constraints. Telegraph Department was entirely a governmental exercise, while the railways were raised on guaranteed profits and depended on wholesalc import from England. The repair-cum-manufacturing establishments were also detached from rest of the country leading to no technological spin-off in the adjacent areas of a railway colony. Mechanical engineering came later, but remained the step-child of the PWD until first half of the twentieth century. The model of a metropolis-colony relationship did not bring a higher form of scientific or technical education to the colonies. It was simply a hybrid budding out of a apathetic merge of industrial and technical education.[29] Headrick rightly points out that colonial rulers educated their subjects only up to a point, beyond that they withheld the culture of technology.[30]

Colonial officials preferred a geographical relocation of technology to its cultural diffusion. Every time a new technological innovation was introduced into a colony, it came with European experts to set it up and to handle it. The colonial government encouraged technical training for the natives up to certain level as it would have been prohibitive to use Europeans in semi-skilled or unskilled jobs. Colonialism usually stops the possibilities of cultural exchange between master and subjects, and prefers a one-way traffic. One may talk of transfer of knowledge or transfer of technology, but it was a transfer guided to achieve certain pre-determined goals.

Europeans found it easy to believe that cultural obstacles prevented Asians from learning to operate Western machinery. They knew that if the colonial subjects were denied the opportunity to study the highest level of technology, they could never compete with the Europeans in the high technology areas.[31] To colonial administrators, native cultural bias was a useful argument.

Despite their cultural ambivalence, many Bengali intellectuals saw Western technology as their key to power and prosperity, and they sought more machinery and knowledge than the British Raj offered them in the province. Unlike the British, they favoured cultural diffusion over the geographic relocation of technology. Even the so-called conservative peasants were not averse to change. They had no objection to the new tools provided these brought profits and were within their means. The problem was not cultural stagnation or social conservatism but finding economically viable and appropriate technological solutions.[32]

Bengali response to the scientific and technical education available in the nineteenth century testifies their awareness of the new phenomenon. From the beginning of the century, Bengali intellectuals recognized the importance of Western science and technology. They had demonstrated their concern for the promotion of technical education among themselves. Here Bengali journals played one of the most crucial parts. An editorial written in 1847, probably by Iswar Chandra Gupta, lamented the closing down of the Calcutta Mechanics Institute due to lack of public interest and noted that industry and technical skills were essential for a nation's progress.[33]

Dinanath Sen, the Head Master of Dacca Normal School, prepared a proposal for a school of industry or practical science in 1876, but remained unheeded.[34] Among the first who successfully raised the issue of technical education was Pramatha Nath Bose in a pamphlet entitled *Technical and Scientific Education in Bengal* in 1886 which attracted very wide notice and is said to have inaugurated the movement for technical education in Bengal. In it he talked about the lack of training in science-based industries and the need to remodel the university curriculum accordingly. Another crusader for the promotion of technical education was Prafulla Chandra Ray. According to him the existing educational system was out of touch with practical needs and was driving students disproportionately towards clerical and legal jobs which were becoming overcrowded, with receding chances for further absorption. Ray endeavoured to make his science directly relevant to the immediate needs of society. His institution sought to put scientific knowledge to immediate industrial use. He tried to encourage the idea of self-sufficiency through his institution. Satish Chandra Mukherjee, the doyen of the national education movement, played an important role for the promotion of scientific and technical knowledge in Bengal. He established the Dawn Society (1902) with a new teaching syllabus and schedule. The courses were divided between general and industrial/commercial with the fourfold objectives of salvaging the worthy elements of traditional science, absorbing the benefits of modern science, spreading science to the masses, and offering job-oriented technical instruction.

We know every action has an equal reaction. The British government wanted to train some Indians in few technical skills to fill up the lower strata of various departments, as literary education led to clerical posts. The real motive behind such a move was the economization of the administration. One interesting feature of the colonial education system was that it did produce political leaders, world famous scientists, and intellectuals, not just office clerks or technicians and overseers. No simple model can help us understand why colonial education had the kinds of effects it had. The British introduced Western scientific and technical education for their own purposes, to assist them at the lower level of administration. But by taking these limited opportunities created by the foreign ruler, India produced many jewels in almost every field, including science and technology. The great champions of 'modern' science, such as Mahendra Lal Sircar,[35] Pramatha Nath Bose, and Prafulla Chandra Ray, realized the importance of the new scientific and technical education and research and devoted themselves to the popularization of the same among fellow Bengalis. They worked ardently for the cause and demanded advanced technical education from the British government. When their calls remained unheeded, the Bengali *bhadralok* community came up with institutions like the Indian Association for the Cultivation of Science (IACS) and the Dawn Society. Both played an important role in spreading scientific and technical education and the latter especially linked technical education with industry. This was a very timely initiative on the part of the Bengali people, as they were repeatedly ignored by the government, which tried to confine technical education to a few artisanal and technical skills. Bengali intellectuals had gradually realized the importance of industrialization through local initiative and had come to see that technical knowledge deserved a central place in the whole project.

The emergence of modern science along with its industrial and commercial applications coincided with colonial explorations and understandings. This was no random coincidence. Both had an intimate, though complex, cause and effect relationship. The development of science, technology, modernization, and domination all marched together. This is the logic of history and this was to change human knowledge and relationship in every conceivable way.[36] Technology, whether tools or forms of knowledge, is not value-free. It always demonstrates political qualities, and in the colonial situation more emphasis was given to its 'use' of technical knowledge than to its 'transfer'. For the educated middle class, in the first half of the nineteenth century, technical education meant only a lucrative job in the lower strata of PWD. However, the situation changed in the second half of that century, when the Bengali intelligentsia, after mastering the new knowledge, demanded a comprehensive techno-scientific education and later worked for industrial upliftment.

The history of technology was almost an uncharted terrain a few decades ago, but its significance is now recognized all over the world. Its concerns and contents have been reflected in academic curricula and research agendas. The history of technology has a wide appeal, to the mainstream of social, economic, and cultural debates in history. Earlier it was seen as an aspect of economic history, but work on the social construction of technology, mainly in the West, virtually revolutionized the field. A social history of technology assumes a mutual relationship between society and technology; it also assumes that changes in one can induce changes in the other. Work related to the context of India is relatively little. Every region has its own distinct flavour and history and the sources and parameters of historical reconstruction also differ with each other. This was especially the case with India where a wide range of existing technologies and a physical and social environment that interacted with an alien culture.[37] The dissemination of new technologies was constrained, we have shown, by the nature of the Raj.

The conclusions made in this study are not final. The field is wide open for further research. Apart from the political debate over the development of technical education in British India, we can ask questions regarding the place of education in economic development and human capital formation. The history of professionals such as engineers and research scientists can be investigated. We also need to look at the history of curricula and the process by which technical knowledge has become institutionalized.

People often talk about medicine in politics and the politics of medicine in British India, but new medical tools and technologies such as the improvement of surgical tools, the development of pathological laboratory, advancement in the field of bacteriology, invention of microscope and X-ray machine also deserve special attention.

The last decade of the nineteenth century saw the electrification of Calcutta, the principal city of Bengal. Until then gas lights were used for the purpose. Electrification was a major technological innovation that rapidly transformed Bengali society. The new technologies behind a miracle like electricity can be an absorbing area of historical research.

NOTES

1. P.N. Bose, *Essays and Lectures on the Industrial Development of India*, Newman & Co., Calcutta, 1906, p. 74.
2. The acronym was popularized by Deepak Kumar in the academic arena. See Deepak Kumar, 'Developing a History of Science and Technology in South Asia', *Economic and Political Weekly*, 7 June 2003, pp. 2248–51.
3. Tapan Raychaudhuri, *Europe Reconsidered: Perceptions of the West in Nineteenth Century Bengal*, Oxford University Press, New Delhi, 1988, p. ix.
4. For more information see Ashis Nandy, *The Intimate Enemy: Loss and Recovery of Self Under Colonialism*, Oxford University Press, New Delhi, 1983; Thomas R. Metcalf, *Ideologies of the Raj*, Cambridge University Press, Cambridge, 1994.
5. For more information see Tapan Raychaudhuri, *Perceptions, Emotions, Sensibilities: Essays on India's Colonial and Post-colonial Experiences*, Oxford University Press, New Delhi, 1999.
6. Haraprasad Sastri, the great Indologist, in his essay on *Bengali Literature of the Present Century*, has written that *Tattobodhini Patrika*, under the editorship of Akshay Kumar Dutt 'was at that

time the missionary of European culture in the whole of Bengal. Akshay Kumar Dutt was the first writer to introduce Western outlook and mentality among Bengali youths. He is the moral preceptor of New Bengal'. Quoted in Arabinda Poddar, *Renaissance in Bengal: Quests and Confrontations 1880–1860*, Indian Institute of Advanced Study, Simla, 1970, p. 148.

7. Deepak Kumar, 'The Culture of Science and Colonial Culture, India 1820–1920', *The British Journal for the History of Science*, vol. 29, no. 2, 1996, pp. 195–209.
8. Gita Chattopadhyay, *Bangla Samayik Patrikapanji*, Kolkata, 1990, p. 3.
9. 'The earth now reveals itself as a mining district, the soil as a mineral deposit. . . . Everywhere everything is ordered to stand by, to be immediately on hand, indeed to stand there just so that it may be on call for a further ordering.' M. Heidegger, 'The Question Concerning Technology', *Martin Heidegger: Basic Writings*, quoted in Gyan Prakash, *Another Reason: Science and the Imagination of Modern India*, Oxford University Press, New Delhi, 2000, p. 159.
10. 'If man is challenged, ordered, to do this, then does not man himself belong ever more originally than nature within the standing-reverse?', Heidegger, op. cit.
11. Langdon Winner, *Autonomous Technology: Technics-out-of-Control as a Theme in Political Thought*, MIT Press, Cambridge, 1977, particularly Chapters 5 and 6.
12. Daniel R. Headrick, *The Tentacles of Progress: Technology Transfer in the Age of Imperialism, 1850-1940*, Oxford University Press, New York, 1988, p. 7.
13. For example, see *Samachar Darpan*, 25 April 1832. There an article described the technological aspects of steam engine.
14. For example *Sambad Purnochandradaya* reported on 16 April 1850: 'For the advancement of the country, especially for trade and commerce, telegraph and railways are very important. Railway deserves special attention, because it can revolutionize the transport system. Railways has been operating in England for long past. After strengthening their Empire in India, the British government now should introduce railways in this country also.'
15. Contemporary Bengali journals were very much aware of such developments and continuously raised their voice for the promo-

tion of technical education among Bengali youths. For example, *Sambad Prabhakar* (13 September 1852) emphasized the need for an engineering college at Calcutta like the Thomason Engineering College, Roorkee.

16. Indeed, all the colleges opened during nineteenth century were called 'civil engineering colleges'. Electrical, mechanical, and mining engineering remained neglected until second decade of twentieth century. See *Quinquennial Review on the Progress of Education in India*, vol. I, Calcutta, Government Press, 1904, pp. 248–9.
17. *Grambarta Prakashika*, 9 September 1876: '. . . the government is now saying that Bengali youths are not efficient in various higher level jobs. Passing an examination does not lead to success in professional life. These are actually excuses on the part of the government to exclude Bengalis from the higher level jobs.'
18. The Bengali journals of the nineteenth century tried to raise awareness about the vital link between science, technical education, and industrialization. They raised their voice for such education which could be used to industrialize the country. For example, *Somprakash* (30 July 1883) in an article 'The Industrial Development of India', gave special importance to technical education.
19. The fall of the Union Bank (1848) was a major setback for the indigenous business houses. After 1850 the international environment was no longer favourable to the growth of big Indian enterprises. In the first half of the nineteenth century the European trading companies employed as compradors the Bengali people who were gradually reduced to the status of petty clerks, then dismissed altogether in favour of young Britishers after mid-century. The Bengali enterprises which flourished during 1830 to 1850 were poorly managed and failed to make the proper use of modern technology. See Rajat Kanta Ray (ed.), *Entrepreneurship and Industry in India, 1800-1947*, Oxford University Press, New Delhi, 1992.
20. The Bengali journals of the nineteenth century were very critical about the Bengali character. The timidity of Bengali entrepreneurs was a recurrent topic in these journals. They criticized those banians who instead of launching their own commercial

ventures, supplied British merchants with capital. These journals condemned the social and religious taboos of the Bengalis which prevented entry into commercial and industrial ventures. See *Sambad Prabhakar*, 23 November 1853.

21. See Amiya Kumar Bagchi, *Private Investment in India 1900-1939*, Cambridge University Press, Cambridge, 1972; Chittabrata Palit, *New Viewpoints on Nineteenth Century Bengal*, 2nd edn., Progressive Publishers, Kolkata, 1980; Amit Bhattacharya, *Swadeshi Enterprise in Bengal 1900-1920*, Readers Service, Kolkata, 1986, etc.
22. We have seen the reasons behind the triumph of the indigenous entrepreneurs over the Europeans after 1914.
23. Sumit Sarkar, *The Swadeshi Movement in Bengal 1903-1908*, People's Publishing House, New Delhi, 1975, pp. 33–4.
24. For example, see *Education Gazette O Saptahik Bartabaho*, 25 January 1889 promoted technical education which was the maiden step towards industrialization.
25. Gauri Viswanathan, *Masks of Conquest: Literary Study and British Rule in India*, Columbia University Press, New York, 1989.
26. Susanta Goonatilake, *Crippled Minds: An Exploration into Colonial Culture*, Vikas, New Delhi, 1982.
27. S. Ambirajan, 'The Content of Science and Technology Education in South India', Roy Macleod and Deepak Kumar (eds.), *Technology and the Raj*, Sage, New Delhi, 1995, pp. 112–33.
28. The dual nature of colonial administration can be seen from the statement of Spilsbury who was writing about Narmada region in a personal letter to his brother. He pointed out that 'they (the natives) are rather barbarous in this part, but I dare say as soon as they get civilized they will become as great scoundrels and villains as they are in our own provinces (Bengal)'. G.G. Spilsbury to E.A. Spilsbury, 25 November 1820, quoted in Deepak Kumar, *Science and the Raj: A Study of British India*, 2nd edn., Oxford University Press, New Delhi, 1995, p. 58.
29. Deepak Kumar, 'Technology, Education and Colonialism in British India 1830s-80s: Convergence or Incongruence?', in Y. Keiji (ed.), *The Transfer of Science and Technology between Europe and Asia, 1780-1880*, International Research Centre for Japanese Studies, Kyoto, 1993, p. 193.
30. Daniel R. Headrick, *The Tentacles of Progress*, p. 345.

31. As Col. George Chesney of the Royal Engineers complained in 1870: 'Qualified students of the Calcutta Civil Engineering College . . . have, I believe, all obtained appointments on completing their course of study, but the class of Bengalee youths which frequents the College is not apt at engineering, and can take the place of European engineers but very gradually.' G. Chesney, *The Civil Engineering College for India*, India Office, 7 October 1870; quoted in Daniel Headrick, *The Tentacles of Progress*, p. 318. Headrick rightly says the arguments of the Britishers that 'non-Europeans had a cultural bias against technology was not an explanation but an excuse, even a weapon', Headrick, p. 309.
32. Taking up the case of Western technologies introduced into India, Sabyasachi Bhattacharya shows that the Bengali peasants would not easily accept the Italian filature system for silk winding. These machines were owned by those who were not the actual users but had money to invest in them. This meant further strengthening of the control of brokers over peasants and the subordination of producers to filature owners. Naturally, the peasants resisted. As Bhattacharya puts it, 'it was not always rejection of change itself, but rejection of a change for the worse'. See S. Bhattacharya, 'Cultural Constraints on Technological Innovation and Economic Development: Some Case Studies', *Indian Economic and Social History Review*, vol. 3, no. 3, 1966, pp. 240–67.
33. *Sambad Prabhakar*, 8 June 1847.
34. Dinanath Sen, *A Scheme for the School of Industry or Practical Science Proposed to be Established in Calcutta, from Funds Raised by the Indian League, with Government Aid, Drawn up, by the Order of the Director of Public Instruction*, Minerva Press, Calcutta, 1876. Although the scheme of technical education was originally made by the Lieutenant-Governor Richard Temple to jeopardize the effort of Mahendra Lal Sircar to establish an institution for original scientific research with the help of wealthy zamindars of India League, the proposal made by Dinanath was really good. But the government rejected the plan.
35. Sircar had underlined the need for 'applied science' and industry in 1890 but insisted that it was in the laboratory that the industry's destiny was decided. He also made it clear that he was never

against technical education and that the ultimate goal of his endeavour was to produce men who would use their training for practical ends. However, a broad scientific substratum had to be created first. Technical pursuits would stand independently on that solid base, without frequently looking to external intervention or imported expertise. See J. Lourdusamy, *Science and National Consciousness in Bengal (1870-1930)*, Orient Longman, New Delhi, 2004, pp. 96–7.

36. Deepak Kumar, 'HISTEM in South Asia: An Overview', in Arun Bandopadhyay (ed.), *Science and Society in India 1750-2000*, Manohar, New Delhi, 2010, p. 31.
37. Institutions established in Roorkee, Calcutta, Poona, and Madras represented an innovation in the history of technical education in British India. Until the end of the nineteenth century, England had no formal technical institutions. The engineering colleges established in India provided the models for replication in England in the late nineteenth century, and the colonial encounter contributed to the development of technical education in Britain. See Russel Dionne and Roy Macleod, 'Science and Policy in British India, 1858-1914: Perspectives on a Persisting Belief', *Proceedings of the Sixth European Conference on Modern South Asian Studies*, CNRS, Paris, 1979, pp. 55–68.

Bibliography*

Primary Sources

I. Bengali Journals

Amrita Bazar Patrika (February 1868–April 1870).
Arya Darshan (October 1875–October 1896).
Balak (October 1885).
Bamabodhini Patrika (October 1864–December 1895).
Bangadarshan (June 1873).
Bharati (January 1877).
Chikitsa Sammilani (April–June 1889).
Dig-Durshun (April 1818–December 1818).
Education Gazette O Saptahik Bartabaho (June 1857–January 1889).
Grambarta Prakashika (June 1876–December 1877).
Jnananeshan (March 1833–November 1834).
Rahasya Sandarbha (August 1873).
Sadhana (April 1892).
Sadharani (March 1873–November 1876).
Sahitya Parishad Patrika (July–October 1894).
Samachar Chandrika (April 1844–February 1846).
Samachar Darpan (June 1831–January 1837).
Sambad Bhaskar (January–June 1857).
Sambad Prabhakar (June 1847–December 1854).

* I have provided names of publishers and locations of publication wherever available. In few instances, full publication details were unavailable in the sources used.

Sambad Purnochandradaya (April 1850–March 1853).
Sibpur College Patrika (August–December 1902).
Somprakash (April 1863–August 1883).
Sulav Samachar (March 1870–February 1874).
Tattobodhini Patrika (May–September 1850).
Vijnan Darpan (September 1884).
Vividhartha Samgraha (January–March 1851).

II. Contemporary English Journals

Bengalee (October 1898–August 1906).
Calcutta Review (February 1895–March 1898).
Hindu Patriot (May 1865–January 1876).
Mukherjee's Magazine (1873–1876).
Reformer (March 1833–August 1835).
The Bengal Hurkaru (February–June 1838, April 1854–February 1861).
The Dawn (July 1898–November 1904).*
The Englishman (January–September 1852).
The Friend of India (August 1851–March 1854).
The Indian Mirror (November 1893–August 1895).
The Statesman (January 1890–October 1899).

III. Official Reports

Bengal Industrial Position Review, Bengal Sect. Book Depot, Calcutta, 1908.

DPI Report, Bengal, 1862–63.

First Quinquennial Review of Education in Bengal, 1892–96, Government Press, Calcutta, 1902.

Indian Industrial Commission-Inspection notes, 1916–18, Government Printing, Calcutta, 1918.

Industrial Education a Report, Supdt. of Government Printing, Calcutta, 1902.

* *The Dawn Magazine* was renamed *The Dawn and the Dawn Society's Magazine* in 1904.

Papers on Technical Education in India, 1886–1904, Calcutta, 1906.

Quinquennial Review on the Progress of Education in India, 1897–1902, vol. I, Government Press, Calcutta, 1904.

Report of the Committee appointed to enquire into the details of a scheme for the establishment of a School of Apprentices in Calcutta in connection with the Mint and other Government Establishments employing skilled mechanical labour, Calcutta, 1875.

Report of the Indian Education Commission, Calcutta, 1882.

Report of Indian Industrial Commission of 1916–1918, Government Printing, Calcutta, 1918.

Report of the Public Service Commission, 1886–87, Government Press, Calcutta, 1888.

Report of the Public Works Reorganization Committee, vol. I, Government Press, Calcutta, 1917.

Report on Industrial Education, Part I by J. Clibborn, C.A. Radice, R.E. Enthoven and Rev. F. Westcott, Office of the Superintendent of Government Printing, Calcutta, 1903.

Report of the Existing Arts and Industries in Bengal by E.W. Collin, Bengal Secretariat Press, Calcutta, 1890.

Report on the Mahanuddy River in Orissa by Arthur Cotton, Calcutta, 1858.

Report on the Indo-European Telegraph Deptt., A History of the Department, 1863–88, Supt. of Govt. Printing, Calcutta, 1890.

Report on Practical and Technical Education by E.C. Buck, Government Press, Calcutta, 1901.

Royal Indian Engineering College Committee Report, Simla, 1903.

Selections from Educational Records, 1840–1859, Part II, J.A. Richey (ed.), Government Printing, Calcutta, 1922.

Selections from the Educational Records of the Government of India, vol. IV (Technical Education in India, 1886–1907), New Delhi, 1968.

IV. Contemporary Tracts and Publications

Adams, M. (ed.), *Memoir of Sir William O'Shaughnessy Brooke, Kt.*, Indian Telegraph Department, Simla, 1889.

Bose, P.N., *Essays and Lectures on the Industrial Development of India*, Newman & Co., Calcutta, 1906.

Bose, P.N. and H.W.B. Moreno, *A Hundred Years of the Bengali Press: Being a History of the Bengali Newspapers From Their Inception to the Present Day*, Calcutta, 1920.

Campbell, George, *Modern India: A Sketch of the System of Civil Government*, J. Murray, London, 1852.

Capper, John, *The Three Presidencies of India: A History of the Rise and Progress of the British Indian Possessions*, Ingram, Cooke & Co., London, 1853.

Carey, W.H., *The Good Old Days of Honorable John Company*, Quins Books, Calcutta, vol. II, 1906.

Chandra, Bholanath, 'A Voice for the Commerce and Manufactures of India', *Mukherjee's Magazine*, 1873–6.

Colebrooke, T.E., *Life of the Hon'ble M. Elphinstone*, vol. II, Parker, Son & Brown, London, 1884.

Cotton, Arthur, *Public Works in India: Their Importance with Suggestions for their Extension and Improvement*, Madras, 1885.

Croft, Alfred, *Review of Education in India in 1886*, Government Printing, Calcutta, 1886.

Cumming, J.C., *Technical and Industrial Instruction in Bengal, 1880–1908* (part I of special report), Office of the Superintendent Govt. Printing, Calcutta, 1908.

——, *Review of the Industrial Position and Prospects in Bengal in 1908—with Special Reference to the Industrial Survey of 1890*, Government Press, Calcutta, 1908.

Deuskar, Sakharam Ganesh, *Desher Katha*, Calcutta, 1904.

Eliot, James. A.G.F., *Indian Industries*, W.H. Allen & Co., London, 1880.

Ewing, J.A., *The University Training of Engineers*, Cambridge University Press, Cambridge, 1891.

Fife, R.E., *The Civil Engineering Profession in India*, London, 1879.

Gangopadhyay, Jadunath, 'Banglar Chikitsak Samaj', *Chikitsa Sammilani*, Calcutta, April–June 1889.

Ghosh, Girish Chandra, *Ramdoolal Dey: The Bengalee Millionaire*, Calcutta, 1868.

Ghosh, Henry Hemantakumar, *The Advancement of Industry*, R. Cambray & Co., Calcutta, 1910.

Havell, E.B., 'Technical Education in India', *The Calcutta Review*, vol. 104, no. 208, 1897, pp. 223–46.

Howell, Arthur, *Education in British India*, Government Printing Office, Calcutta, 1872.

Hughes, James L. and L.R. Klemm, *Progress of Education in the Nineteenth Century*, The Linscott Publishing Company and W. and R. Chambers Limited, Edinburgh, 1907.

Indian Industrial Exhibition (a handbook), Calcutta, 1906.

Iyer, G. Subramanya, 'Our Artisans and Mechanics: Or Indian Arts and Crafts', *The Dawn*, vol. VII, no. 9, April 1904.

Kale, V.G., 'The Present Economic Condition of India', *The Indian Review*, XI(5), May 1910.

Long, James, *The Catalogue of Bengali Books*, Sanders, Cones & Co., Calcutta, 1855.

Majumdar, Kedarnath, *Bangla Samayik Sahitya*, Mymensingh, 1917.

Marx, Karl, 'The Future Results of British Rule in India', *New York Daily Tribune*, 8 August 1853.

Moitra, Kalidas, *Electric Telegraph Ba Tarit Bartabaha Prakaran: Electric Telegraph for the Telegraph Office Assistant's Manual etc.*, Serampore, 1855.

Mitra, Kissory Chand, *Mutty Lal Seal*, Calcutta, 1869.

Mukherjee, Satish Chandra, 'The Indian Economic Problem', *Dawn*, vol. III, March–June 1900.

Muir, Ramsay, *The Making of British India, 1756-1858*, Manchester University Press, Manchester, 1915.

O'Shaughnessy, W.B., *Notes of Lectures on Natural Philosophy, 1st Series: On Galvanic Electricity*, Baptist Mission Press, Calcutta, 1841.

Prinsep, G.A., *An Account of the Steam Vessels and of Proceedings Connected with Steam Navigation in British India*, Calcutta, 1830.

Sandemann, H.D. (ed.), *Selections from Calcutta Gazette 1816–1823*, Calcutta, 1869.

Sen, Dinanath, *A Scheme for the School of Industry or Practical Science*

Proposed to be Established in Calcutta, from Funds Raised by the India League, with Government Aid, by the Order of the Director of Public Instruction, Minerva Press, Calcutta, 1876.

Shastri, Shibnath, *Ramtanu Lahiri O Tatkalin Banga Samaj* (in Bengali), 2nd rev. end., New Age Publishers, Calcutta, 1904.

Smith, George, *The Life of William Carey: Shoe Maker and Missionary*, Everyman's Library, Calcutta, 1885.

Sircar, Mahendra Lal, *On the Desirability of a National Institution for the Cultivation of the Sciences by the Natives of India*, Calcutta, 1869.

——, *The Indian Association for the Cultivation of Science*, Calcutta, 1877.

Spring, J.E., *Technical Education in Bengal*, Government Press, Calcutta, 1886.

Stocqueler, J.H., *The Handbook of India*, 2nd edn., Wm. H. Allen, London, 1845.

Strachey, John, *India: Its Administration and Progress*, London, 1903.

Tagore, Rabindranath, *Jibansmiti*, Calcutta, 1912.

Trevelyan, C.E., *On the Education of the People of India*, Longman, Calcutta, 1838.

SECONDARY SOURCES

I. Articles

Barnes, Barry, 'The Science Technology Relationship: A Model and a Query', *Social Studies of Science*, vol. 12, no. 1, 1982, pp. 166–72.

Basalla, George, 'The Spread of Western Science', *Science*, vol. 156, no. 5, 1967, pp. 611–22.

Basu, Aparna, 'Technical Education in India, 1900–1920', *Indian Economic and Social History Review*, vol. 4, no. 4, 1967, pp. 361–74.

Bhattacharya, Durgaprasad, 'A Preliminary Note on Survey of Books on Science and Technology in Major Indian Languages in the Last Quarter of the 19th Century', Paper presented at the seminar on *Science and Empire*, NISTADS, New Delhi, January 1985.

Bhattacharya, Durgaprasad, Ranjit Chakravarty and Rama Deb Roy, 'A Survey of Bengali Writings on Science and Technology 1800–1950', *Indian Journal of History of Science*, vol. 24, no. 1, 1989, pp. 8–66.

Bhattacharya, Sabyasachi, 'Laissez Faire in India', *Indian Economic and Social History Review*, vol. 2, no. 1, 1965, pp. 1–22.

——, 'Cultural Constraints on Technological Innovation and Economic Development: Some Case Studies', *Indian Economic and Social History Review*, vol. 3, no. 3, 1966, pp. 240–67.

Bowers, J.Z., 'The Odyssey of Smallpox Vaccination', *Bulletin of the History of Medicine*, vol. 55, 1981, pp. 17-33.

Bridge, J.A., 'Sir William Brooke O'Shaughnessy, M.D., F.R.S., F.R.C.S., F.S.A.: A Biographical Appreciation by an Electrical Engineer', *Notes and Records of the Royal Society of London*, vol. 52, no. 1, 1998, pp. 103–20.

Buchanan, R.A., 'The Diaspora of British Engineering', *Technology and Culture*, vol. 27, no. 3, 1986, pp. 501–24.

Chakravarty, A.K., 'Three 19th Century Calcutta Astronomers', *Indian Journal of History of Science*, vol. 30, no. 2-4, 1995, pp. 151–8.

Chakrabarty, Dipesh, 'The Colonial Context of the Bengal Renaissance: A Note on Early Railway-Thinking in Bengal', *Indian Economic and Social History Review*, vol. 11, no. 1, 1974, pp. 107–11.

Chakraborty, Pratik, 'Science, Morality, and Nationalism: The Multi-faceted Project of Mahendra Lal Sircar', *Studies in History*, vol. 17, no. 2, 2001, pp. 245–74.

Das, Jnanendramohan, 'Sarvapratham Bangali Engineer Nilmony Mitra', *Pravasi*, Aswin 1332 (1925), pp. 17–23.

Dionne, Russel and Roy Macleod, 'Science and Policy in British India, 1858-1914: Perspectives on a Persisting Belief', *Proceedings of the Sixth European Conference on Modern South Asian Studies*, CNRS, Paris, 1979, pp. 55–68.

Foltz, Franz A., 'Technology within Society', *The Journal of the Technology Studies*, vol. 12, no. 1, 1991, pp. 23–9.

Ghosh, Amitabha, 'Introduction of Steamboats in India', *Bulletin of the Victoria Memorial*, vol. IX, 1975, pp. 32–44.

——, 'Some Eminent Pioneers in the Field of Technology', *Indian Journal of History of Science*, vol. 29, no. 1, 1994, pp. 63–75.

Ghosh, Birendranath, 'Sargiyo Motilal Seal', *Bharatbarsha*, Jyaistha 1338 (1931), pp. 994–5.

Ghosh, Hemendraprasad, 'Shivchandra Nundy', *Masik Basumati*, Kartik, 1360 (1953), pp. 107–14.

Ghose, Saroj, 'Technology: What is it?', in Jyoti Bhusan Das Gupta (ed.), *Science, Technology, Imperialism and War*, vol. XV, part 1, *History of Science, Philosophy and Culture in Indian Civilization*, General Editor D.P. Chattopadhyay, Pearson Longman, New Delhi, 2007, pp. 197–259.

Ghosh, Siddhartha, 'Calcutta's Industrial Archeology', in Sukanta Chaudhury (ed.), *Calcutta: The Living City*, vol. I: *The Past*, Oxford University Press, Calcutta, 1990, pp. 246–55.

Ghosh, Suresh Chandra, 'The Utilitarianism of Dalhousie and the Material Improvement of India', *Modern Asian Studies*, vol. 12, no. 1, 1978, pp. 97–110.

Gorman, Mel, 'Sir William O'Shaughnessy, Lord Dalhousie, and the Establishment of the Telegraph System in India', *Technology and Culture*, vol. 12, no. 4, 1971, pp. 581–601.

Gowing, Margaret, 'Science, Technology and Education: England in 1870', *Oxford Review of Education*, vol. 4, no. 1, 1978, pp. 3–17.

Habib, Irfan, 'Colonization of the Indian Economy, 1757–1900', *Social Scientist*, vol. 3, no. 8, 1975, pp. 23–53.

Headrick, Daniel R., 'The Tools of Imperialism: Technology and the Expansion of European Colonial Empires in the Nineteenth Century', *The Journal of Modern History*, vol. 51, no. 2, 1979, pp. 231–63.

Hughes, Thomas P., 'The Seamless Web: Technology, Science, Etcetera, Etcetera', *Social Studies of Science*, vol. 16, no. 2, 1986, pp. 281–92.

Inkster, Ian, 'Prometheus Bound: Technology and Industrialization in Japan, China and India prior to 1914: A Political Economy Approach', *Annals of Science*, vol. 45, 1988, pp. 399–426.

Jaggi, O.P., 'Diseases as Seen by Early European Physicians in India', in D.P. Chattopadhyay and Ravinder Kumar (eds.), *Science, Phi-*

losophy and Culture: Multi-disciplinary Exploration, Pearson Longman, New Delhi, 1997, pp. 54–126.

Joseph, G.G., V. Reddy and M. Searle Chatterjee, 'Eurocentrism in the Social Sciences', *Race and Class*, vol. 31, no. 4, 1990, pp. 1–26.

Kennedy, R.E., 'The Protestant Ethic and the Parsis', *American Journal of Sociology*, vol. 68, 1962, pp. 16-20.

Kling, Blair B., 'Entrepreneurship and Regional Identity in Bengal', in David Kopf (ed.), *Bengal Regional Identity*, Michigan State University, Michigan, 1969, pp. 21–37.

Kopf, David, 'The Brahmo Samaj Intelligentsia and the Bengali Renaissance: A Study of Revitalization and Modernization in 19th Century Bengal', in R.I. Carne (ed.), *Transition in South Asia*, Duke University Press, Durham, 1970, pp. 7–48.

Kranzberg, Melvin, 'Technology and History: "Kranzberg's Laws"', *Presidential Address*, SHOT, Henry Ford Museum in Dearborn, Michigan, 19 October 1985.

Kumar, Deepak, 'Racial Discrimination and Science in Nineteenth Century India', *Indian Economic and Social History Review*, vol. XIX, 1983, pp. 63–82.

——, 'Technology, Education and Colonialism in British India 1830s-80s: Convergence or Incongruence?', in Y. Keiji (ed.), *The Transfer of Science and Technology between Europe and Asia, 1700-1880*, International Research Centre for Japanese Studies, Kyoto, 1993, pp. 183–96.

——, 'Calcutta: The Emergence of a Science City (1784-1856)', *Indian Journal of History of Science*, vol. 29, no. 1, 1994, pp. 1–8.

——, 'The Culture of Science and Colonial Culture, India 1820–1920', *The British Journal for the History of Science*, vol. 29, no. 2, 1996, pp. 195–209.

——, 'Medical Encounters in British India, 1820-1920', *Economic and Political Weekly*, vol. 32, no. 4, 1997, pp. 166–70.

——, 'Science and Society in Colonial India: Exploring an Agenda', *Social Scientist*, vol. 28, no. 5/6, 2000, pp. 24–46.

——, 'Developing a History of Science and Technology in South Asia', *Economic and Political Weekly*, 7 June 2003, pp. 2248–51.

——, 'Investigating the Histories of Technology and Medicine in South Asia', *Proceeding of the Indian Association for Asian & Pacific Studies*, Kolkata, 2006, pp. 32–57.

——, 'HISTEM in South Asia: An Overview', in Arun Bandopadhyay (ed.), *Science and Society in India 1750-2000*, Manohar, New Delhi, 2010, pp. 29–47.

Kumar, Krishna, 'Colonial Citizen as an Educational Ideal', *Economic and Political Weekly*, 28 January 1989, pp. 45–51.

Lehmann, Fritz, 'Great Britain and the Supply of Railway Locomotives to India: A Case Study of "Economic Imperialism"', *Indian Economic and Social History Review*, no. 2, 1965, pp. 297–306.

Long, Pamela O., ''The Annales and the History of Technology', *Technology and Culture*, vol. 46, no. 7, 2005, pp. 177–86.

Macleod, Roy, 'Scientific Advice for British India: Imperial Perceptions and Administrative Goals, 1898–1923', *Modern Asian Studies*, vol. 9, no. 3, 1975, pp. 343–84.

Mayr, Otto, 'The Science Technology Relationship as a Historiographic Problem', *Technology and Culture*, vol. 17, no. 4, 1976, pp. 663–73.

Nair, P. Thankappan, 'Civic and Public Services in Old Calcutta', Sukanta Chaudhury (ed.), *Calcutta: The Living City*, vol. I: *The Past*, Oxford Unversity Press, Calcutta, 1990, pp. 230–8.

Nicholas, Ralph W., 'The Goddess Sitala and Epidemic Smallpox in Bengal', *Journal of Asian Studies*, XLI, 1981, pp. 24–39.

Palit, Chittabrata, 'Indigenous Business Enterprise in Bengal: 1780–1880', in *New Viewpoints on Nineteenth Century Bengal*, 2nd edn., Progressive Publishers, Kolkata, 2006, pp. 44–61.

Park, Robert Ezra, 'Reflections on Communication and Culture', *Canadian Journal of Economics and Political Science*, vol. 6, 1940, pp. 135–52.

Raha, Bipasha, 'Kangal Harinath' (in Bengali), *Parikatha*, vol. 10, no. 2, 2008, pp. 404–19.

Raina, Dhruv and S. Irfan Habib, 'Copernicus, Columbus, Colonialism and the Role of Science in the 19th Century India', *Social Scientist*, vol. 17, no. 3/4, 1989, pp. 51–66.

——, 'Technical Content and Social Context: Locating Technical

Institutes', in Patrick Petitjean et al. (eds.), *Science and Empires*, Kluwer Academic Publishers, Dordrecht, 1992, pp. 121–36.

——, 'The Unfolding of an Engagement: The Dawn of Science, Technical Education and Industrialization in India, 1896–1912', *Studies in History*, vol. 9, no. 1, 1993, pp. 87–117.

——, 'Bhadralok Perceptions of Science, Technology and Cultural Nationalism', *Indian Economic and Social History Review*, vol. 32, no. 1, 1995, pp. 95–117.

Ranger, T.O., 'From Humanism to the Science of Man: Colonialism in Africa and the Understanding of Alien Societies', *Transactions of the Royal Historical Society*, vol. XXVI, 1976, pp. 123–31.

Raychaudhury, Tapan, 'A Re-Interpretation of Nineteenth Century Indian Economic History?', in M.D. Morris (ed.), *Indian Economy in the 19th Century: A Symposium*, Hindustan Publication, Delhi, 1969, pp. 56–71.

Roach, J.P.C., 'Victorian Universities and the National Intelligentsia', *Victorian Studies*, vol. 3, no. 2, 1959, pp. 131–50.

Rooney, David, 'A Contextualizing, Socio-Technical Definition of Technology: Learning from Ancient Greece and Foucault', *Technology and Culture*, vol. 27, no. 3, 1998, pp. 27–44.

Roy, Rama Deb, 'The Great Trigonometrical Survey of India in a Historical Perspective', *Indian Journal of History of Science*, vol. 21, no. 1, 1986, pp. 22–32.

Sangwan, Satpal, 'Indian Response to European Science and Technology 1757–1857', *The British Journal for the History of Science*, vol. 21, no. 2, 1988, pp. 211–32.

——, 'Science Education in India under Colonial Constraints, 1792-1857', *Oxford Review of Education*, vol. 16, no. 1, 1990, pp. 81–95.

Sarkar, Sumit, 'Rammohan Roy and the Break with the Past', in V.C. Joshi (ed.), *Rammohan Roy and the Process of Modernization in India*, Vikas, New Delhi, 1975, pp. 46–68.

Sarkar, Suvobrata, 'Technical Content and Colonial Context: Situating Technical Knowledge in Nineteenth Century Bengal', *Social Scientist*, vol. 38, nos. 1-2, January–February, 2010, pp. 37–52.

——, 'Technological Momentum: Bengal in the Nineteenth Century', *The Indian Historical Review*, vol. 37, 1 June 2010, pp. 89–109.

Sen, S.N., 'The Character of Introduction of Western Science in India During the 18th and the 19th Centuries', *Indian Journal of History of Science*, vol. 1, no. 2, 1966, pp. 112–21.

Sen, Subhas, 'Bengal Providential Rail Company: Hooghly-r Zamidarbarger Akti Swadeshi Udyog (1890–1906)', *Itihas Anusandhan 7* (in Bengali), K.P. Bagchi & Co., Kolkata, 1993, pp. 341–53.

Sinha, Narendra Krishna, 'Indian Business Enterprise: Its Failure in Calcutta (1800–1848)', *Bengal Past and Present*, Diamond Jubilee number, July–December 1967, pp. 121–48.

Staudenmaier, John M., 'Recent Trends in the History of Technology', *The American Historical Review*, vol. 95, no. 3, 1990, pp. 715–25.

Thorner, Daniel, 'The Pattern of Railway Development in India', *Far Eastern Quarterly*, vol. XIV, no. 2, 1955, pp. 201–6.

Tomlinson, B.R., 'Colonial Constructs and Technical Education in India, 1880–1914', paper presented at the *20th Conference of International Association of Historians of Asia*, JNU, New Delhi, 14–17 November 2008.

II. Theses

Ghose, Saroj, 'The Introduction and Development of Electric Telegraph in India', Ph.D. thesis, Jadavpur University, 1974.

Kumar, Arun, 'Engineering Education and Public Works Department', Ph.D. thesis, University of Delhi, 1989.

Sarkar, Sarmila (Nee Mitter), 'The Urbanization of Calcutta in the Nineteenth Century: A Case Study of City-Lighting', M.Phil. dissertation, Jadavpur University, 1991.

Sarkar, Poulami, 'Towards Swadeshi Technology: A Comparative Study between the Bengal Engineering College (Sibpur) and the Bengal Technical Institute (Jadavpur) 1843-1947', M.Phil dissertation, Jadavpur University, 2000.

III. Books

Acharya Prafulla Ray Birth Centenary Volume, Calcutta University, Kolkata, 1962.

Adas, Michael, *Machines as the Measure of Men: Science, Technology and Ideologies of Western Dominance*, Oxford University Press, New Delhi, 1990.

Arnold, David, *Colonizing the Body: State Medicine and Epidemic Disease in Nineteenth Century India*, University of California Press, Berkeley, 1993.

——, (ed.), *Imperial Medicine and Indigenous Societies*, Manchester University Press, Manchester, 1988.

——, *The New Cambridge History of India: Science, Technology and Medicine in Colonial India*, Cambridge University Press, Cambridge, 2000.

Baber, Zaheer, *Science of Empire: Scientific Knowledge, Civilization and Colonial Rule in India*, Oxford University Press, New Delhi, 1998.

Bagal, J.C., *Pramatha Nath Bose*, P.N. Bose Centenary Committee, Kolkata, 1955.

Bagchi, Amiya Kumar, *Private Investment in India 1900–1939*, Cambridge University Press, Cambridge, 1972.

Bala, Poonam, *Imperialism and Medicine in Bengal: A Socio-Historical Perspectives*, Sage, New Delhi, 1991.

Bandopadhyay, Bajendranath, *Sambadpatre Sekaler Katha*, vols. I & II (in Bengali), Bangiya Sahitya Parishad, Kolkata, 1932 and 1933.

——, *Bangla Samayik Patra*, vols. I & II (in Bengali), Bangiya Sahitya Parishad, Kolkata, 1935 and 1951.

Bandopadhyay, Sekhar, *From Plassey to Partition: A History of Modern India*, Orient Longman, New Delhi, 2004.

Banerjee, Chittaranjan (ed.), *Dui Sataker Bangla Mudrana O Prakashana*, Ananda Publishers, Kolkata, 1981.

Basu, Aparna, *Essays in the History of Indian Education*, Concept Publishing Company, New Delhi, 1981.

Basu, Swapan (ed.), *Sambad Samayik-Patre Unis Sataker Bangali Samaj*, Paschimbanga Bangla Academy, Kolkata, 2000.

Basu, Swapan and Mamun Muntasir (eds.), *Dui Sataker Bangla Sambad Samayikpatra*, Pustak Biponi, Kolkata, 2005.

Basu, S.K., *The Managing Agency System*, Government of India Publication Division, New Delhi, 1957.

Bhattacharya, Amit, *Swadeshi Enterprise in Bengal 1900–1920*, Readers Service, Kolkata, 1986.

——, *Business, Politics and Technology*, Readers Service, Kolkata, 2005.

Bhattacharya, Arabinda (ed.), *Satabarsha-purti Smarak Patrika P.M. Bagchi & Co. 1883-1983*, Kolkata, 1983.

Bhattacharya, Arupratan, *Bangalir Vijnan-Bhabhana O Sadhana*, Dey's Publishing, Kolkata, 2006.

Bhattacharya, Buddhadev, *Banga Sahitye Vijnan*, Paschimbanga Bangla Academy, Kolkata, 1960.

Bhattacharya, Sabyasachi (ed.), *The Contested Terrain: Perspectives on Education in India*, Orient Longman, New Delhi, 1998.

Basalla, George, *The Evolution of Technology*, Cambridge University Press, Cambridge, 1988.

Bengal Engineering College Centenary Souvenir, Calcutta, 1956.

Bernal, J.D., *Science and Industry in the Nineteenth Century*, Oxford University Press, London, 1953.

——, *Science in History*, Watts, London, 1954.

Bernstein, H.T., *Steamboats on the Ganges: An Exploration in the History of India's Modernization through Science and Technology*, Orient Longman, Bombay, 1960.

Bijkar, Wiebe E., Thomas P. Hughes & Trevor J. Pinch (eds.), *The Social Construction of Technological Systems: New Directions in the Sociology and History of Technology*, The MIT Press, Massachusetts, 1987.

Bishee, Pramathanath (ed.), *Bhudev Rachana Sambhar*, 2nd edn., Kolkata, 1962.

Biswas, Arun Kumar (ed.), *History, Science and Society in the Indian Context*, The Asiatic Society, Kolkata, 2001.

Bose, D.M, S.N. Sen and B.V. Subbarayappa (eds.), *A Concise History of Science in India*, INSA, New Delhi, 1971.

Bose, Pradip Kumar (ed.), *Health and Society in Bengal: A Selection from the Late 19th Century Bengali Periodicals*, Sage, New Delhi, 2006.

Cardwell, D.S.L., *The Organization of Science in England*, Heinemann, London, 1980.

Chakraborty, Pratik, *Western Science in Modern India: Metropolitan Methods, Colonial Practices*, Permanent Black, New Delhi, 2004.

Chakraborty, Ranjan, *Terror, Crime and Punishment: Order and Disorder in Early Colonial Bengal, 1800-1860*, Readers Service, Kolkata, 2009.

Chandra, Bipan, *The Rise and Growth of Economic Nationalism in India*, Anamika Publishers, New Delhi, 1966.

Chattopadhyay, Gita, *Bangla Samayik Patrikapanji*, Kolkata, 1990.

Chattopadhyay, Partha, *Bangla Sambadpatra O Bangalir Nabajagoran*, Dey's Publications, Kolkata, 1977.

Crook, Nigel (ed.), *The Transmission of Knowledge in South Asia*, Oxford University Press, New Delhi, 1996.

Cowan, Ruth Schwartz, *A Social History of American Technology*, Oxford University Press, New York, 1997.

Das Gupta, Anil Chandra (ed.), *The Days of John Company: Selections from Calcutta Gazette 1824-1832*, West Bengal Government Press, Kolkata, 1959.

Dasgupta, R.K., *Concept of National Education in India, National Council of Education, Bengal*, National Council of Education, Kolkata, 1970.

De, S.K., *History of Bengali Literature 1800-1825*, University of Calcutta Press, Kolkata, 1919.

Dimock, E.C (ed.), *Bengal Literature and History*, Michigan University Press, Michigan, 1967.

Dutt, Paramananda, *Memoirs of Moti Lal Ghose*, Amrita Bazar Patrika, Kolkata, 1935.

Ellul, Jacques, *The Technological Society*, tr. & ed. J. Wilkinson, Vintage Books, New York, 1964.

Forbes, G.E., *Positivism in Bengal: A Case Study in the Transmission and Assimilation of an Ideology*, Minerva Associates, Kolkata, 1975.

Fox, Robert (ed.), *Technological Change: Methods and Themes in the History of Technology*, Harwood Academic Publisher, Amsterdam, 1996.

Gadgil, D.R., *The Industrial Evolution of India in Recent Times 1860-1939*, Oxford University Press, New Delhi, 1924.

——, *Origins of the Modern Indian Business Class*, Institute of Pacific Relations, New York, 1959.

Ghose, Binay, *Samayikpatre Banglar Samajchitra 1840-1905*, 5 vols., Bengal Publishers Pvt. Ltd., Kolkata, 1962–8.

Ghosh, Siddhartha, *Karigari Kalpana O Bangali Udyog*, Dey's Publishing, Kolkata, 1988.

——, *Kaler Shahar Kolkata*, Ananda Publishers, Kolkata, 1991.

Goonatilake, Susanta, *Crippled Minds: An Exploration into Colonial Culture*, Vikas, New Delhi, 1982.

Gupta, S.P., *Modern India and Progress in Science and Technology*, Vikas, New Delhi, 1979.

Harrison, Mark, *Public Health in British India: Anglo-Indian Preventive Medicine 1859-1914*, Cambridge University Press, New Delhi, 1994.

Hasan, Mushirul (ed.), *Knowledge, Power and Politics: Educational Institutes in India*, Lotus Collection, New Delhi, 1998.

Headrick, Daniel R., *The Tools of Empire: Technology and European Imperialism in the Nineteenth Century*, Oxford University Press, New York, 1981.

——, *The Tentacles of Progress: Technology Transfer in the Age of Imperialism, 1850-1940*, Oxford University Press, New York, 1988.

Hughes, Thomas P., *Networks of Power: Electrification in Western Society 1880-1930*, Johns Hopkins University Press, Baltimore, 1983.

Hunter, L.C., *Indian Railways: One Hundred Years, 1853-1953*, Railway Board, New Delhi, 1953.

Inkster, Ian, *Science and Technology in History: An Approach to Industrial Development*, Palgrave Macmillan, London, 1991.

Innis, Harold A., *Empire and Communications*, Dundurn Press, Toronto, 1950.

Jolepalyam, Mangamma, *Technical and Agricultural Education: A Study of Madras Presidency*, Kumar Publishing House, Delhi, 1990.

Kerr, Ian J., *Building the Railways of the Raj, 1850–1900*, Oxford University Press, New Delhi, 1995.

—— (ed.), *Railways in Modern India*, Oxford University Press, New Delhi, 2001.

Kling, Blair B., *Partner in Empire: Dwarkanath Tagore and the Age of Enterprise in Eastern India*, University of California Press, Berkeley, 1976.

Kranzberg, Melvin and Carroll Pursell (eds.), *Technology in Western Civilization*, Oxford University Press, New York, 1967.

Kumar, Anil, *Medicine and the Raj: British Medical Policy in India, 1835-1911*, Sage, New Delhi, 1998.

Kumar, Deepak (ed.), *Science and Empire: Essays in the Indian Context*, Anamika Prakashan, New Delhi, 1991.

——, *Science and the Raj: A Study of British India*, 2nd edn., Oxford University Press, New Delhi, 1995.

Lands, David S., *The Unbound Prometheus: Technological Change and Industrial Development in Western Europe from 1750 to the Present*, Cambridge University Press, Cambridge, 1969.

Lourdusamy, J., *Science and National Consciousness in Bengal (1870-1930)*, Orient Longman, New Delhi, 2004.

Macleod, Roy and Deepak Kumar (eds.), *Technology and the Raj: Western Technology and Technical Transfers to India 1700-1947*, Sage, New Delhi, 1995.

Mahindra, Kailash Chandra, *Sir Rajendra Nath Mookerjee*, Kolkata, 1933.

Majumdar, B.B., *History of Indian Social and Political Ideas*, Firma KLM, Kolkata, 1967.

Metcalf, Thomas R., *Ideologies of the Raj*, Cambridge University Press, Cambridge, 1994.

Misra, B.B., *The Indian Middle Class: Their Growth in Modern Times*, Oxford University Press, London, 1961.

Mital, K.V., *History of Thomason College of Engineering*, University of Roorkee, Roorkee, 1986.

Mukherjee, Haridas, *Satish Chandra Mukherjee and the Dawn Magazine*, Calcutta, 1953.

Nandy, Ashis, *The Intimate Enemy: Loss and Recovery of Self under Colonialism*, Oxford University Press, New Delhi, 1983.

Pacey, Arnold, *Technology in World Civilization: A Thousand Years History*, MIT Press, Oxford, 1990.

Palit, Chittabrata and Subrata Pahari, *Satish Chandra Mukherjee, the*

Dawn Society and National Science, Readers Service, Kolkata, 2002.

Palit, Chittabrata and Amit Bhattacharya (eds.), *Science, Technology, Medicine and Environment in India: Historical Perspectives*, Bibhasa, Kolkata, 1998.

Poddar, Arabinda, *Renaissance in Bengal Quests and Confrontations 1800-1860*, Indian Institute of Advanced Studies, Simla, 1970.

Prakash, Gyan, *Another Reason: Science and the Imagination of Modern India*, Oxford University Press, New Delhi, 2000.

Priolkar, A.K., *The Printing Press in India: Its Beginning and Early Development*, Marathi Samsodhan Mandala, Bombay, 1958.

Raina, Dhruv and S. Irfan Habib, *Domesticating Modern Science: A Social History of Science and Culture in Colonial India*, Tulika Books, New Delhi, 2004.

—— (eds.), *Social History of Science in Colonial India*, Oxford University Press, New Delhi, 2007.

Raj, Kapil, *Relocating Modern Science: Circulation and the Construction of Scientific Knowledge in South Asia and Europe Seventeenth to Nineteenth Century*, Permanent Black, Delhi, 2006.

Ray, Jitendranath Ray, *Banglar Kalkarkhana O Karigari Bidyar Itihas*, Dey's Publishing, Kolkata, 2004.

Ray, Prafulla Chandra, *Life and Experiences of a Bengali Chemist*, vol. 1, Chuckervertty, Chatterjee & Co., Kolkata, 1932.

Ray, Rajnarayan, *Atma-Charita* (in Bengali), Kolkata, 1961.

Ray, Rajat Kanta (ed.), *Entrepreneurship and Industry in India, 1800–1947*, Oxford University Press, New Delhi, 1992.

Raychaudhuri, Tapan, *Europe Reconsidered: Perceptions of the West in Nineteenth Century Bengal*, Oxford University Press, New Delhi, 1988.

——, *Perceptions, Emotions, Sensibilities: Essays on India's Colonial and Post-colonial Experiences*, Oxford University Press, New Delhi, 1999.

Roderick, G.W. and M.D. Stephens, *Scientific and Technical Education in 19th Century England*, David and Watts, London, 1972.

Roy, Sharadindu Sekhar (ed.), *Bangla Bhasay Vijnan Charcha 1818–1860*, The Asiatic Society, Kolkata, 2007.

Rungta, R.S., *The Rise of Business Corporations in India 1851-1900*, Cambridge University Press, Cambridge, 1970.

Sangwan, Satpal, *Science, Technology and Colonization: An Indian Experience 1757–1857*, Anamika Prakashan, Delhi, 1991.

Sarkar, Benoy Kumar, *Education for Industrialization: An Analysis of Forty Years of Jadavpur College of Engineering and Technology, 1905–45*, Chuckervertty, Chatterjee and Co., Kolkata, 1946.

Sarkar, Sumit, *The Swadeshi Movement in Bengal 1903–1908*, People's Publishing House, New Delhi, 1975.

Sarkar, Susobhan, *On the Bengal Renaissance*, Papyrus, Kolkata, 1979.

Sen, Adinath, *Sargiya Dinanath Sener Jiboni O Tatkalin Purbobanga*, vol. 2, Kolkata, 1948.

Sen, Asok, *Iswar Chandra Vidyasagar and His Elusive Milestones*, Riddhi-India, Kolkata, 1977.

Sen, S.N., *Vijnanacharya Dr. Mahendra Lal Sircar*, Kolkata, 1985.

——, *Scientific and Technical Education in India 1781-1900*, INSA, New Delhi, 1991.

Sen, Sunil Kumar, *Studies in Industrial Policy and Development of India*, Kolkata, 1964.

Shridharani, Krishnalal, *Story of the Indian Telegraph: A Century of Progress*, Post & Telegraph Department, New Delhi, 1953.

Sinha, N.K., *The Economic History of Bengal 1793-1848*, vol. 3, K.L. Mukhopadhyay, Kolkata, 1970.

Sinha, Nirmal (ed.), *Freedom Movement in Bengal, 1818-1904, Who's Who*, Government of West Bengal, Kolkata, 1968.

Souvenir of 125th Anniversary of Bengal Engineering College, Sibpur, 1981.

Viswanathan, Gauri, *Masks of Conquest: Literary Study and British Rule in India*, Columbia University Press, New York, 1989.

Weber, Max, *From Max Weber: Essays in Sociology*, tr. H.H. Gerth, and C. Wright Mills, Oxford University Press, New York, 1946.

——, *The Rational and Social Foundations of Music*, tr. & ed. D. Martindale, J. Riedel and G. Neuwirth, Southern Illinois University Press, Southern Illinois University, 1958.

Winner, Langdon, *Autonomous Technology: Technics-out-of-Control as a Theme in Political Thought*, MIT Press, Cambridge, 1977.

——, *The Whale and the Reactor*, University of Chicago Press, Chicago, 1986.

Zaidi, A.M. (ed.), *The Encyclopaedia of the Indian National Congress*, vol. II, Indian Institute of Applied Political Research, New Delhi, 1978.

IV. Website

The Official Website of CESC: http://www.cescltd.com

Index